Praise for *The Perfect Pass*

"The most entertaining book on football this decade . . . [Gwynne] writes with the enthusiasm of a fan and the scope of a historian."
—Allen Barra, *The Dallas Morning News*

"A thrill-a-minute book . . . Along with his protégé Mike Leach, now the head coach at Washington State University, Mr. Mumme revolutionized their sport in ways that, frankly, dwarf the legacy of Billy Beane and his gang from *Moneyball*."
—Will Leitch, *The Wall Street Journal*

"Informative and entertaining and a must-read for anyone interested in the inner game of football strategy . . . If you are a football coach, football fan, or simply a guy who likes a good story, S. C. Gwynne scored a touchdown."
—Tony DeMeo, *American Football Monthly*

"The tale of Hal Mumme and how he changed American football is a David and Goliath story with similarities to Michael Lewis's *Moneyball: The Art of Winning an Unfair Game*. . . . That was a different sport and era, but both Beane and Mumme found themselves in underdog positions and used creative, out-of-the-box thinking to level the playing field."
—*Houston Press*

"Being a football coach who goes against the way the game has long been played is deeply challenging. S. C. Gwynne captures perfectly how Hal Mumme's Air Raid offense helped change the landscape of college football forever. It's a great story."
—Bruce Arians, head coach, Arizona Cardinals

"When we played against a Hal Mumme offense, our defense had to be changed dramatically. You had to throw away everything you knew or you were going to get beat. Every offensive coordinator and defensive coordinator in football better study this book to find out why."

— Jerry Glanville, former NFL and college head coach

"Hal Mumme has always been a true American genius, and every year teams running his offense are among the tops in yards and points. I know, because I would've liked to have hired him. He has a brilliant football mind, and here at last is his amazing story, told in full."

— Bob Stoops, head coach, University of Oklahoma

"*The Perfect Pass* is a perfect book about football—and the transformative power of innovation. S. C. Gwynne brings the same remarkable reporting and storytelling skills he used in *Empire of the Summer Moon* and *Rebel Yell* to reveal the dramatic history behind the passing revolution that disrupted and forever changed America's favorite sport. His portrait of Hal Mumme, the unknown underdog coach who unleashed the Air Raid offense on the modern game, is superb, at once capturing the passion and genius that made him an unsung hero of his generation."

— *Texas Monthly*

"If you are a coach, a manager, an entrepreneur, an executive, an MBA student, etc., looking for a real-life example of thinking way outside the box and changing your industry or field completely, then *The Perfect Pass* is the book for you. Read it, digest it, and then apply it to your life's work."

— *Texas History Page*

"[An] illuminating history."

— *The New Yorker*

"Rich, well-told story of Hal Mumme, who spent years losing before inventing the Air Raid offense, which has swept football."

—*Sports Illustrated*

"It is undeniable that the Air Raid, the fast passing game, and the frequency of the forward pass are now imprinted on football, especially, as Gwynne notes, on the college level, though also in the NFL. That makes his subtitle all the more fitting, for undeniably, the two coaches changed the game—and brought glory to their institutions. A superb treat for all gridiron fans."

—*Kirkus Reviews* (starred review)

"Excellent sports history . . . an inspiring reminder that great ideas don't automatically permeate the existing ideology. Sometimes a devoted few must pursue their principles with diligence, even if they don't get the glory."

—*Publishers Weekly*

"A rousing tale of innovation finding success in the face of the gale-force winds of convention."

—*Booklist*

"Gwynne masterfully reports how this eccentric offensive genius . . . followed his own path and put passing at the forefront to runaway success. His stamp is everywhere, even in the NFL."

—*Austin American-Statesman*

"The most fun football book I've read in some time."

—Chris Brown, SmartFootball.com

THE

AMERICAN GENIUS

PERFECT

AND THE

PASS

REINVENTION OF FOOTBALL

S. C. GWYNNE

SCRIBNER
New York   London   Toronto   Sydney   New Delhi

SCRIBNER

An Imprint of Simon & Schuster, Inc.

1230 Avenue of the Americas

New York, NY 10020

First Scribner paperback edition September 2017

SCRIBNER and design are registered trademarks of The Gale Group, Inc.,
used under license by Simon & Schuster, Inc., the publisher of this work.

For information about special discounts for bulk purchases,
please contact Simon & Schuster Special Sales at 1-866-506-1949
or business@simonandschuster.com.

The Simon & Schuster Speakers Bureau can bring authors to
your live event. For more information or to book an event,
contact the Simon & Schuster Speakers Bureau at 1-866-248-3049
or visit our website at www.simonspeakers.com.

Interior design by Kyle Kabel

Manufactured in the United States of America

5   7   9   10   8   6

The Library of Congress has cataloged the hardcover edition as follows:

Names: Gwynne, S. C. (Samuel C.), 1953– author.
Title: The perfect pass : American genius and the reinvention of football / S. C. Gwynne.
Description: New York, NY : Scribner, 2016. | Includes bibliographical references
and index.
Identifiers: LCCN 2016012980 (print) | LCCN 2016038320 (ebook) |
ISBN 9781501116193 (hardback) | ISBN 9781501116216
Subjects: LCSH: Football—United States—History. | Football—Coaching. |
Passing (Football) | Leach, Mike, 1961– | Mumme, Hal | BISAC: SPORTS &
RECREATION / Football. | SPORTS & RECREATION / Coaching / Football. |
HISTORY / United States / 20th Century.
Classification: LCC GV950 .G99 2016 (print) | LCC GV950 (ebook) |
DDC 796.3320973—dc23
LC record available at https://lccn.loc.gov/2016012980

ISBN 978-1-5011-1619-3
ISBN 978-1-5011-1620-9 (pbk)
ISBN 978-1-5011-1621-6 (ebook)

Photograph credits: pp. 95 and 179: Kalen Henderson; p. 151, courtesy of
Hal Mumme; and p. 245, University of Kentucky Football Media Guides, courtesy of
University of Kentucky Libraries Special Collections Research Center.

For my wife, Katie, who encouraged me to write this book, and for my daughter, Maisie, who came up with its title

We decided that since football is a game with a ball in it, we should use the ball, we should let the boys play with the ball, we should put the ball in the air, we should let people see the ball.

—Glenn "Tiger" Ellison
Head Football Coach
Middletown (Ohio) High School,
1945–1963

Now and then we had a hope that if we lived and were good, God would permit us to be pirates.

—Mark Twain

Contents

CONTENTS

1

The Mad Pirate's Revenge

The Red Raiders are almost out of time.

With 1 minute and 23 seconds left in the game, Texas Tech's football team trails the University of Texas, 33–32. They have the ball on their own 38-yard line, 62 yards from the end zone. They have one time-out left, but the clock is just one of their problems. Texas is the top-ranked team in the country, loaded with future NFL draft picks. In the previous three weeks the Longhorns have beaten, consecutively, the first-, eleventh-, and seventh-ranked teams in the nation, on whom they have hung a collective 129 points. Texas's Heisman-candidate quarterback, Colt McCoy, has just engineered a textbook-perfect, 11-play, 80-yard touchdown drive to take the lead. On the Texas sideline you can see that the Horns are juiced. They are chest-bumping. They are jumping up and down. They are screaming.

So are the 56,000 Red Raiders fans in the stands, who have watched, agonizingly, as their team's 22–6 lead has steadily vaporized in the second half. They are desperate to win. Tech is ranked sixth—a rare occurrence in itself—and has never beaten a number-one-ranked team in its 85-year history. The game has been wildly hyped. The West Texas campus has been turned into a giant, free-floating pep rally. ESPN's *College GameDay* carnival has trundled into town with its 15,000 hangers-on. An elaborate tent city with 2,000 residents has sprung up around the stadium, loaded with so much digital technology and generator-powered electricity that it glows at night.

But as the clock ticks perilously toward 0, the feeling in Lubbock on this warm November night in 2008 goes much deeper than that. In spite of the odds, Tech fans *believe,* as an article of unwavering faith, that they will win. They do not doubt it. That is not just because their football team is having an exceptional year. The real reason is that they are the possessors of what is, by the traditional standards of the Big 12 Conference and the rest of the NCAA, a sort of gridiron black magic, a brand of offense so profoundly different from what their opponents play, so alien to the conventions of the rest of American football, and so astoundingly effective that for almost a decade it has consistently defied the best efforts of the best defensive minds in football to stop it. They call it the Air Raid. That's because the magic is in the air: balls thrown and balls caught. In their hearts, the citizens of Red Raider Nation do not believe that it can be stopped.

Most of America is seeing the offense's oddities for the first time, as Texas Tech sets up at the line of scrimmage. Conventional wisdom holds that offensive linemen should position themselves close together so that there is no more than a foot or foot and a half between them, creating the effect of an impenetrable wall. Often they are closer than that. Texas Tech's offensive linemen are, as one amazed commentator puts it, "strung out from here to Amarillo." There are four or more feet between the center, guards, and tackles, creating a line that looks, when viewed from the end zone, shockingly porous. As though any self-respecting linebacker could just walk right through those vast open spaces and kill the quarterback. Nobody lines up like this. The linemen, moreover, do not get down in the normal three- or four-point stance, ready to fire out, like everybody else. Instead, they stand, hands resting lightly on their thighs, looking like men waiting for a bus. Nor do they even position themselves on the line of scrimmage. They are set back from it, deeper than the center. Football traditionalists would tell you that they look like a group of fat men who are about to be knocked backward onto their Buick-sized hindquarters, while the defensive tackles and linebackers ravage the backfield. Tech has been setting up this way for years. Hardly anyone, anywhere, does any such thing.

Where did this madness come from? The simple answer is, Texas Tech's coach, a slender, mild-mannered man of average height who never played football in college. His name is Mike Leach. He is the proximate antithesis of the beefy, square-jawed drill sergeants who have populated American football since the 19th century. He has a law degree from Pepperdine University. His intellectual interests range from history—Apaches, pirates, Wyatt Earp, the Vikings, Winston Churchill, Daniel Boone, Napoleon Bonaparte—to the tango, the philosophy of John Wooden, the music of Jimmy Buffett, and, because he is a surfer, the dynamics of offshore breaks in San Onofre, California. When recruiting players, he does card tricks and tells pirate stories. In conversation he generally wants to talk about anything other than football.

But when he does think about football, interesting things happen. During his nine-year tenure at Texas Tech, he has compiled a 73-37 record. But those numbers tell you nothing. He has accomplished that while playing in one of the nation's toughest conferences and using players that few or no other elite college football programs wanted. In five of those nine years, Texas Tech—running its mysterious, pass-crazy Air Raid system—led the nation in offense, routinely hanging ungodly numbers of points on the opposition. Leach's first quarterback, Kliff Kingsbury, set the all-time NCAA record for career completions. His second, B. J. Symons, passed for the most yardage in a single season in NCAA history. His third and fourth, Sonny Cumbie and Cody Hodges, also led the nation in passing. Symons, Cumbie, and Hodges, moreover, were all *fifth-year seniors who only started for a single season.* Leach's current quarterback, Graham Harrell, who has actually played three years, was the first quarterback in NCAA history to have multiple 5,000-yard-plus seasons. His completion rate is an astonishing 70 percent. (He will soon set the all-time NCAA record for career touchdown passes, with 134.) Tech never huddles and plays blazingly fast, running as many as 90 plays a game compared with the NCAA and NFL average of 65. The Red Raiders throw 50 or 60 passes a game. Sometimes more. They rarely punt, even on fourth-and-4 from their own 35-yard line. They disdain field goals.

To say that Tech's Air Raid offense can score quickly is to understate the point. In 2004 the Red Raiders were trailing a good TCU team, 21–0, with 8 minutes to go in the second quarter. It looked like a blowout. One of the TCU defensive backs was even captured on camera saying, "They aren't going to score." Texas Tech won the game 70–35, behind five touchdown passes and 441 yards of spectacular aerial offense. That same year Tech rang up 70 points on Nebraska, the most that had been scored against the Cornhuskers in their 114-year history. In the 2006 Insight Bowl, trailing Minnesota, 38–7, in the third quarter, Texas Tech rallied to win 44–41 in overtime—the greatest comeback in NCAA bowl history. This is why Raiders fans believe. When Tech lost, it was often no fault of the offense. In 2007 the Raiders went down to Texas, 59–43, and to Oklahoma State, 49–45. Air Raid is an offensive, not a defensive, system. Leading up to the Texas game in 2008, Tech is undefeated and averaging 48 points a game. Ten of its scoring drives this year took less than 1 minute and 30 seconds.

Which is just a little bit more time than Mike Leach has now, facing a dazzling, adrenaline-pumped array of all the talent he has no access to.

With 1:23 to go, Harrell zips an 8-yard pass over the middle to running back Baron Batch. He follows it with a swing pass for a first down, then an 11-yard dart to wideout Detron Lewis at the 38-yard line. With 28 seconds to go, Harrell, dead calm in the pocket, hits the other wide receiver, Edward Britton, down the left sideline for 10 yards and another first down.

Unbeknownst to almost everyone watching this game, two of the four passes Harrell has thrown are actually the same play, known as Four Verticals, a sort of backyard, "everybody go deep" play that has been adapted to the Air Raid attack. The Texas defensive coaches, on the other hand, know all about Four Verticals. They can diagram it in their sleep. They know exactly what Tech is doing, but they can't stop it. This is the true beauty of the Air Raid; the reason it will be written about in history next to the single wing and the wishbone. With 15 seconds to go, Leach calls Four Verticals again. This time the ball is deflected off the hands of Texas defensive back Blake Gideon.

There are 8 seconds left. The crowd is hysterical, a stadium full of shimmering, dancing patterns of red and black. Fifty-six thousand fans scream in unison.

The ball is on the 28-yard line. It's second down. Tech, playing with its single time-out, needs to move the ball maybe 5 yards downfield, putting it within the range of its kicker. A field goal wins the game.

But the Air Raid is not about kicking field goals or punting or doing anything except scoring touchdowns. The Red Raiders' shorthand for Four Verticals, in fact, is simply the number "6"—the number of points they believe they are going to get every time they run it. And now Leach wants one more touchdown. He's not going short, he's going long. He calls . . . *Four Verticals*. Tech sets up, Harrell in the shotgun flanked by a single running back, four receivers spread wide. On the far right is Michael Crabtree, the best receiver in the nation, winner of two consecutive Biletnikoff Awards, a lightly recruited high school quarterback whom no college coach other than Leach knew what to do with.

Eight seconds.

Harrell waits, standing on the 36-yard line. The ball is snapped. Crabtree streaks down the right sideline. Texas Tech quarterbacks are taught to make quick reads, and Harrell sees more or less instantly that—for some reason known only to God, Texas head coach Mack Brown, and his defensive coordinator, Will Muschamp—Texas has elected to use single coverage on Crabtree. That single defender is freshman cornerback Curtis Brown. As Brown sprints to keep up, Crabtree, running full tilt, turns to find Harrell's eyes, and in a flash they both know what is going to happen. Crabtree is going to slow down and let Brown run by him, then he will spin to his right. Harrell's pass will travel 30 yards in the air, as Leach later puts it, "to Crabtree's outside ass cheek."

Harrell hits his target. Crabtree catches it at the 6, spins to the outside, and, instead of stepping out-of-bounds with 3 seconds to go to set up an easy field goal, shucks Brown milliseconds before the safety arrives and tightropes into the end zone with 1 second on the clock. It is impossible to fully express the depth of happiness Texas Tech fans feel at this moment. Years of perceived disrespect by Texas and everybody else are obliterated. They go crazy. The extra point is an afterthought, as is Texas's last play from scrimmage. Tech wins, 39–33.

The victory over Texas marked the moment that Mike Leach and his radical Air Raid offense stepped into the full glare of the national spotlight. Since his arrival in Lubbock in 2000, he had always been seen as a marginal, pass-happy guy who played a sort of anti-football and scared the hell out of everybody—an eccentric uncle who was entertaining but in the end was never going to win anything big. There was always a suggestion, too, sometimes spoken aloud but often implied, that this wasn't real football anyway.

Beating Texas changed all that. It was no longer possible to dismiss Leach as a refugee from a Jimmy Buffett concert, or his passing attack as a sort of cheap novelty item that would soon vanish in the heat mirages of the High Plains. Here was a coach in the bone-dry wastes of West Texas, where few top-rated recruits would willingly choose to go, putting together teams that consistently piled up huge yardage against the nation's elite football schools. He did it with fifth-year senior quarterbacks with weak arms, and he did it with slow receivers and running backs and offensive linemen whom no one else wanted. Just exactly what this "system" was few could say.

Only a handful of people inside the football community really understood how it worked. The rest of the world could only theorize about what sort of mad-professor schematics could allow a team of second-raters from Lubbock to hang 70 points on Nebraska. But the proof that this was a "system," commentators all agreed, was that hardly any of Leach's players, and none of his quarterbacks, ever made it in the NFL. They were merely products of a scheme that magically spun dross into gold, mediocre quarterbacks into NCAA record-holders. It was a nice conceit, but it still didn't explain how the thing worked.

Amid all this new interest in the Air Raid—which would grow as the system began to dominate huge swaths of American football in the following years, from the pee-wees to the pros—was the obsession, as old as the game of football itself, with the "unstoppable" play. Such a thing was not entirely mythical. It had existed, for several brilliant, flashing moments in history. There was Harvard's weird, lethal (and later outlawed) flying wedge in 1892. Pop Warner's sweep off his radical single wing at the Carlisle Indian Industrial School and Clark Shaughnessy's counterplay from the T formation at Stanford both had long moments of invincibility. When it was unveiled to the world in 1969, no one could stop Darrell Royal and Emory Bellard's triple-option play out of the wishbone, which started at the University of Texas and tore through American football in the 1970s and early 1980s.

Defenses eventually caught up, of course, as unstoppable objects finally met immovable forces. You could only fool people so long. That is the story of the game of football. But the myth lingered. Everyone wanted to see the Four Horsemen ride again. And it was not lost on the coaching community, once their noses had been fully rubbed in it at the Texas game, that Leach had been running *exactly* the same offense—featuring the same handful of basic plays, including his favorite, Four Verticals—in the Big 12 for nearly a decade. And that, after a decade's worth of intensive film study and game experience and much grinding of teeth and cogitation and marking of dry-erase boards, defensive coaches in one of the nation's toughest conferences *still could not stop it*. The Texas game was the perfect case in point: How could Tech possibly call the same play four out of six times with everything on the line and use it to beat a number-one-ranked team in the biggest game of the year? Was that not the very definition of the unstoppable play? Leach had others like it, too, that haunted the nightmares of defensive coordinators. They had names like Y-cross, Y-sail, and mesh. Nobody had figured out a foolproof way to stop *them* either. Only a handful of coaches in the country even understood the concept behind them.

Mike Leach was not the inventor of the Air Raid offense, though he had played a major role in its development. What fans saw at Texas Tech in the miraculous season of 2008 was merely the final flowering of an American sports technology that had its origins a quarter century before, in a small town on the rolling plains of Central Texas, with a coach nobody had ever heard of, at a high school that couldn't beat anybody, with an idea that the football world thought was somewhere between crazy and suicidal.

2

A Job You Wouldn't Want

In the annals of the American workplace, there are few jobs as thankless, unforgiving, underpaid, overworked, lacking in security, destructive to marriages, and mercilessly competitive as coaching college football. Yes, there is the warm glow that comes from making an impact on the lives of impressionable young athletes, teaching them the virtues of courage, discipline, teamwork, etc.

But for the dewy-eyed idealists and everyone else, the more immediate reality is this: The college football coach is the one with the cell phone pressed firmly to his ear in the delivery room, at parent-teacher conferences, on family vacations. His job requires him to miss weddings, funerals, marriages, the births of his children. College football coaches work all the time. The football season is filled with coaches' meetings, film and training sessions, practices, team travel, games, meetings with irate parents, and the complex logistics of running a large organization. The average football coach clocks 100 hours a week, in season, often sleeping in his office.* Nor is there anything "off" about the off-season. After the final game, they take to the road to recruit new players, traveling for weeks at a time, staying in Best Westerns, eating at Arby's, and spending untold hours in living rooms trying to sell parents, athletes, high

* Study by the website jobmonkey.com, cited in an article titled "College Football Coaching Jobs."

school coaches, and guidance counselors on the excellence of their programs. For many of them the money is lousy. Their job security is a joke. Nobody gets fired or changes location more than a college coach. A dozen moves in twenty years is common. (High school coaches work hard and move frequently, too, though turnover there is much lower. They are also paid significantly more money at junior levels. But mainly they are spared from the bane of most college coaches' lives: the ceaseless task of recruiting new players.)

If they win, they are loved and celebrated. That is the good part. That is the first noble truth about coaching. The second noble truth is that, in this cruelly Darwinian world, coaches who lose have their houses egged, their cars keyed, and their wives shunned at church functions. Losing consistently is nothing less than proof that you, your school, its athletes, and all of its alumni are simply not as tough, talented, brave, or smart as your opponents. You're all losers. That's the message. The difference between being loved and being run out of town is the difference between 7-4 and 5-6. A couple of injuries, some bad calls, a missed field goal, a few poorly timed turnovers. It's the sort of high-risk, low-return job that many people would not want.

Which brings us to a young man named Hal Mumme. (His last name is pronounced "mummy.") On Good Friday of the year of our Lord 1986, he is 33 years old. He is a trim 6 feet 2 inches tall, handsome, with a head full of thick blond hair that falls down across his forehead in a way that reminds you of a *Three Days of the Condor*-era Robert Redford. He has a broad, toothy smile and a deep tenor voice with an accent that originates somewhere in the live oak savannas of south-central Texas, where he was born, and can explode unexpectedly into a high-pitched laugh. He is—or was—a college football coach.

On this day Hal and his family are taking a trip across Texas, though it is not one of those happy vacation excursions that include stops at barbecue joints, snake farms, and spring-fed swimming holes. Until a few months ago, Hal was the offensive coordinator for the University of Texas at El Paso (UTEP) football team. He'd taken the job four years earlier, at the age of 29, which, at the time, made him the youngest offensive coordinator in Division I-A. He had made the sort of lightning-quick career jump from a smaller college that most young coaches could only dream about.

But the title, he soon learned, was one of the few good things about the job.

UTEP was a kind of French Foreign Legion of major college football, a desert outpost in the sun-scorched Mexican borderlands of West Texas with a team full of misfits and rejects and players no one else wanted. UTEP had long been the worst team in the Western Athletic Conference, the sort of patsy that decent teams in more-powerful conferences could open their seasons against and beat 66–6. That was the team's most useful purpose, in fact, in the college football ecosystem. Most of its facilities, from its locker rooms, to the gyms and nonexistent weight room, were not what you would want to show prospects.

Because El Paso wasn't near any place anyone cared about, recruiting trips were difficult, frequent, and long. During the season, Hal would fly to Dallas on Thursday to scout high school players and watch their Friday-night games, then return Saturday and go straight to his own game. He would spend the entire month of May recruiting in California because UTEP could not afford to fly him back and forth. His schedule was so unforgiving that, in order for him to be there for his daughter Leslie's birth, in October 1983, his wife, June, had to schedule an induced labor.

Not that any of that brutally hard work made much difference. From 1982 to 1985 UTEP won 7 games and lost 39. In 1985 the team won only 1 of 11. The coaching staff, under head coach Bill Yung, was deeply unpopular. Fans said nasty things; the press was relentlessly negative. To boost morale, Yung and his wife held potluck parties after home games in a room in the stadium. Instead of happy social occasions, they ended up being gloomy, despondent affairs. The team had usually lost, and the simultaneously depressed and wound-up husbands brought the losses with them to the parties, where they hovered in the air above the chips and queso like a bad odor.

And then, predictably, the ax fell. And of course it fell on Thanksgiving, which is when football axes fall, and in a matter of moments it was the end of Bill Yung and all his staff and the end of the line for the youngest offensive coordinator in Division I-A. The timing could not have been worse. The mass execution happened to coincide with the demise of the short-lived, professional United States Football League, whose unemployed coaches flooded the college market and immediately sucked up most of the good jobs.

The result of this run of bad luck is that Hal has been unemployed for four months; he has looked hard but in vain for a job, while the family moved to a rental house and the bank account dwindled. The "courtesy" car, given to him by the booster club, was abruptly repossessed, as though Hal and June were deadbeats. Casual acquaintances told June they "couldn't believe" she was still hanging around, as though Hal's firing meant that they were pariahs who could not possibly live in El Paso anymore. She sometimes came home crying.

This is why the children—Matt, 10, Karen, 8, and Leslie, 2—have been pulled out of school and why the family is traveling on Good Friday. With no money and no prospects, they are moving to June's parents' ranch in Brenham, between Houston and Austin, using Hal's unemployment check to pay for the move. Their future at this point—entirely in keeping with the storied traditions of college football coaching—is about subsisting on the last of their savings and on the charity of June's mother and stepfather. It is the only thing they can think of to do.

Something in Hal Clay Mumme had always wanted to be a football coach. He had always loved the game. When he was young, his grandmother had let him pick out his Christmas present from the

Sears catalog. The only thing he ever wanted was a pair of football spikes. When he wasn't shooting at squirrels with a single-shot 410 on his grandparents' ranch near San Antonio, he was dreaming of playing and, even at a young age, of coaching. He played wide receiver for Jefferson High School in Dallas and was good enough to win scholarships at New Mexico Military Institute, a two-year college, and later at Tarleton State University, in Stephenville, Texas, from which he graduated. In 1974, while he was still in college, he married the former June Leishman, a striking Louisiana State University coed from Houston. They were opposite personalities: She was serious-minded and personally conservative; Hal was boisterous, fun-loving, and adventurous, eager to pursue the great worlds of possibility that shimmered beyond the walls of the class-rooms at Tarleton State. Their first meeting tells you everything about them. While she was lifeguarding at a pool in Houston, Hal swam up and delivered the line "What does a person have to do to get saved around here?" She considered him arrogant and ignored him for a full year. Eventually she was persuaded to date him, and then marry him, anyway. When he graduated, in 1975, he took a job selling agricultural equipment for his father in Corpus Christi. He was a natural salesman and made decent money.

But Hal still dreamed of football. Against the wishes of his wife and parents, he took a job as quarterbacks and receivers coach at Foy H. Moody High School, in Corpus Christi. His salary was $9,000. While Hal labored long hours, June worked as a substitute teacher. Hal was so busy that June's mother had to take her home from the hospital after the birth of their second child, Karen. June, who had been furious that he had taken the job, was told point-blank by the school's principal that her husband had "made a poor decision" and that "he'll never amount to anything." Moody had three los-ing seasons while he was there. Things were even worse at nearby Aransas Pass High School, where Hal got the head coaching job in 1979, making $13,000 a year. His team went 1-9. The other coaches held meetings in Spanish from which he was excluded. Fans egged his house. Nine unpleasant months later, he took a job coaching quarterbacks and receivers at West Texas State University under head coach Bill Yung.

The college was located in Canyon, south of Amarillo, a pretty little town surrounded by breathtaking scenery and some of the largest—and most malodorous—cattle feedlots in the world. That sounded like a step up. What didn't was the salary: $500 a month with no benefits. Though that kind of money was common enough in the hardscrabble world of collegiate sports—where for young coaches it was always a buyer's market—the salary was alarmingly small for a 28-year-old man with a wife and two children. It was so small that the team's offensive coordinator tried to talk Hal out of taking the job. He failed. June went to work, which was the only way the family survived. She did alterations and babysat to make ends meet and eventually opened a small sewing shop. The family struggled financially, ate Hamburger Helper for dinner, with large portions of Helper. Sometimes they got checks from June's parents. Hal worked long days.

But this time the hard work paid off. The first year, West Texas was 5-6 but beat a couple of very good opponents. The second year, 1981, the team went 7-4. Hal had gotten a raise—to $16,000 a year—and June's sewing business was bringing in enough to allow them to buy a $50,000 house. Things were finally looking up for the Mumme family; they were settling in.

Then, on December 15, June received a call from one of her friends. "When are you moving?" she asked. "Moving?" June replied. "We're not moving." The woman said: "Turn on your television." On the news was a report that Yung had just accepted the head coaching job at UTEP. And of course in the world of college football that meant that most of his coaching staff, including Hal, would go with him and share in his good fortune. And of course the wives were not consulted. Not only that, but so great was the magnitude of the task they were about to undertake, and so desperately were they needed—this was *so* college football—that the men were leaving for

El Paso on a plane *that very day*. That meant they were leaving their wives to handle all the messy details of the move, worrying about the logistics of selling houses and getting out of rental leases and pulling children from school in the middle of the year. The wives also had to figure out how to pay for all that since these wonderful new jobs came with no money to cover moving expenses or real estate fees.

Hal was coming home only to pack a bag. He would begin recruiting immediately for next year's class in his assigned areas of Los Angeles and Dallas. This time at least the money was better: $33,000. June had managed to save $600 for the honeymoon they had never taken. Now she used that money to fly with the kids to see her mother and stepfather in Houston for Christmas. Hal was able to get a day off from his desperately important work to join them.

Almost four and a half years later, with the wreckage of their dreams of victory and happiness left behind in El Paso, with few savings, no job, and no income, the Mumme family finally arrived in Brenham on that Good Friday in 1986, followed by the moving van with all their belongings. While they were unloading, Hal drove to the small Central Texas town of Copperas Cove, in the shadow of the gigantic Fort Hood, the country's largest military base. The high school there was looking for a head football coach and director of athletics. Copperas Cove was a sort of high school version of UTEP, one of the worst programs in Texas, a perennial loser in one of the state's toughest districts. The school's administrators were desperate for something to change their luck. By the time Hal got back, he had the job. The Mumme family had not even unpacked and they were moving again. This time there was a $36,000 salary waiting for them, with a moving allowance and full health benefits.

It would not have been clear to an impartial observer, however, that Hal was making a wise career move. For one thing, it was going to make a simple, unavoidable firing seem like a spectacular career dive, from Division I offensive coordinator to head coach at a dead-end high school. There was the inescapable fact, too, that in 10 years of coaching Hal had experienced *only two winning seasons.* Taking the new job suggested that the UTEP job—the 29-year-old prodigy and all that—was some sort of mistake, an aberration that was now being corrected in the marketplace. On paper Hal was beginning to look like one of those career losers, of whom there are thousands in the coaching world, well-meaning, somewhat sad men with a bit of wistfulness in their voices who lack whatever it is that makes teams win.

Hal didn't see it that way at all. He was ecstatically happy. The money was fine and the benefits were fine and his family would be happy enough in Central Texas. All that was true. But his optimism was rooted in something deeper. In the early 1980s, while he was coaching in West Texas, he experienced a series of events that together amounted to a revelation about how he could change the game of football. It didn't matter how good or bad Copperas Cove High School was or whether it had won any games or whether he liked the town and the people or they liked him. What mattered to him was that he had a vision and he was going to be able to try his vision out. He was going to be able to put it on the field. And because he was head coach and athletics director, no one could tell him that he couldn't do it. No one could tell him—though many would eventually try—that what he wanted to do was, by football standards of the day, crazy and that he would never get away with it. His vision would have sounded wildly impractical if not outright wrong-headed to people who did not know any better, which would have been just about everybody.

Hal's grand, icon-shattering idea was that he was going to *throw the ball.*

He was going to make *passing* the centerpiece of the game.

He was going to throw the football more often and for more yardage than anyone in history. He was, moreover, going to change not only the way football was played but the premise of the game itself. He was going to smash more than a century of football tradition.

No one knew or cared about this except Hal.

No one was waiting for such a vision. No one would have given him the slightest chance of success.

To understand what he was about to try to do, and the world in which he was about to do it, one must first grasp the peculiar, hostile, and seemingly irrational relationship that has persisted between the game of football and the forward pass since the sport began in the latter 19th century.

3

A Brief History of
Men Throwing Balls

In the beginning there was the Civil War, in which 750,000 men died and whole sections of the country were wrecked and burned and devastated. In the years immediately afterward, it was hard to see much glory in all that ghastly killing and wholesale destruction. But as time passed and no more wars occurred—except the minor Spanish-American War, whose paltry 2,000 American casualties were equivalent to about an hour at Antietam—citizens of the North and the South, peering backward, began to consider that in spite of its horrors there was something redeeming about war, something principled and character-building, something that toughened your fiber and endowed you with the sort of moral and physical courage that the next generation seemed to lack. Americans began to see that there was a link between the violence, discipline, and hardship of war and the development of upright, courageous, productive, and God-fearing citizens. They began to see something that was missing in a country that would not fight a major war between 1865 and 1917—fully 52 years.

Thus arose a legal form of intimate, savage violence to fill that need: the game of American football. Baseball was mostly a game of speed and finesse and timing. Football was pure combat. The first contest took place in 1869 between Princeton and Rutgers and was more like soccer than football. But the rules soon changed to allow the ball to be carried by a man, which in turn allowed for a far more violent style of tackling, which was what everyone really wanted. Its supporters saw it as a cross between social Darwinism and military science: It required intelligence, strategy, and collaboration as well as pure strength. From its humble start in an open field bounded by split-rail fences, the sport soon became wildly popular.

It also became dangerous to human health. The early game of football was all about sheer, crunching force. Speed and deception were largely irrelevant. The contests consisted of men colliding in a tightly packed scrum in a very small area of the field. The few rules that existed were broken routinely. There were punches to the face, elbows to the throat, knees to the groin, kicking, biting, gouging, and throwing dirt into players' eyes. All while wearing minimal or no protective equipment. Often the game consisted of simply pushing, or pulling, the ballcarrier forward, while the other team piled on and arms and ribs and legs snapped underneath all those layers of vulnerable flesh. A common ploy was to try to maim or cripple the opposing team's star player. The center of the action was known as "the pile," and players who came out of it with dislocated joints or broken collarbones were expected to rub some dirt on their wounds, grit their teeth, and play on.

The game's early violence soon became codified in elaborate "massed" plays. The first of these was Princeton's V-trick, invented in 1884, which consisted of a moving "V" with the apex forward and the ballcarrier in the middle, rumbling slowly and inexorably down the field. Its purpose was to bring enormous force and human tonnage to bear at a single point of the opposing team's line. It worked brilliantly and soon became one of the most popular plays in the game. But the formation was not invulnerable. The following year Yale's legendary star William Walter "Pudge" Heffelfinger took a running leap, vaulted the human wall, and landed with his knee in the back of the Princeton ballcarrier. That marked the beginning of the end of the V-trick's dominance.

But Harvard soon made a stunning improvement on the basic concept by adding speed to the V-trick. On kickoffs and other plays in the open field, two lines of players would converge like Canada geese, moving at full speed with the ballcarrier shielded inside the chevron from would-be tacklers. Thus was invented perhaps the most spectacular football play of all time: the flying wedge. Recently two researchers, Allen St. John and Ainissa Ramirez, used Newtonian physics to assess its power. Assuming a very modest average of 200 pounds per player, they calculated that the change in momentum after impact—the collision, often between a single player and the point of the apex—was *2.5 tons,* the equivalent of being hit by a modern-era sport-utility vehicle moving at 25 miles per hour.

In this world of gritty, intimate violence there was no such thing as a forward pass. It was, specifically, illegal. The game, by modern standards, was a monotonous and often-low-scoring contest involving line plunges, mass momentum plays, and kicking, none of which seemed to affect its popularity. To many of the fans, games ending in scores of 5–2 seemed hugely exciting.

This status quo might have held but for the inescapable truth that by the turn of the century the sport had become increasingly *lethal.* Men were actually killing one another at the bottom of the pile. In the 1905 football season there were 18 deaths and 149 severe injuries, which led to a national outcry over violence in the sport. And since football's rise in popularity coincided with the dawn of the Progressive movement in America, it was only logical that the same activists who had taken on child labor, the trusts, and the railroad monopolies would eventually turn their attention to America's most troubled sport. They were convinced that the game of football was both ignorant and barbarous, like cockfighting or bullfighting or the old sports of the Roman arena. Much of the national press corps bought this line. The result: The prohibition of football became a social and political crusade. Its supporters included such odd bedfellows as Harvard president Charles W. Eliot and former Confederate general John Singleton Mosby.

Theodore Roosevelt himself was soon drawn into the debate. Roosevelt, who was president from 1901 to 1909, had been too small to play football at Harvard, but he believed in the "doctrine of the strenuous life," loved the game, and wanted to save it. He believed, moreover, that the people who wanted to ban football were misguided idealists who would, if left to their own devices, "feminize" the hardy youth of America and turn them into "mollycoddles instead of vigorous men." He also realized that the status quo could not hold; something had to be done to placate the pacifists, to reduce the violence.

One of the main issues in this fight was what to do about the exotic and highly illegal forward pass. The players all had fun tossing the ball around, rugby-style, in practice. But all attempts to make it legal in games had been soundly defeated. To listen to the run-only diehards of the era talk about it, you would think that throwing a leather ball down the field was some kind of satanic ritual. Opponents such as Yale coach Walter Camp, one of the dominant forces in the early history of football, believed that passing would "sissify the game." To Camp and his cohort there was something not quite right about the idea of passing, something delicate and a bit too feminine and possibly even un-American. The big, bloody pile at the line of scrimmage, on the other hand, merely reflected both the violence of the world and the natural selection of life. Such close combat, which recalled an Iron Age world that predated horses, guns, and bows and arrows, "prepares [the player] to be a man in the best sense of the term," according to Ed Poe, Edgar Allan Poe's grand-nephew, who quarterbacked Princeton's undefeated team in 1889. "It implants in him courage . . . and lays the foundations of an iron constitution." The reformers argued that passing would open the game up, utilize more of the field, discourage massed formations, and result in something other than a bleeding heap of human beings at the line of scrimmage on every play. Passing was the single rule change, they argued, that had the best chance of opening the field and busting up the bloody scrum.

They eventually won the argument. In a deal brokered in part by

Roosevelt—in an era when Americans had become enthralled with the idea of things that flew, from biplanes to zeppelins—football rules changed to allow the forward pass for the 1906 season. The change came with severe restrictions. The passer had to be 5 yards behind the line, an incomplete pass resulted in a loss of possession, and a pass could not cross the goal line for a touchdown. The shape of the ball would remain unchanged, watermelon-like and difficult to throw. There were other rule changes, too: The game assumed its modern 60-minute length; unsportsmanlike conduct was defined more precisely and penalized more severely; to reduce mass momentum plays, no more than five men were allowed in the backfield.

Still, the rules did not say teams *had* to pass, merely that they could. And, overwhelmingly, they chose not to. But there were exceptions, and the new rules inevitably gave rise to history's first forward pass. On September 5, 1906, in a game between St. Louis University and Carroll College, a quarterback named Bradbury Robinson threw the first downfield overhand spiral pass. The first team to really grasp the significance of the rules changes was the Carlisle Indian Industrial School, in Carlisle, Pennsylvania, which had been founded in 1879 as the first federally funded, off-reservation boarding school for Native Americans. The school's football team was coached by a man named Glenn Scobey "Pop" Warner, considered to be the father of the modern game of football. Using speed, deception, forward passes—the Indians had somehow figured out how to throw short spirals with the unaerodynamic ball—and Warner's brilliant new single wing formation, the Carlisle School became one of the most exciting teams in the country. In a landmark 1907 game against the fourth-ranked, unscored-upon University of Pennsylvania, the Indians completed an unheard-of 8 of 16 passes, gained 402 yards to Penn's 76, and won 26–6. This was in spite of Penn's huge size advantage. A Sac and Fox Indian named Jim Thorpe made his debut in that game, threw a complete pass, and cut loose on a 45-yard run. Two months later Carlisle beat perennial powerhouse Harvard, spawning a near riot on the field.

Despite such successes, the main body of the game clung tightly to tradition. Harvard and Penn took no particular lessons from the pass-happy Indians, other than the idea that they were running a screwy novelty act. Hardly anybody else did either. Predictably, the game's mortality rate started to rise again. Between September 1908 and the summer of 1909, the *Chicago Tribune* reported 31 deaths related to football. Two in particular shocked the nation. On October 16 Navy's star quarterback suffered a fractured spine, which led to paralysis and death. Two weeks later, as Harvard bulldozed downfield in one of its trademark massed formations, an Army tackler dived headlong into the oncoming mass, breaking his neck and upper spine. He died two days later. Army and Navy both canceled the rest of their seasons. Those deaths, at such prominent schools, sparked renewed controversy, and rules were changed again, to require only seven men on the line of scrimmage and to allow only one offensive player in motion in the backfield.

Passing's real breakthrough into the national consciousness came in 1913, after even more rules were changed and the ball was made less blunt and more airworthy. On November 1, Army, thought to be the best team in the country, took on upstart Notre Dame, a small regional college in Indiana that no one in the East took the least bit seriously. In fact if anyone at Army or in the eastern press had cared to look, they would have seen that the Fighting Irish's statistics that season were downright scary. They had scored 174 *points* on their last four opponents—an unimaginable number to the East Coast football powers—and they had done it by throwing passes in addition to the usual runs. The East Coast press and football powers tut-tutted and rolled their eyes and rationalized it all by saying that this little-known Catholic school had beaten a bunch of nobodies. The New York newspapers added to the general dismissal of Notre Dame, reporting that West Point would be playing *a* team from South Bend, *Illinois.* The boys from Army, of course, were sticking to their old rough-and-tumble ground game.

They would soon have cause to rethink their assumptions. In

the middle of the first quarter, with the game tied, 0–0, Notre Dame quarterback Charles Emile "Gus" Dorais took the snap from center, dropped back five steps, and launched a perfect spiral that traveled 40 yards and hit receiver Knute Rockne at a full run for a touchdown. It is impossible to fully appreciate today the shock that this single play produced. Neither the Army team nor the spectators had ever seen anyone throw a football 40 yards, much less a perfect strike to a sprinting receiver. "Everybody seemed astonished," recalled Rockne, who would go on to become the 20th century's most famous college football coach. "There had been no tackling, no plunging, no crushing of fiber and sinew. Just a long-distance touchdown by rapid transit." It was as though, in that split second, when the ball had landed in Rockne's outstretched hands, the men on the field were suddenly playing a completely different game, one that involved speed and deception and movement through open space instead of the usual bloody grind. Dorais mixed long and short passes with the usual runs, and Notre Dame not only upset the favored team but completely outmaneuvered the Black Knights, 35–13. (On the Army bench that day sat an injured, deeply frustrated halfback named Dwight David Eisenhower. Next to him sat his injured roommate, Omar Bradley.)

At this point you might expect to hear that, after such a stunning demonstration of this new technology, the forward pass soon became a central feature of the game of American football. But that did not happen, thus establishing an odd and counterintuitive pattern of behavior in American football that would persist for three-quarters of a century. Though some teams continued to experiment for a while with the pass, they were almost all in the "West"—schools like Michigan, under Fielding Yost; the University of Chicago, under Amos Alonzo Stagg; and Illinois, under Bob Zuppke—and therefore far away from the East Coast power centers of football and arbiters of football taste and practice. Passing, in fact, would continue to be mostly a phenomenon of the American West. The dominant teams—Harvard, Penn, Yale, Princeton—did not pass. They saw it very much the way Walter Camp saw it: as a sort of sissified gimmick, a cheap trick that would soon fade away. It is interesting to compare that 1913 Army–Notre Dame game to the Harvard-Yale game of the same year. The latter was a typical slog-fest, and the players did what they usually did when the running game bogged down: They kicked the ball. Kicking, in fact, was the innovation that everyone preferred over passing. The hero of the game was Harvard's Charles Brickley, who kicked five field goals in a 15–5 victory. Fans were thrilled and sportswriters awed by this game, in which no touchdowns were scored. "Try to find anything to beat it!" said one coach.

As years went by, the game proved remarkably resistant to passing in spite of periodic proof that it could actually win games. There was quarterback Benny Friedman at Michigan, for example, the first truly modern passer, who cocked the ball behind his ear and threw tight, overhand spirals with a follow-through like a baseball pitcher. In 1925, behind Friedman's crisp, accurate passing, the University of Michigan walloped Yale, 54–0. In the 1930s Texas Christian University coach Leo Robert "Dutch" Meyer introduced a spread formation that featured two wide receivers, two slot receivers, and a substantial amount of passing. Meyer often used his full legal allotment of five receivers, a tactic that was virtually unheard of at the time. With his tailback Sammy Baugh slinging mostly short passes from a formation that looked like the modern shotgun, TCU tore through opposing defenses. Though Baugh passed only an average of 15 times a game, completing 7 of them, and the team ran the ball twice as often as it passed, the passing numbers were still radical for the age. Sometimes Meyer would seem to take leave of his senses and let Baugh throw the ball 40 or more times. Baugh went on to an even greater career in the NFL. Playing for the Washington Redskins in 1943, he completed an unprecedented 133 passes in 239 attempts for 23 touchdowns and 1,754 yards.

But once again, no lesson was learned. The Meyer Spread, years ahead of its time, had few imitators, and never caught on. Meanwhile the single wing, a run-heavy offense that relied both on power and on deception, continued to dominate football into the 1940s. The most famous single wing tailbacks, like Michigan's Tom Harmon, threw the ball reasonably well. But the essence of the game was still the old ground-and-pound attack. The game was about running, and about stopping the run. The forward pass was a bit of filigree, something you did on third-and-long if you were desperate. It usually did not determine outcomes. Halfback tosses and fullback dives did.

The successor to the single wing was yet another ground attack: the full-house T formation with three backs stacked horizontally behind the quarterback. Stanford rode it to the national championship in 1940 under coach Clark Shaughnessy. That same year George Halas and his Chicago Bears (with help from Shaughnessy) used it to obliterate the Washington Redskins in the NFL Championship Game, 73–0. The leading college football teams of the 1940s, Army and Notre Dame, both ran the T and won games with speed and power on the ground.

When there were isolated advances in aerial offense, such as the brief flowering in the NFL led by quarterbacks Bob Waterfield and Norm Van Brocklin of the Los Angeles Rams in the early 1950s and their contemporary Otto Graham of the Cleveland Browns, the result was not a league that was finally persuaded to adopt passing on a large scale. Instead the needle swung the other way. The great innovation that came out of the 1950s and launched itself full-blown into the 1960s was not a passing scheme but the devastating Lombardi sweep, a thing of raw physical beauty that drew on the same geometries of motion and vectors of force that had made the single wing so effective. The presence, in the mid-1960s, of Sid Gillman's prolific San Diego Chargers passing offense featuring quarterback John Hadl and receiver Lance Alworth barely dented the trend. Even teams that were famous for throwing the ball were not, by contemporary standards, really doing that much passing. A supposed "gunslinger" quarterback like the Oakland Raiders' Ken Stabler actually threw the ball only 18 times a game for 152 yards in an offense that preferred running two to one.

In the college ranks, the story was the same, only there the killer ground game that emerged in the 1960s and 1970s was the wishbone, a spectacular triple-option offense invented by offensive coordinator Emory Bellard at the University of Texas. The quarterback, moving to his left or right, could hand the ball off to his fullback, keep it himself, or pitch it to his halfback. Texas ran off 30 consecutive victories with the wishbone and won two national championships. Alabama and Oklahoma also won national championships with it, which was copied by everyone in college football for two decades. It was not accidental that none of the quarterback's three options involved passing. In 1969, the year Texas beat Arkansas for the national championship, the Longhorns passed an average of 12 times a game and completed 6 of those passes for a total of 50 yards. This was the offense—in which passing was nearly completely irrelevant—that almost everybody in high school and college wanted to emulate. When it faded in popularity, it was succeeded by the grind-it-out, run-heavy power-I.

By the late 1970s it was apparent that the forward pass was not only failing to catch on as a productive and entertaining feature of the game, but was actually declining in popularity. Football was reverting to type. Football—college and pro—was regressing to its primordial origins. The most visible evidence of this was the so-called dead-ball era in the NFL, in which scoring finally bottomed out at 17.1 points per game in 1977, the lowest total since 1942.* Pass attempts per game were down from almost 30 in the early 1970s to 25. Once again, the game was devolving into a low-scoring affair of stacked defenses and halfback plunges. There was something instinctive in American football that wanted to return to the old bloody scrum.

* Not to be confused with the "dead ball" era in professional baseball, the end of which was famously heralded by the debut of Babe Ruth. In both sports the effect was the same: low scoring.

This may have been fine for the steely-eyed men who hated the idea of balls traveling through the air. But it was emphatically not good for the game. The NFL was so alarmed at how boring football was becoming that it put in rule changes in 1978 to allow offensive linemen to use their hands when they blocked. This would give the quarterback more time to throw, among other things. It also became illegal for defenses to bump receivers more than 5 yards from the line of scrimmage. It was almost like 1906 all over again: People were trying to save the sport by relaxing the passing rules. Colleges showed little interest in exploiting those changes. They still ran the ball most of the time, passed downfield on third-and-long if they had to, and every so often ran a play-action pass on first down. A comparison of some of the country's traditional college powers well after the rule changes shows the persistent preeminence of the ground game:

1984			
School	Passes/Game	Rushes/Game	Yards Passing/Game
Oklahoma	16	60	108
Nebraska	13	58	107
Alabama	25	47	143
Florida	19	49	154
Notre Dame	23	43	174
USC	24	51	154

The corollary was that the percentage of teams that featured a predominant passing offense, or that even threw the ball around much, was absurdly small. One could count them on two hands. In the vast world of football in America, which included three dozen professional teams, 620 college teams, and more than 12,000 high school teams, this was an extremely small group. Seven decades after Gus Dorais hit Knute Rockne on the run with that astounding 40-yard dart, the idea of opening up the passing game was still not percolating into the American heartland.

This was most clearly visible at high school games, where tens of millions of Americans focused their hopes and dreams, and where often 50 percent or more of the student body was out on the playing field in the form of players, band members, cheerleaders, and kick line dancers. Most of these games were showcases of conservative, old-school football. Though the passing technology was more than half a century old, there was still something morally thrilling about watching the quarterback toss the ball to the tailback, while the guard or tackle pulled and the fullback crashed down on the defensive end and the whole team seemed to move en masse in that swinging, lovely rightward arc of pure power followed by the popping sounds of all of those helmets and pads and the scream of the crowd as the whole thing disintegrated into a mass of bodies on the turf.

What was going on here? Why was there such resistance to what had been apparently proven many times over six decades to be a good idea? The truth was that most coaches still regarded passing as a sort of feminized football, an approach to the game that seemed to willfully and systematically discount the value of brute force, replacing it with something that seemed airy, light, delicately tactical, and even balletic. Coaches who threw the ball a lot—the key term being "a lot"—were still deemed subversive, somehow not tough or spiritually sound enough to play the real game of football, which was meant to be fought out violently and in close quarters. This was pure superstition, of course, but most everyone believed it anyway.

Then, too, there was the fear, neatly captured in the old chestnut "There are three things that can happen when you pass, and two of them are bad." Running forward through the line of scrimmage was a measured, predictable, rational approach to moving the ball 10 yards. Passing, on the other hand, was an exercise in vulnerability. Your passes could be intercepted, returned for touchdowns. There could be deflections. Quarterbacks and receivers were uniquely vulnerable when throwing or catching the ball, prone to fumbles. The quarterback could be crippled by headhunting defensive ends.

By opening up the field you introduced risk. Above all, risk. Unnecessary risk. Risk that you, as a coach, could not teach the forward pass to the linemen, running backs, receivers, and quarterbacks necessary to its execution. Even the brilliant aerialist Sid Gillman saw his quarterbacks intercepted at high rates. In 1965 his San Diego Chargers quarterbacks threw 26 interceptions against only 23 touchdowns. Coaches who wanted to keep their jobs ran the ball.

The magic of passing, moreover, seemed fragile at best. It had to be intensely *taught*, for one thing. It relied heavily on one player. And even if you could figure out how to teach it, the fact was that passing's greatest advocates had not been able to sustain it. One of the most famous examples of this took place in the early 1980s at Mississippi Valley State University, which was for a while one of the most pass-crazy teams in the country. A wideout named Jerry Rice, who would become the greatest receiver in NFL history, was paired with a rifle-armed quarterback named Willie Totten. Together the two drove an offense that in 1984 threw an average of 54 passes a game for 58 touchdowns and 5,043 yards. Those numbers were—and are—at or near the top of all historical rankings of offensive production. The method was simple enough. Either Totten threw to Rice, or, if Rice was double- or triple-teamed, coach Archie Cooley stacked three receivers on the other side of the line and overloaded the zone, allowing the defense to choose the means of its own destruction. Nobody could stop them. But Mississippi Valley State's victorious run did not last. What happened there was mostly driven by Jerry Rice and Willie Totten, an accident of time and place. Before Rice and Totten came to MVSU, there had been no great passing attack. After they graduated there was no great passing attack. Suddenly the enchantment was gone, like dust on the wind.

Which illustrated the simple point: You could maybe get a piece of that magic, a Jerry Rice or a Benny Friedman or a Sammy Baugh, but you could never hold on to it for more than a few years. Or, if your gunslinger quarterback or speed-burner receiver got hurt, more than a few games. Over the years the forward pass became an intermittent phenomenon, the work of individual practitioners who arose like mayflies, flourished briefly, then passed from view. Meanwhile, the rest of the football world soldiered on as it always had, and most of the game took place in a relatively small area in the middle of the field. As football lumbered into the 1980s, Walter Camp himself would have been pleased to note how successful the traditionalists had been in fighting off the rabid feminizers who wanted to ruin the game.

4

Secrets of the Air

Hal Mumme's big idea about the forward pass came to him in a sequence of epiphanies. There were other, lesser bits of information in that vision, but at its core lay four separate pieces of truth that, when fitted properly together, added up to a full-scale, Saul-on-the-road-to-Damascus revelation.

The first took place in the fall of 1980, when Hal was coaching quarterbacks and receivers at West Texas State University. He was 28 years old. He dreamed of building a true passing team, but had very little idea of how to do it. He knew that it did not mean simply throwing or catching passes, or designing clever pass patterns. Everybody threw passes. There was nothing special about that. All coaches had sections of their playbooks where they kept the aerial stuff. They all had long passes and screen passes and passes where the receivers' routes intersected in order to mess up the defensive coverage. What Hal needed was a grand theory, something bigger and better and different from simply sending a receiver to beat a linebacker on third-and-long. He needed a single, integrated theory of some sort that would make the "total scheme," as he thought of it, fit. This was his problem.

Lacking such a theory, and isolated in the remoteness of the High Plains, he scavenged. He attended clinics when he could, grilled coaches he knew on their techniques, read whatever football books he could get his hands on, and experimented on live receivers and quarterbacks when the rest of the coaches were busy. He spent much of his free time diagramming pass plays. He would often do this on scraps of paper or whatever he could find to write on, scrawling down ideas about how to freeze this or that defensive back, how to flood a zone defense, how to throw a curl/flat combination, how to protect against a blitz. He did this everywhere he went, day and night, so much so that he trailed these little artifacts of ambition and desire behind him at his home and office. They were tiny pieces of the master plan he didn't have yet. June actually picked them up and put them in boxes. She soon discovered that he didn't need to keep them. The writing itself was the mnemonic device. He worked long hours, and was often distracted by his thoughts.

For a man who dreamed of throwing passes, however, Hal was in the wrong place. Head coach Bill Yung was a run-it-up-the-gut guy from the oldest of the old schools, playing in a league with like-minded coaches. He ran the ball out of a traditional I formation and he ran it three-quarters of the time. He called the plays. The exception was when he was badly overmatched, and then he would let Hal, who sat up in a box high above the field with headphones on, call the passing plays. The first time that happened was in September. West Texas State was playing Oklahoma State, a Division I-A power with a fast-rising coach named Jimmy Johnson and a fearsome defensive end named Dexter Manley, both of whom would go on to exceptional careers in the NFL.* Oklahoma State, playing at home in Stillwater, was expected to make sausage out of West Texas State. The score was likely to be 70-0.

Hal, who had been stealing practice time to teach his quarterbacks and receivers more-advanced routes, had developed a modest repertoire of passing plays. And now Yung was giving him some scope, letting him do what he wanted. Hal could see, as the game

---

* Johnson won two Super Bowls as head coach of the Dallas Cowboys. Manley played for several NFL teams, including the Washington Redskins, with whom he won Super Bowls XVII and XXII.

progressed, that Johnson was staying with a conservative zone defense. So he went to work, probing for weaknesses. If the Oklahoma State cornerbacks stayed back, he would call quick outs to wide receivers in the flat. If the corners came up, the receivers would run patterns that would drop them into holes between the corners and the safeties. Hal systematically exploited slow linebackers and cheating safeties. He found unoccupied seams. His plays worked. And he quickly discovered that Johnson's zone defense could not stop them. For some reason he never came out of his Cover 2 and Cover 3 formations, perhaps because he could not quite believe what was happening to him. Hal made him pay for this conservatism. West Texas quarterback Matt Patterson threw for 209 yards and a touchdown and West Texas won, 20–19, in what remains one of the greatest victories in school history. Hal believed that, had Yung allowed him to throw the ball more, he could have gained 400 yards through the air.

For Hal it was more than a thrilling win. So much of what he had drawn up over the years was theoretical, unproven. The Oklahoma State game offered tangible evidence that he could read the shifting patterns of a Division I-A pass defense—with defensive backs who were bigger and faster than his receivers—and find their weaknesses. He had never doubted that he had this talent. He had never lacked self-confidence. But here was proof that he could do it.

Three months after the victory over Oklahoma State, on December 19, 1980—this will be the second epiphany—Hal happened to tune his home television to the Holiday Bowl, a post-season game that had been started to give the Western Athletic Conference—which meant, in effect, its best team, Brigham Young University—an automatic bid to a bowl game. BYU was the very definition of an odd duck, a Mormon school in the Utah desert with a team populated by ultra-clean-cut 24-year-olds who had done two-year mission trips abroad. They were coached by a man seemingly just this side of crazy named LaVell Edwards, whose quarterbacks threw the football more than anyone else in major college football and routinely gained vast yardage through the air. The previous year, BYU quarterback Marc Wilson had led the nation in completions, attempts, and passing yards. In spite of this, the football establishment persisted in viewing BYU the way Yale and Army had looked at the Carlisle Indians 70 years earlier: as purveyors of cheapjack novelty items that nobody else was interested in and that would soon disappear. It didn't help that BYU played in the Podunk-friendly WAC, with such middle-of-nowhere football schools as Hawaii, Utah, and Wyoming, that seemed to score a lot of points on one another but did less well against national opponents. It was another reason to ignore the Mormons and keep them off the airwaves. That didn't alter the fact that BYU scared the hell out of everybody.

BYU's opponent in the Holiday Bowl was Southern Methodist University, a team that was its antipode in almost every possible way. The Cougars had led the nation in passing that season, averaging a dazzling 405 yards a game. SMU had the NCAA's most dominant running game, featuring twin All-Americans Eric Dickerson and Craig James, who were known as the Pony Express.* SMU ran the ball almost 50 times a game; on a good day their quarterback might complete eight passes. Where BYU had a squeaky-clean program, SMU's was thoroughly corrupt, using illegal slush funds to make secret payments to players and routinely violating all sorts of NCAA rules and regulations. For its transgressions, in 1986 SMU's football program would receive the "death penalty" from the NCAA, canceling an entire season of play. But in 1980 none of that was known. The game was a rare matchup of two radically divergent football philosophies.

The few people who tuned in saw one of the greatest contests in collegiate history. For the first three quarters the momentum was all SMU's. The Pony Express ran wild. BYU's defense

---

* Dickerson and James would both go on to stardom in the NFL. Dickerson played for the Los Angeles Rams, Indianapolis Colts, Los Angeles Raiders, and Atlanta Falcons. He still holds the NFL's single-season rushing record. James played for the New England Patriots.

had no answer for them. James and Dickerson controlled the ball, ate up the clock, and kept BYU's offense, under its brash quarterback, Jim McMahon, off the field.* By the end of the third quarter, SMU was leading 38–19 and pulling away. With four minutes to go the score was 45–25. It was just around that time, when all hope seemed to be lost and television viewers had long since switched channels and many of the fans had left the stands, that McMahon and the rest of the BYU offense went completely berserk. They scored three unanswered touchdowns, two of them through the air.

BYU won, 46–45, on a last-second pass. The media quickly christened the game the Miracle Bowl. Dickerson and James together had run for a blistering 325 yards, but McMahon had outdueled them. The box score, moreover, showed that BYU had beaten SMU *entirely through the air*: BYU's net rushing yardage was negative 2. McMahon, who completed 32 of 49 passes for 446 yards, had put on a virtuoso passing performance, the likes of which America had rarely witnessed. He spread the ball all over the field, from sideline to sideline, with short and long passes. While the game rolled by on-screen, an amazed and profoundly excited Hal sat on his couch taking notes on formations and patterns. He knew that on some level he was watching a redefinition of the game. But he had no idea how it was being done. How could BYU protect its quarterback if everybody in the Western Hemisphere knew he was going to pass? What was that astonishingly successful play where the two receivers crossed over the middle and seemed to run directly at each other? BYU was clearly running a meticulously plotted system of some sort. But what were its components?

Hal's third revelation occurred in 1981, after his first season at West Texas State. That spring Hal had persuaded head coach Bill Yung to let him attend the 49ers' training camp in California to

---

* McMahon would later win a Super Bowl with the Chicago Bears.

learn more about the passing game. The camp was being run by Bill Walsh, who had been the head coach of the San Francisco 49ers for the previous two years. Walsh's teams had gone 2-14 and 6-10 and seemed headed for yet another bad season, though his recently promoted quarterback, Joe Montana, was showing promise. Hal was there because Walsh seemed to be one of the few professional football coaches who had any interest in experimenting with the forward pass.

Walsh had been a case study in the failure of innovation to pierce the thick, conservative hide of the NFL. He had played college football at San Jose State and had coached briefly with the Oakland Raiders and with a short-lived semi-pro league. In 1968 he landed a job as receivers coach with the American Football League expansion Cincinnati Bengals under head coach and part owner Paul Brown and was later named quarterbacks coach. He quickly turned an inept passing team into an extremely efficient one. Using an offense characterized by short, quick passes, his quarterback, Virgil Carter—a weak-armed passer whose trademarks were 20-yard wounded ducks—led the league in completion percentage in 1971. Walsh had, in effect, designed a system around Carter's weakness. Carter's successor, Ken Anderson, performed even better. In 1973 the Bengals went 10-4. In 1975 they went 11-3 and qualified as the AFC wild card team for the playoffs.

But in spite of the extraordinary things Walsh had done, he and other coaches who were perceived to be innovators of the forward pass were still not welcome in the NFL (which the Bengals had joined in 1970). In 1975 he was skipped over by Paul Brown for promotion to head coach. As Walsh later discovered, Brown had not only snubbed him but had actively worked against his candidacy for other head coaching jobs in the league. Brown—a man sitting astride the old and new worlds of football—thus seemed oddly torn: He wouldn't promote Walsh but wouldn't let anyone else have him either. Walsh left the Bengals, coached briefly with the San Diego

Chargers and then at Stanford, where, as head coach, his quarter-backs led the nation in passing in 1977 and 1978.

At the close of their losing 1980 campaign, the 49ers had won three games in a row and three of their last five, most notably a game against the New Orleans Saints when they had come back from a 35–7 halftime deficit to win, 38–35. Hal saw how quickly the team was improving, and how Walsh was making great progress with a lot of players with ordinary physical skills, starting with Joe Montana. As Hal saw it, there was a reason Montana was drafted 82nd overall in 1979 and so many teams had passed on him: He did not have the physical skills they were looking for. They wanted big, strong throwers, and scouts had given Montana's arm uniformly poor ratings. Receivers like Dwight Clark—a 10th-round pick—were competent but not very fast, with nowhere near the speed that some of the other teams' burners had.

What Hal saw at Walsh's training camp completely changed the way he thought about football. It turned out that Walsh, who had originally crafted his offense to compensate for the weak arm of Virgil Carter, had actually made a major discovery: that he could operate a fully integrated *system* based on precise timing and short passes that ordinary players could execute. This led to an even more radical concept: that players, and even quarterbacks, were not as important as the system itself. This was just the sort of big idea that Hal was looking for.

The root of what would soon become famous as the "West Coast offense" was timing. Walsh designed plays so that the steps taken by the quarterback in his three- or five-step drop and the steps the receivers took running their routes were perfectly synchronized. When Montana's right foot hit the ground on his fifth step, the ball was in the air; he knew exactly where the receiver would be and threw to that spot. He had a progression of reads that told him which receivers to look for, and in which order. The passes were mostly short; they were also meant to stretch the field horizontally. Most offenses measured passing by vertical depth: Walsh was happy to beat defenses with 2- and 5-yard passes. On some of his routes, he let his receivers read the field, settling in seams and gaps in zone coverage or running like mad if they saw they were covered one-on-one.*

The idea underlying it all was strikingly simple. Find a quarterback with a fast release, then get as many completions as you could to receivers who could run with the ball, using the full width of the field. Even more amazing than the concept's excruciating obviousness was that no one had ever thought of it before. Walsh's West Coast offense brought the term "yards after catch" into the lexicon of American football.

What Walsh was doing was not easy. It required many repetitions and much practice. But once mastered a team could do something that no one since Sammy Baugh had done well: control the ball and dominate time of possession using passes the way teams usually use their run games. You could win 17–14 on ball control. It wasn't necessarily pretty. It wasn't a glamorous vertical passing attack with balls arcing magnificently 40 or 50 yards downfield (though Walsh did have a deep game, too). And it was roughly balanced with the running game. But Walsh proved that you could win with passing in an entirely different way than had ever been conceived before.

He preached other heresies, too. One that Hal particularly loved was that you could win without paying much attention to what your opponents' defense was doing. What mattered was the perfect

---

* In the years following Walsh's first Super Bowl win, his continued success would prove the point again and again. When Montana was injured in 1986, he was replaced by an undersized Dartmouth graduate named Jeff Kemp, who had had an unimpressive career, completing less than 50 percent of his passes. But in 10 games for Walsh that year he completed almost 60 percent and ended up with one of the highest passer ratings in the NFL. When he got hurt, his journeyman fill-in, Mike Moroski, completed 57.5 percent of his passes, among the best in the NFL. The next year Walsh replaced Montana with Steve Young, Jim McMahon's understudy at BYU, who was immediately sensational, calling into question just how singular Montana really was and at the same time proving what an efficient machine Walsh had built.

execution of *your* scheme. This was of course deeply subversive; coaches spent at least half their time worrying about the elaborate schemes their opponents had concocted to defeat them.

Hal was among the first coaches to understand what Walsh was doing, to realize that you could structure your passing game in such a way that the system itself trumped individual ability and performance, that you could build a consistently good team out of ordinary players. But in 1981, coaching at a run-heavy college in the Texas Panhandle, there was little he could do with this new knowledge, no way to put the information to work. In any case, his instincts were quickly proved out. Later that same year Walsh used his systematized offense to win his first Super Bowl.

Hal's final revelation—the one that tied everything else together— was vouchsafed to him in the form of another BYU football game. This one took place in 1985, and this time BYU's opponent was the University of Texas at El Paso, whose offensive coordinator was Hal Mumme. Though coaching football at UTEP was usually a thankless task, there was one aspect of it that Hal loved: He got to watch all the BYU film he wanted. In college football, before a game, coaches exchange film of their team's last three games with their upcoming opponent. Because UTEP and BYU were in the same conference, Hal would get to see BYU film every year. When other WAC teams sent their films to Hal, they often included their games with BYU, too. In its archives, UTEP had BYU game film going back many years.

Thus Hal had been in a position to do what few coaches had the opportunity to do, even if they had wanted to: watch and analyze, in depth, one of America's greatest passing offenses. Though UTEP was still a running team, head coach Yung had begun to let Hal call passes more often, and as Hal began to understand some of BYU's methods, more and more of the passes he called came straight from BYU's playbook. Or rather, straight from Hal's concept of what BYU's playbook might look like. No one had ever explained any of this to him or helped him understand it. He simply tried to copy what he saw on film. He was like a man who had found a radio and taken it apart and was now trying to figure out how to put it back together and make it work again.

On October 26, 1985, the BYU Cougars took the field in El Paso fully expecting to slaughter the hapless Miners. Everybody else had. UTEP had not won a game that year. The Cougars were the defending national champions. They had won 30 of their last 31 games. They were undefeated and ranked seventh in the nation. They were a 35-point favorite.

What happened next stunned the 22,061 diehards who had shown up to watch the national champs obliterate their opponent. Except for the first quarter, the Miners dominated the game. They won, 23–16, in what sportswriters called one of the biggest upsets in college football history. For BYU it was a full-blown disaster. The team was hurt by turnovers that included a 100-yard interception return for a touchdown. The Cougars missed field goals. They became flustered when Yung, in a classic backyard maneuver, rushed only two men and left nine back in pass coverage. But something else happened in that game—something with far greater consequences for the evolution of American football—and only a handful of people in the world saw it.

Hal had by this time spent years studying BYU passing plays. There was one in particular called Y-cross, in which three of the five receivers ran routes on one side of the field at different depths, while the other two ran short routes on the opposite side of the field. The idea was to flood and overwhelm the zone defense, and to give receivers multiple options on how to run their routes. It was BYU's favorite play—one that drove defensive coaches to nervous breakdowns—often well disguised by switching receiver roles or putting men in motion. Hal had been experimenting with it, trying to figure out how it worked.

And now he and his quarterback, Sammy Garza, unleashed Y-cross and its various cloaked versions against the team that had perfected it. To their amazement, they tore through the Cougar secondary. The play worked beautifully. They ran other BYU plays, too. One of them in particular bore BYU's proprietary stamp. That year the Cougars had played Boston College. While watching film of the game, Hal had noticed that BYU's All-American quarterback Robbie Bosco kept throwing what looked like bad passes to his receivers running vertical routes. They looked like underthrows, and the receivers had to slow down and turn around to catch them. Except that Bosco usually didn't make mistakes like that. Hal soon understood that Bosco was deliberately throwing just behind the receiver, to his back shoulder; any defensive back sprinting downfield and scared of being beaten deep would, in effect, be beaten shallow, as the receiver faded back to the ball. It was a difficult throw. But done right the play was nearly unstoppable. Because only the quarterback and his receiver needed to understand how the pass worked, Hal kept it out of team meetings and coaches' meetings. No committee was going to decide whether he was going to throw this pass. And he had Garza and receivers Larry Linne and Eric Anderson work on it every day in practice for a few minutes, running the route and trying to get the defensive backs to bite.

Early in the BYU game Garza had thrown a deep ball for a touchdown, over the outstretched hands of the cornerback. Realizing that this was the perfect setup, the first play Hal called on the next set of downs was the back-shoulder pass. Garza threw it deep, and just behind the receiver. The defensive back, fearing the same outcome as the previous pass, overran it, and Linne caught it. No one in the stands or in the television audience had any idea of what had just happened. To the rest of the world Garza had gotten a lucky completion on an underthrown pass.*

But there were a few other people in the stadium who knew exactly what Hal had done. They were all BYU coaches. The first

---

* Today this is a bread-and-butter pass in professional, college, and high school football. In 1985 BYU may have been the only team doing it; Hal had never seen it or heard of anyone else using that particular back-shoulder technique.

one to figure out what was happening was LaVell Edwards. The other coaches soon caught on, too, among them a linebackers coach named Claude Bassett, whose job it was to stop the nation's best passing offense in practice every week. He was flabbergasted by what he saw. BYU's staff came to the same startling conclusion: *The Cougars' own offense was being used against them by the worst team in the country.*

The result was not only UTEP's amazing victory, but a phone call to Hal after he had been fired at the end of that season. It came from Bassett, who said that BYU's quarterbacks coach, Mike Holmgren, was leaving to join Bill Walsh's high-powered San Francisco 49ers, and the school was looking for a replacement.* Would Hal like to come up to Provo and get to know Coach Edwards and the guys? "We have lost some games here," said Bassett, "but we have never lost to someone who was doing to us what we do to them."

Hal was of course thrilled to hear this. It was the first real validation of his talent as an offensive football coach. He would go to Provo as soon as he could, though that would not be for another year. For now he was jumping back into the ultracompetitive world of Texas high school football, with a team that couldn't beat anybody.

As he does so, in the spring of 1986, it is worth taking inventory of America's great passing offenses. There were remarkably few of them. The coaches who were approaching the forward pass seriously and systematically constituted an extraordinarily tiny group in the immense landscape of American football.

There were probably three teams in the NFL that could be considered passing innovators, one in the USFL, and three in college. Under head coach Don Coryell, the San Diego Chargers—the NFL version of BYU—were setting NFL records with quarterback Dan Fouts. (Hal had attended two of their camps in San Diego in 1980 and 1981, where he had learned to shorten the short routes that

---

* Holmgren would later win two Super Bowls, one as offensive coordinator for the San Francisco 49ers, one as head coach of the Green Bay Packers.

accompanied deep passes.) There were the Miami Dolphins, whose quarterback Dan Marino had set the single-season NFL passing record in 1984, and of course there were Bill Walsh's 49ers. In the USFL the Houston Gamblers under offensive coordinator Mouse Davis and quarterback Jim Kelly were out-throwing everybody. In the college ranks the radical passing attacks were pretty much limited to BYU, Mississippi Valley State, with its receiver prodigy Jerry Rice, and the University of Idaho, where Dennis Erickson's receivers were spreading the field.

That was it.

Though Hal had chosen Copperas Cove High instead of pursuing opportunities at the college level, what seemed to be a road not taken was really not at all. His decision to move to Cove, in fact, was only the beginning of career-defining relationships with Edwards and the other brilliant men who ran the wide-open, pass-crazy football program at BYU—relationships that would change everything.

5

Ballad of the Lonesome Polecat

Copperas Cove doesn't look like much. Like so many small cities in Texas, it seems to organize itself around resolutely drab commercial strips of fast-food joints, mattress stores, muffler shops, check-cashing operations, car dealerships, and convenience stores that run along the flanks of four-lane state roads. It is neither cute nor cozy, as its name might suggest, though once you get out of town, the land opens up and you find yourself in more pleasant surroundings: the big, lazy, green hills of Central Texas. What the town does have is close proximity to the country's largest military base, Fort Hood, which covers 340 square miles and supports 50,000-odd soldiers and 9,000 civilian employees.

You might think that such a socioeconomic engine would have produced tough, gritty football teams. But back in 1986 the opposite was true. Copperas Cove High School couldn't beat anybody. The student body wasn't much interested in football anyway, and the players who did show up to play tended to lack size, speed, and strength. And because they were often the sons of soldiers, they also tended to disappear and reappear at seemingly random intervals. Copperas Cove High played in one of the toughest high school districts in the state, which by extension meant one of the toughest districts in America, featuring such perennial juggernauts as Waco High and Temple High. During the previous season, Temple had beaten Copperas Cove 70–0 using mostly second- and third-stringers after the second quarter. No one had been surprised.

Yet it was here that Hal would spend the next three years in what amounted to a research-and-development tank for his scheme to master the forward pass. Because of the nature of Cove, Hal's challenge—and it was a very large one in a football-mad state that fully embraced the dogma of nonairborne offenses—necessarily had two parts. First, he had to teach teenagers to throw the ball and catch it and run with it. And he simultaneously had to show small, weak, slow players how to beat big, strong, fast ones. The two problems, he would soon learn, had a single solution. To beat Goliath, David had no choice but to throw, and if he could throw well enough, he would always have a chance of winning. Of course, the whole thing might backfire, too: Copperas Cove might end up being the ultimate proof that Hal couldn't coach anybody to do anything, and that passing itself was a bad idea.

In spite of the progress he had made, Hal was still an apprentice of the forward pass, a collector of bits of information about how it worked. To this point he had learned mainly by observation. In the games against Oklahoma State and BYU he had demonstrated a striking ability to use what he had observed. But to find what he was looking for he was going to have to sit, literally or metaphorically, at the feet of the masters. The problem was that, of the tens of thousands of football coaches in America, you could count the masters of the forward pass on one hand.

There was, however, one coach who had not only espoused wildly innovative ideas about the passing game and implemented them on the field, but had also managed to do what few football coaches have ever been able to do: articulate them brilliantly on paper.

His name was Glenn "Tiger" Ellison. He had been head football coach at Middletown High School in Middletown, Ohio, from 1945 to 1963. He had published a book in 1965 called *Run and Shoot Football: Offense of the Future* about a radical experiment he had conducted with his team, starting in the late 1950s. Somehow a well-worn copy had fallen into Hal's hands. At first glance, Ellison's methods seemed so extreme—sometimes almost humorously so—that they could never possibly work on the field. They represented a complete reordering of how the game of football worked, in particular how the forward pass worked. And yet Ellison had made them work stunningly well. Hal was enthralled by the book, and was astounded to find a kindred spirit. Many of Ellison's ideas were very close to his own, which had been deeply influenced by what he had seen in the BYU films. Tiger Ellison and LaVell Edwards seemed to view the open spaces in the field the same way. Many of BYU's plays seemed to rely on the same principles Ellison's did.

For Hal, the Ohio coach's 20-year-old theories amounted to a road map to an entirely new way of thinking about the game.

Sometime in the middle of the 1958 season, Tiger Ellison had a revelation. This was not one of those minor illuminations that persuade a coach to replace his starting quarterback. This was a five-star, shift-the-axis-of-the-universe, change-the-course-of-your-destiny manifestation. Ellison had been coaching football at Middletown High School for 25 years, 13 of them as a head coach. He was exceptionally good at it. He believed in the value of brute force. His motto, he said, was "Hit 'em so hard and so often with so much that they simply cannot stand up in front of us." His teams had operated most of the fashionable run-based offenses of the era: from Pop Warner's single wing to Don Faurot's split-T (Missouri) to Bobby Dodd's belly-T (Georgia Tech) to Woody Hayes's 3-yards-and-a-cloud-of-dust pulverizing T (Ohio State). His practices were brutal. His players did wind sprints until they threw up. Middletown ran the ball all the time, dominating and physically destroying its opponents. Passing was a minor diversion from the real game.

Then something unusual happened. The team stopped winning. All of a sudden the once-fearsome Middletown Knights were 0-4-1. They had not had a losing season since football began at Middletown, in 1911. One more loss would guarantee one, even though the boys had practiced longer and harder and sweated more than any team Ellison had ever coached. Instead of cheers from the stands came catcalls and demands for Ellison's resignation. Team morale had fallen so low that, after watching film of one game, its quarterback spent the night on the banks of the Miami River contemplating suicide.

One day a despondent Ellison happened to pull his car up next to a vacant lot where a group of elementary school students were playing a backyard variant of football called aerial. The passer was a slender boy who would scramble around while his receivers cut right and left, deep and short, trying to get open. That night Ellison got a scant three hours of sleep. He woke up in a fever, sat up straight in bed, and in a single blinding flash of insight saw the solution to all his problems and the salvation of the Middletown Knights football team. In the morning he rushed to his office to tell everyone about it. They all thought he'd taken leave of his senses. They thought he had finally buckled under the enormous emotional pressure of his own failure as a coach.

Tiger Ellison had, in fact, just come up with one of the most brilliant ideas in the 89-year history of the game. It just didn't look that way. For his idea involved far more than just Xs and Os, though those were quite brilliant, too. It was an *attitude*, a way of thinking that transcended the mud and mayhem, snot and slobber of the game on the field. It was, in fact, a way of thinking about life. "We forgot about work; we began to play," he wrote in *Run and Shoot Football*. "We quit being serious; we commenced having fun. We stopped our blood and thunder pep talks; we started telling funny stories." He immediately stopped everything they were doing and got to work teaching the boys his new scheme.

At the core of the idea was a formation, a way of lining up on the field. At first glance it really did seem like the product of a deranged mind, or what football might look like if it were run by early-20th-century Cubists. It looked, moreover, as though it would not even work on a lunchtime playground. One of Ellison's skeptical assistant coaches dubbed it the Lonesome Polecat, "because it stinks." In the formation the players were arranged like this:

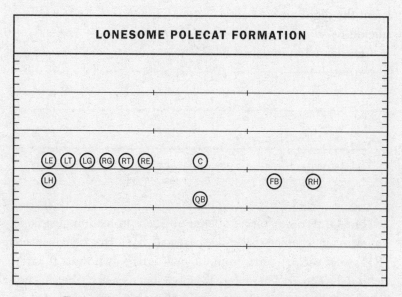

The Lonesome Polecat formation, with its wild innovations, became the vehicle for Tiger Ellison's "escape from reality."

Even casual fans can understand that this is not what they see on their television sets on Saturday and Sunday: The fullback and right halfback are spectacularly alone on the right side of the center, and the rest of the team is grouped, apparently irrelevantly, on the far left, with yawning empty spaces between them. For comparative purposes, a standard pro-set formation, in which the quarterback and running backs are fronted and protected by the wall of an offensive line, looks like this:

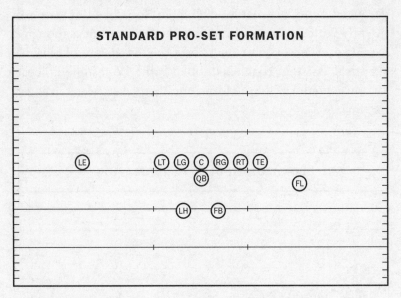

This standard pro-set—i.e., a normal-looking offensive formation—shows how weird, by contrast, the Lonesome Polecat was.

The Lonesome Polecat offered no such protection, just large chunks of unoccupied space. The left end (LE) and the right halfback (RH) were each 17 yards from the quarterback, who was 11 yards behind the center. There were five potential receivers, the left end, left halfback, center, fullback, right halfback. (Since the center was positioned on the far right of the line, he was an eligible receiver; the right end—RE—was not.) The whole contraption was wildly porous.

And on every play the five receivers sprint to the far corners of the field, opening up even more space. The following play, operated out of the basic Lonesome Polecat formation, was called the Dead Polecat.

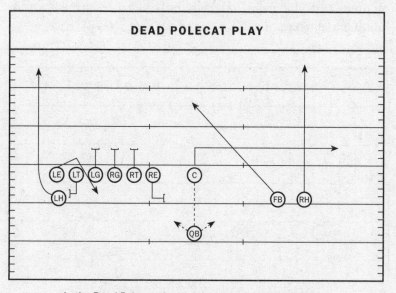

DEAD POLECAT PLAY

In the Dead Polecat play, receivers ran routes that forced
the defense to cover every part of the field.

The quarterback could throw to his left end, who'd make a jog step back toward the middle—this was his first read. But he could also throw to receivers streaking down both sidelines, running shallow outpatterns and zipping across the middle.

This all looks eccentric enough. But as the following diagram shows, the play begins to look even more outlandish once it snaps into motion. That's because four of the receivers can alter their routes *in as many as five different ways.* Their instructions are straight from the sandlot: If the defender was on his left, he'd break right; if the defender was on his right, he'd break left; and if the defender was in front of him at a distance of 5 yards or more, the receiver would make a tight curl and settle right there. If the defender was directly in the receiver's path and covering him closely, the receiver would stick to the original route, running as fast as he could. You can see the effect. Suddenly the defenders are facing what looks like a swarm of angry hornets coming at them, doing strange and unpredictable things, even though the basic routes themselves are quite straightforward.

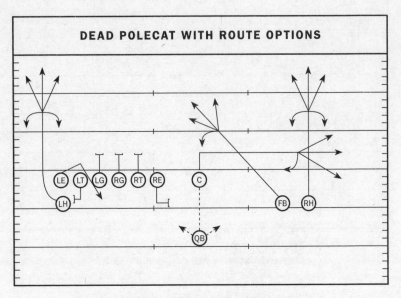

DEAD POLECAT WITH ROUTE OPTIONS

The most lethal thing about the Dead Polecat was that each receiver had as many as five options.

So what exactly was happening here? Mainly, Ellison was trying to replicate the joy and simplicity that he had seen in that vacant lot. He wanted the opposite of what he called the "graveyard seriousness" that had come to dominate his practices and games. This was it. Pure pandemonium held together by the precious logic of the schoolyard.

Ellison's unconventional scheme redefined the field of play itself. Instead of the tightly packed, massed violence of the traditional running game, with heavy bodies colliding in small spaces and snarling middle linebackers filling the gaps, there were now receivers spread clear to the sidelines, stretching the field obliquely with crossing routes or dashing deep into the secondary. The field was suddenly very large, and the appearance of all of this unclaimed real estate created serious problems for the defense. Instead of defending a relatively small, tightly circumscribed box in the middle of the field, defenders would now be forced to cover *all of it*.

The team's transformation was immediate and total. The Knights won their last five games easily, passing most of the time and completing 63 percent of their passes. Teams that thought they would take advantage of the apparently huge holes in the line of scrimmage were quickly schooled. The first team the Knights played after adopting the Polecat mounted a furious six-man rush, blasting right through those big holes. Middletown won easily, 34–0. Another team placed two of the district's fastest runners on either side of the center, sending them against the passer on every play. For their efforts they got no sacks and one deflected pass. By mounting a big rush in the middle, a defensive team was neglecting the sides, which were full of potential trouble. A quick pass to the left end, as in the Dead Polecat play, suddenly set the receiver up in front of a mass of blockers, who now greatly outnumbered their opponents. The Lonesome Polecat was also designed to allow the quarterback to scramble, rolling right or left and creating even more fluid chaos in the defensive ranks.

Perhaps the most important advantage the Polecat offered was that Ellison could take average players with average talents and beat much better players. This new game was all about finesse and not brute strength or even, necessarily, speed. It took the bludgeon out of the bully's hands. That was an astonishing concept all by itself.

For all of its innovation, the Lonesome Polecat was still an odd formation, and Ellison never viewed it as a permanent solution. As he himself pointed out, "we do not wish to sell the Lonesome Polecat as a basic offense. That would be a departure into insanity. We used it basically for half a season because we needed to escape from reality." But that offense became the precursor to Ellison's full-scale reinvention of offensive football, which he installed the following season. He named it the run-and-shoot.

The basic formation that Ellison's revamped run-and-shoot used for every play looked nothing like the Lonesome Polecat, though the underlying principles of the two systems were similar. The run-and-shoot featured a quarterback under center, a single running back, two wide receivers (WR), and two slot receivers (SR)—a total of four pass-catchers at all times and no tight ends. (See diagram below.) The set was perfectly symmetrical. The run-and-shoot also featured more runs than passes, though all plays were launched from the identical spread formation. Its trademarks were a quarterback who began each play rolling to the right or left; blocking that looked the same for both runs and passes; a willingness to pass on any down, anywhere on the field; and, the most important lesson of the Polecat, receivers who would adjust on the fly to what the defense was giving them. And like the Polecat, it was all about optimism and happiness and fun. The Knights believed they could score from anywhere. They hated to punt. They loved the freedom of open spaces.

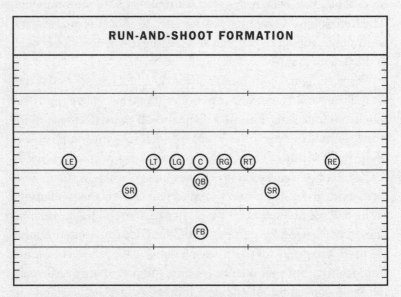

Operating out of the run-and-shoot formation—two wide receivers, two slot receivers, and no tight ends—the Middletown High Knights destroyed their opposition.

One of the run-and-shoot's classic plays, which inflicted enormous damage on opposing defenses, was known simply as the automatic pass. The play had its origins in the raw mathematics of the game. In this system, if the defensive back lined up 3 yards or more *inside* the offensive end's position, whatever other play had been called was automatically canceled. The quarterback said nothing but signaled for the ball by slapping the center's leg. While everyone else waited for the snap count, the quarterback took one step back and fired the ball to the receiver's inside shoulder.

The play was not only devastating to opponents who stubbornly refused to come out of their 5-4 defenses (common for the time). It was also structurally brilliant. When Ellison's ends saw the defender out of place, they were instructed to run at a 90-degree angle to the imaginary line linking them to that defender. This meant, in effect (as diagrammed below), that the ends were running one leg of a right triangle while the linebacker was running the hypotenuse. As any high school geometry student can tell you, the hypotenuse is the longer of the two. *Which meant that a receiver with average speed would win the race to the ball.* It is impossible to understate how revolutionary this idea was, though it would take many years before more than a few coaches understood it. It would become one of the key concepts in the great passing offenses of the late 20th and early 21st centuries.

Ellison saw triangles all over the open spaces on the defensive side of the field and systematically exploited them. For the next four years, he ran the run-and-shoot with phenomenal success. Playing in one of the most competitive high school leagues in the country, the Knights won 38 games and lost 7. They averaged almost five touchdowns a game, or one touchdown every 10 plays. The team was such a scoring machine that it was often hard to shut off, even after the third-stringers were put in. Middletown once piled up 98 points against longtime rival Portsmouth High School, in Portsmouth, Ohio.

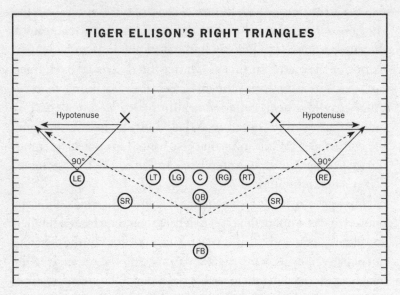

Tiger Ellison saw the field in geometric terms, where the elemental laws of triangles gave his receivers an advantage.

Because of his success, Ellison was celebrated among his peers in schoolboy football as well as in the college game. He received mail from all over the country. *Run and Shoot Football* sold more than 40,000 copies. But in spite of the book's popularity, Ellison wasn't able to build a large following among his peers. Many of them were happy, as coaches always are, to pirate individual plays. One of the few coaches to take his system seriously was Stewart "Red" Faught, who was the head coach at Franklin College, a small school in southern Indiana, from 1957 to 1988. He ran many run-and-shoot plays but never subscribed to the full orthodoxy, tampering with the system, mixing in wing-T plays, rocket sweeps, and play-action passes. Though he did well with it (his record at Franklin was 120-99-4) and his quarterbacks threw for impressive yardage, Faught labored in isolation and in obscurity.

Another coach who took selective lessons from Ellison's book was Jack Neumeier at Granada Hills High School, in Southern

California. In the early 1970s, Neumeier built what was probably the latter 20th century's first spread offense, usually deploying one back and four widely spread receivers. He liked the same read-option routes that Ellison did. He won a Los Angeles city title using the one-back offense and gained even more renown from 1976 to 1978, when John Elway was his quarterback. (Elway's father, Jack, would adopt this offense in 1979 as the head coach at San Jose State and run it with his assistant Dennis Erickson.) But Neumeier in no sense ran Ellison's run-and-shoot.

In spite of the book's brilliance, and Ellison's obvious success on the playing field, it had remained one of those allegedly influential but curiously impractical texts. True to form, the football establishment had watched yet another brilliant passing innovator rise from the undifferentiated mass of gridiron mediocrity, had nodded a few times in appreciation, then had gone back to the more important business of running the ball in the cramped spaces in the middle of the field. The magic, as always, was a delicate, fragile thing. Tiger Ellison had a huge piece of it, obviously, but like anything fragile, it was hard to sustain.

Ellison himself was, ironically, a classic example of what happened to his innovations. He ended his career coaching quarterbacks under Woody Hayes at Ohio State, the self-described "non-passing-est coach that ever lived." Ellison thus effectively buried himself under Hayes's cloud of dust for the last years of his coaching life. He did manage, after several years of badgering, to convince Hayes to run a few old run-and-shoot plays. But always out of Hayes's arch-conservative, full-house basic formation. Ellison never ran his old system again.

There was, however, one coach who not only believed deeply in the gospel according to Tiger Ellison, but also, through his remarkable personality and coaching talents, had the ability to introduce the run-and-shoot to a vastly larger world.

6

Of Mouse and Mormons

In the winter of 1984, Tiger Ellison's run-and-shoot ceased to exist in Hal's mind as a theoretical abstraction and suddenly became completely real. This profound change entered Hal's life in the form of a diminutive man who walked into his office at UTEP one day during the off-season. His full name was Darrel Davis, but from the time he was a 5-foot-6-inch, 160-pound quarterback for the Oregon College of Education, everybody called him Mouse. Even to his players, he was never Mr. Davis, or Coach Davis. Just Mouse. He had grown up in Independence, Oregon, with siblings named Birdie, Blackie, Teancie, and Tickie. Mouse was the youngest. It sounded as if he had been raised in a *family* of mice. In a 1979 article, *Sports Illustrated* suggested that "their mother's call to dinner sounded like an appeal for an exterminator."

He got his first head coaching job in Oregon in 1958. He was soon employing a basic run-oriented I formation—two backs stacked vertically behind the quarterback with a halfback in the slot. Coach John McKay had won a national championship at USC running the I, and the copycat world of football fell immediately and predictably in line, Mouse included. But he was frustrated. He wanted to make use of what he called "little pissant" players—like he'd been—small, fast guys who could make plays in what football coaches liked to call "space," which just meant all that green grass out there beyond the slugfest that was taking place at the point of scrimmage.

In 1965 one of Mouse's colleagues gave him Tiger Ellison's book, which had just been published, and it changed Mouse's life. Ellison's ideas were everything he had been looking for. He immediately installed the run-and-shoot and ran it continually for the next twelve years in three different Oregon high schools. Along the way, he produced some of the most deadly offenses the state had ever seen. He compiled a 79-29 record, culminating in a state championship with Hillsboro High in 1973. He did so well that he was eventually offered a job as offensive coordinator at Portland State University in 1974 and as head coach there in 1975.

Mouse was even more successful at the college level. In his first season at Portland State, his quarterback, June Jones, threw for a Division II record 3,518 yards. Neil Lomax, Mouse's second quarterback at Portland State, passed for 8,044 yards and 63 touchdowns in his last two years. By the time Lomax left he owned 90 NCAA offensive records. (Portland was a D-II school when Jones played, a D-IAA school when Lomax played.)* He once threw 7 touchdowns in a single quarter. From 1975 to 1980 Portland State averaged 485 yards and 36 points per game.

Some of the scores seemed to come from the world of pinball. Portland State beat Delaware State 105–0, Cal Poly Pomona 93–7, and Weber State 75–0, a game in which Lomax went 32 for 55 for 558 yards passing. No one anywhere was passing this much for this sort of yardage.

Mouse changed the run-and-shoot, too. Most of the fundamentals were still there, and the attitude certainly was, but where Ellison had operated an attack that used more runs than passes, Mouse made it a pass-first, majority-pass system. He sometimes threw the ball 60 or 70 times in a game. Lomax threw it 77 times in a loss to Northern Colorado in 1979. That same year he averaged 47 attempts

---

* Lomax later played for the St. Louis Cardinals of the NFL; Jones played for the Atlanta Falcons and Toronto Argonauts and was head coach of the Atlanta Falcons from 1994 to 1996.

per game, passing the ball more than twice as often as he ran it. By the standards of the second decade of the 21st century, when this book was being written, that may not seem extraordinary (though it exceeded those levels, too). But at the time Mouse did it, such a thing had never happened at a major college or on an NFL team in American history. Not on a season-to-season basis and not on that scale.

As it turned out, the frequency with which a coach passed the ball defined everything. At 10 to 20 percent, he was in the antediluvian slime with most of the retrograde coaches in America. At 55 percent, he was at the evolutionary cutting edge of the aerial world. His run/pass ratio defined how he practiced, whom he recruited, how much risk he was willing to take, whether he passed on first and second downs. It defined, really, what he thought about the game of football. In 1980—Mouse's fifth and last year at Portland State—the NFL featured a roughly even balance of passing and running: 31 passes per game, 32 runs. Even the so-called pass-happy offenses were relatively balanced or even favored the run slightly. From 1980 to 1984, years that included two Super Bowl victories, Bill Walsh's 49ers averaged 32 carries per game and 33 passes. Even the most prolific NFL and college passing attacks of the late 1970s and early 1980s, such as Air Coryell and BYU, threw the ball at most 55 percent of the time (think: 35 to 38 times per game). Mouse, who threw it 70 percent of the time, represented the first full-scale commitment to the forward pass.

The critical feature of the system, and the main takeaway for coaches who hoped to emulate it, was that *the receivers were allowed to make adjustments to their routes in the middle of the play*. This was the screwy backyard component of the run-and-shoot that most defensive coaches never managed to fathom. "He go right, I go left; he go left, I go right; he's deep, I go short"—as Ellison put it—was just too off-the-wall, too random, and ultimately too unsophisticated for men who prided themselves on fat, demonically complex playbooks. Though they would watch hours of Portland State film, they never could understand that Mouse was running only 10 plays (3 run, 7 pass). They thought they were seeing 40.

The importance of Ellison's innovation—and Mouse's improvements on it—cannot be exaggerated, though at the time few other coaches understood it or incorporated it into their passing games. One of the first to do so was Don Coryell of the San Diego Chargers, whose receivers often ran option routes—Kellen Winslow was the best example—and whose quarterback, Dan Fouts, led the NFL in passing. But Air Coryell itself was never widely understood, and for the most part nobody in the NFL or anywhere else allowed receivers to read the defensive coverage. Doing so meant that coaches were allowing *imprecision* into their systems, something they hated to do. And it meant allowing players to make their own decisions, something coaches *really* hated to do. As always, football technology moved slowly and imperfectly through the larger system. If the playbook said run a hitch or a slant, that generally is what the receiver did, no matter where the defenders were, and the receivers were yelled at if they changed the route. What those traditional offenses were doing was science. What Tiger Ellison and Mouse Davis did was something much closer to art.

When Hal met Mouse, the latter was traveling through El Paso on a recruiting trip. Mouse was coaching for the Houston Gamblers of the United States Football League, where he had landed as offensive coordinator and where head coach Jack Pardee had given him a free hand to install his beloved offense. That year his offense had the same sort of success it had at Portland State, only now it was happening on a national stage and under klieg lights. In 1984 his quarterback Jim Kelly (who would go on to play in four Super Bowls with the Buffalo Bills) threw for an astounding 5,219 yards and 44 touchdowns. He completed 63 percent of his passes, and was named Most Valuable Player of the USFL.

Hal was thrilled to speak with one of the few living masters of the pass—of an *integrated system* of passing, no less. Mouse, in fact, was not hard to corral. He was gregarious and full of energy and loved to talk. On this day he showed Hal in detail how the run-and-shoot worked, marking up a chalkboard while he told stories in his funny, volatile way. Hal listened, took notes, and tried to contain his excitement. The two men spent seven hours together, taking turns scratching out pass patterns and formations.

Hal was so interested in what he had heard that in the summer of 1986 he took his entire staff at Copperas Cove to a clinic Mouse gave in San Antonio. What happened there was an object lesson in the innate traditionalism of the football establishment. As Mouse spoke, describing the revolutionary principles of the run-and-shoot, the high school coaches began to walk out, first one by one, then in groups. There was nothing subtle about it. Their disapproval was crushingly obvious. They had no use for anything the diminutive coach was saying. Heresy was heresy. When the time came to take a lunch break, Mouse gazed out at the few remaining coaches, and said, as much to the coaches who were still there as to the ones who were walking away: "Well, when you all come back after lunch, we're going to talk more about these route adjustments and throwing the ball on every play and all that. If you want to learn that, come back. If you don't, well, fuck you." After lunch only Hal's staff and the staff of his friend Rusty Dowling, another passing zealot, who coached at Mission High in South Texas, returned. It was the same problem all over again: Coaches were not interested in such elemental changes to the game of football. All they could see was risk, and they hated risk. Mouse, like Tiger before him, was just too radical for everybody.

In his first year at Copperas Cove, using what Mouse had told him and what he had learned from Ellison's book, Hal installed an offense that took most of its plays from the run-and-shoot. He added a few plays from BYU and some of his own inventions. His team threw the ball far more than anyone ever had at Cove and in ways that had never been done before. The result was a 5-5 season. For most high schools that would have been nothing to brag about, but for Cove it was a small miracle. Over the past 10 years its teams had won a total of 14 games. They scored more points in their first game under Hal (34) than they had in the entire preceding season. He occasionally opened up the passing throttle; in one game quarterback Dustin Dewald threw the ball 40 times, and in another, 37, which, for a 48-minute high school game, was extremely rare. (Only a handful of Texas's 1,000-plus high schools ever threw anywhere near that much.) There was real output, too. Dewald threw for more than 200 yards four times.

There were moments, too, when Hal and his team saw glimpses of the power that the passing game gave them, even when they were at a physical disadvantage. In a late-season game against traditional powerhouse Westlake High, from Austin, Hal and Dewald had noticed that Westlake was blitzing the outside linebackers on every play. Though Hal called the plays, he allowed Dewald to override him when he saw that receivers were not being covered. He was allowed to call a "hot read" from the line of scrimmage, much like Ellison's old automatic pass. Blitzing linebackers, of course, meant that somebody was not being covered in the secondary. So Dewald would take one step back and hit his slot receiver in the space vacated by the linebacker. Over and over. Dewald kept hitting those hot reads while Westlake kept on blitzing. It was as though something in the circuitry of the team's coach, the legendary Ebbie Neptune, would not allow him to understand that he was repeating the same mistake. The result was a 53–10 rout and Cove's first win against Westlake. Dewald got so bored throwing the hot routes that in the second half he asked Hal if he could do something else.

This was progress, but it was a long way from a dominant passing offense. The total number of passes was still roughly equal to the number of runs; Hal was not yet running anything like a wide-open, "pass-first" offense. And as much as Hal liked the attitude of the run-and-shoot, its optimism, aggressiveness, and ability to adapt to defenses, there was much about it that he did not like. He was not comfortable with the strict formation requirements:

one back in the backfield, two slot receivers, no tight ends, which he thought left his quarterback vulnerable to a pass rush. He also found the run-and-shoot's methods of reading the defense to be too complicated. He preferred stark, reductive instructions, like the one he always gave his quarterbacks: "Never pass up an open receiver, never throw to a covered one." He was all about simplicity. That idea would, above all others, define his coaching style for the next three decades. The run-and-shoot was a stunning piece of technology. For Hal and a few other innovators, it reset the baseline ideology of the forward pass, and really of the game of football itself. And no one could deny the amazing things Mouse had done with it. But for Hal it was only the first piece of the magic he was looking for.

In the spring of 1987, Hal finally took LaVell Edwards up on his invitation to visit BYU's training camp. His relationship with the BYU coaches there had deepened during the preceding year. He had helped them with their high school recruiting in Central Texas and had introduced them to local coaches. At BYU's campus in Provo he found a warm reception—the masters of the pass welcoming a kindred spirit. He met the staff, which included offensive coordinator Roger French; quarterbacks and receivers coach Norm Chow; former quarterback Robbie Bosco, now an assistant; and the head man himself, LaVell Edwards. The team opened its doors to the young coach; he was given the run of the practice field, locker room, and coaches' offices. He was given full access to BYU's film room and—even more important—to their "cut ups," the team's own fully edited collections of their plays. That spring there were no other coaches with anything like that sort of access. That was partly because the BYU coaches admired Hal, and partly because, safely stashed away at Copperas Cove High, he posed no threat to them.

One afternoon Hal found Edwards alone on the sideline and

asked him about the origins of his offense. Edwards told him a story about how, during his first 18 years of being an assistant coach—8 in high school and 10 at BYU—he had experienced only three winning seasons. Then he made his discovery: BYU was never going to win by running the ball against physically superior teams, which most of their opponents were. What he needed was a "total concept" of a passing game that would use passes of all kinds—screens, sprintouts, sideline patterns, and verticals—to force the defense to defend the entire field, which Edwards pointed out was 53.33 yards wide in addition to being 100 yards long. BYU loved to stretch the field horizontally. The ultimate key to success, Edwards told the awestruck Hal, was that as the team got better and could recruit better players, "we resisted the temptation to become conservative." He said it twice, and Hal, though it would take several years before he fully understood what it meant, did not forget it.

Hal knew what Edwards and his offensive prodigy, Doug Scovil, had done in the larger sense. They had taken inspiration from one of the NFL's premier passing gurus, Sid Gillman, who had experienced his own revelation several decades earlier: If you spread receivers all over the field at different distances from the line of scrimmage, it was mathematically impossible for any zone defense to cover them. The challenge—and it was a very large one—was how to exploit that. Edwards and Scovil turned Gillman's idea into an integrated system that was based on vertical, horizontal, and oblique stretches and also on timing. The quarterback drops and receiver routes were synchronized so that the quarterback could throw the ball in what Edwards called "a specific timed sequence." If the defense disrupted that, BYU would revert to what Edwards blandly called "route adjustments." The latter were the read-on-the-fly components. The Cougars wanted to control the ball with the pass; they also wanted to hit all the big plays they could.

Hal also knew that BYU's magic had more to do with what Edwards called "commitment" than with schematic black magic.

To play like BYU, you had to fully dedicate yourself to the pass, to being better at it than anyone else. Which meant you had to drill it all the time and drill it at the expense of everything else, which meant that the average coach had to give up his long rambling practices in which a little bit of everything was rehearsed. You had to practice routes and quarterback reads over and over—endless reps—until you got it right. The secret to BYU's passing success, Hal realized, lay in simple execution. Minutely coached, repetitive practice. Hal also loved the Cougars' arrogance, the belief among the players that they could not be stopped, that they could score at will. They threw deep on third-and-1 with the game on the line. The players saw offensive penalties against them simply as a way to run up that many more yards, to burnish their already-dizzying stats.

Hal was so thrilled with his trip to BYU that he returned the next year, twice. The result was that he abandoned the run-and-shoot's plays and formations—though not its ideas—and installed a system like BYU's based on its standard two-back, one-tight-end, three-wide-receivers package. Though he made progress in reordering the way Cove played the game, he lost many more games than he won. The team was 3-6-1, and the next year it was 4-6. In Cove terms, this was success. Hal won a total of 12 games in three years, which the fans thought was a significant achievement. His players had beaten three district rivals they had never before beaten, including Temple (28–21 in 1988). They had their first-ever All-State player. Their quarterback in 1988, Billy Parks, ranked fifth in the state for total yardage.

But they were still far from Hal's goal of the sort of pass-first offense Mouse Davis operated, and Hal could not see, based on the talent available to him, that he could do much more than he had done. Hal's Cove teams remained roughly balanced between run and pass. In 1988 Parks passed the ball an average of 25 times per game, well above the Texas high school average, but nowhere near the 40-plus times a game that a quarterback named Lupe Rodriguez at Mission High was throwing. (Rodriguez led the nation in passing in 1987 and 1988 under coach Rusty Dowling, a close friend and collaborator of Hal's, who had taken his system from a coach at Long Beach State.*)

But Hal was learning. One sign of his evolution in the Copperas Cove years was a pass play he installed with an innocuous-sounding name: quick screen. To say that he invented it is not accurate. Football is a game where hardly anything is invented anymore, and that has been true for a long time.† But it is absolutely true that he discovered it, recognized it for what it was, pulled it from obscurity, modified it brilliantly, and turned it into a play that soon became a staple of American football at all levels.

The quick screen was actually a synthesis of two radically different concepts. In the early 1980s, Hal had heard USC coach John Robinson speak in Los Angeles. During the speech, he talked about what was probably USC's most famous play: the sweep right, known to millions of football fans as Student Body Right. The idea was to bring overwhelming force to bear on one side of the line. The quarterback pitched the ball to the tailback, who followed everyone

---

* In the vast high school football landscape of Texas in those days, only a few teams were running pass-heavy offenses. One was Southwest High School, in San Antonio, coached by Sonny Detmer and featuring his Heisman-to-be son, Ty. In the late 1970s a coach named Ronnie Thompson at Jefferson High School, in Port Arthur, had been considered "pass happy." (His offense, too, had featured an outstanding quarterback: Todd Dodge, who would go on to play at the University of Texas.)

† It is a cliché of the football business that nothing is ever invented; everything is copied, stolen, or, more politely, *synthesized*. Though Clark Shaughnessy gets credit for "inventing" the revolutionary T formation in 1940, it was actually created by Walter Camp in the 19th century. Though the spread offense is widely considered to be a development of the late 20th and early 21st centuries, Dutch Meyer was deploying a formation with four spread receivers at TCU in the 1930s, and according to Meyer it was already old by then. (One of the pioneers of this style of offense was actually a home for orphans in Fort Worth, Texas, in the 1930s.) "Option" offenses were around for more than two decades before Emory Bellard and Darrell Royal "invented" the triple-option wishbone in the late 1960s.

but the soda vendors around the right end. Its brute elegance is apparent even in diagrammatic form, below.

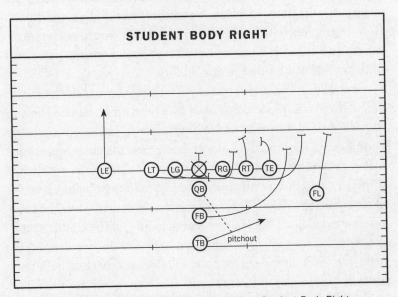

STUDENT BODY RIGHT

Hal turned USC's sweep right, also known as Student Body Right, into an innovative passing concept.

But it was not the raw power of the play that interested Hal. He was more interested in Robinson's description of what happened when the sweep right *did not work.* As Robinson told it, when the Trojans played good teams, they would call the sweep, and invariably the tailback—say, Ricky Bell—would take the toss, try to sweep wide around the right end, and be cut off by the defense. He would gain few or no yards. And the next time Robinson called the sweep right, the same thing would happen. And so on. Robinson would continue to call the play. And then sometime just before the half, the slightly gassed linebackers would get there just a split second late, and Bell would go 80 yards for a touchdown. Robinson's point: Even if you got no yardage out of it, you were making everybody from the nose tackle to the safeties *pursue* the play. They would take their pursuit angles and run like crazy until the whistle blew. That was what they were coached to do. They didn't want to be the ones in the film room who failed to appear in frame ready to gang-tackle the runner. Defensive coordinators loved gang-tackling. Robinson's play, whether it got yardage or not, forced 11 players to run at least 10 yards. Over and over. It took a cherished defensive tactic and turned it into a major liability.

Several years later Hal was at a coaching clinic when he saw a video of a play that was being used by a head coach named Darrell Mudra at the University of Northern Iowa. There was nothing complicated about it. The quarterback took the snap, spun, and threw a horizontal pass to his wide receiver on the right or left, who turned upfield and ran with it. The play had the obvious benefit of stretching the defense and making the defenders cover the field sideline to sideline. But Hal also saw instantly that he could use the quick screen the same way Robinson had used the sweep right: to make the defenders and especially the linebackers chug back and forth in their angles of pursuit until they were good and tired. He could turn the massed power play that looked like something from the 1920s into a sideways pass that would rearrange the geometries of the field and put the ball into the hands of his fastest receiver.

The alchemy was lovely. The play, moreover, was not really a screen at all. Screens were thrown by quarterbacks to backs in the backfield, sometimes just in front of the quarterback, sometimes just off to one side or the other. In any case it was a short, lobbed throw. A quick screen, by contrast, was often a *25- or even a 30-yard pass,* thrown very quickly and thrown very hard. A ball launched that far down the field would be considered a long pass. It was a pure horizontal stretch of the defense in the best tradition of LaVell Edwards and Bill Walsh. It was a way of making the defense worry about a much larger piece of real estate than it had ever dealt with in practice. If the corners hung back, they would be burned shallow. If they tried to correct that by pressing the wide receivers, they would be burned deep. The play also required meticulous execution. From the moment of the snap, the quarterback had just over one second to get the pass into the hands of the wide receiver; to do that he had to begin to turn his hips before the snap, then pivot like a second baseman turning a double play. It was a brilliant little scheme. Hal once called it five times in a row, just to make those hard-ass linebackers run themselves out of breath. Hal added a zone-blocking scheme, where the whole offensive line slid crabwise down the line, picking up defenders with oblique blocks. Hal called this "elephants on parade." The halfback had the critical block, picking up the cornerback, and the fullback slid forward just before the snap, then swung into the backfield to pick up the free safety. At the time Hal installed it at Copperas Cove, no one else was running it.

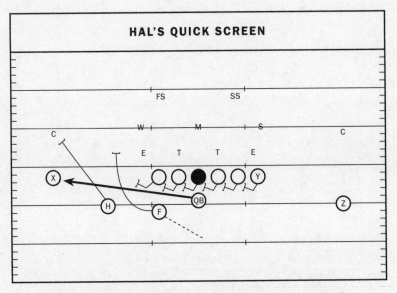

In Hal's hands, the quick screen—which, distance-wise, was really a medium-long pass—became a devastating horizontal stretch of the field.

With all the progress Hal had made, however, there was the inescapable truth that he had now experienced only three winning seasons in 13 years of coaching. He was full of ideas and some of those ideas were working. There was no arguing with statistics. He was not discouraged; Hal was a stubbornly optimistic person. But he knew two things as the 1988 football season came to an end: first, that he would likely never win more than half of his games at Copperas Cove—and he wanted many more wins than that—and second, that his apprenticeship at the feet of LaVell Edwards, Doug Scovil, Roger French, Norm Chow, Mouse Davis, Bill Walsh, and others was over. He would continue to learn from them. But he believed he already knew enough to build his unified system. He did not really harbor any doubts about this. He was ready to do something. He just was not quite sure yet what, or where, that was going to be.

7

Maybe the Worst Team
in America

Bob Prins had a problem. From his office in the administration building of Iowa Wesleyan College, where he was president, he looked out across a school that was steadily dwindling in size. In the 1950s there had been as many as 1,000 students enrolled at the campus in Mount Pleasant, Iowa. Now, in 1988, that number had dropped to 466 full-time students and a total enrollment of 750. The school had a minimal endowment; old and shopworn facilities; cinder-block dorms that looked like something out of the old Soviet bloc; a hulking, decayed gym built in the early 20th century; and an academic reputation somewhere between decent and unexceptional. The college boasted a bit of history. It had been founded in 1842. Abraham Lincoln's son, daughter-in-law, and grandchildren had spent summers in a house on campus. But even the school's claim of "uniqueness" had to be deeply hedged. On its brochures Iowa Wesleyan proclaimed itself to be "the oldest four-year, coeducational, church-related, liberal arts college west of the Mississippi *in continual existence on the same campus!*" (italics theirs). The school had a few lovely old redbrick buildings, which appeared in leafy settings on the covers of its brochures. From the right angles, it could look like any number of small liberal arts colleges in the Midwest.

But IWC was in trouble. Not immediate-bankruptcy sort of trouble, but trend-line sort of trouble. As though you could see the end looming on the far horizon. Lacking large reserves or alumni donations, it relied heavily on students' tuition for its income. That was slowly draining away. And the revenue problems translated into faculty problems. Many of the professors made $20,000 a year or less. The school had recently lost two popular business professors because the salaries were so low. Revenues were being squeezed, junior colleges were on the rise and competing for applicants, and the place in the world of regional, small-scale purveyors of higher education, like IWC, was being challenged. Prins was all too aware that a comparable small college, Parsons, in nearby Fairfield, had gone bankrupt in the 1970s and had been taken over by, horror of horrors, the Maharishi Mahesh Yogi.

Prins, a big, gregarious man with a goatee who smoked a pipe and whose manner reminded some people of Burl Ives, had been working hard on a solution. He had made a number of trips to recruit students from Japan and China and had succeeded in luring some paying customers to the windswept plains of southeastern Iowa. ("Asia is where the money is," he would tell friends.) But he needed more. He had recently shifted his gaze to the small town of Pella, where a tiny liberal arts school with Protestant traditions named Central College had figured out the secret to prosperity. Central's brilliant solution was, in a word, *football*. The school lodged a permanent group of 125 players on campus, which accounted for a large percentage of its student body. And the theory went that if you got those young men to come to your school, you would probably get their girlfriends to come, too. Other schools were using football to pad enrollment. Greenville College, a small school across the border in Illinois, had started up a football program a few years earlier and had immediately boosted its student numbers.

Football, then, became the keystone of Prins's new plan to turn Iowa Wesleyan around. There was just one large obstacle in the way: IWC had one of the worst, if not the very worst, football teams in the entire Midwest. Since its epic 91–0 loss to the University of Iowa in its debut game in 1890, IWC had compiled a long and storied tradition of getting murdered on the gridiron, interrupted by brief and inexplicable spurts of winning. In 81 years of continuous football, IWC had 60 losing seasons. In recent years the team had gone from bad to pathetic. The previous season, running a prehistoric single wing offense, IWC had gone 0-10, though its win-loss record didn't reveal the full depth of its incompetence. The purple-clad Tigers were often beaten by whopping margins: 40–0, 41–2, 52–0, 39–0. Their opponents scored 316 points to their 76. In one three-game stretch they scored only 8 points. IWC's other sports teams were losers as well. That year not one of them had a winning record.

The football team's performance on the field was just one problem among many. IWC had some of the worst sports facilities in the country, while many of the colleges it competed with for athletes—Iowa schools such as Drake, Coe, Central, and Simpson—were building sparkling-new student centers and athletics complexes. Hardly anyone, least of all Iowans, wanted to come to IWC to play football.

In the fall of 1988, Prins fired the football coach. He had enlisted the help of Chicago Bears special teams coach Steve Kazor. Kazor also happened to be a friend of Hal's. By coincidence, Hal had sent a résumé to Prins. When Kazor saw it, he called Hal immediately.

"Are you really sure you want to be head coach at Iowa Wesleyan?" Kazor asked.

"Well, I am not even sure I know where Iowa is, exactly," Hal replied. "But tell me about the deal. Do they want to win?"

"Oh, yeah," Kazor replied. "They are desperate to win. The president is a good guy, and very embarrassed at how bad the team is."

"How bad is it?" Hal asked.

"It's the worst football team I've ever seen," said Kazor.

A few weeks later Hal was in a car with Prins on the way to the airport in Cedar Rapids, being offered the job. Considering the team's performance, the facilities, and the utter lack of popular support (100 fans or fewer attended the games), Hal figured this was because Prins could not find anyone else. Iowa coaches certainly weren't lining up for the job, which had "career killer" written all over it. Prins, smoking his pipe, offered Hal $24,000 a year. In addition to that very low salary, which was a shade over half what Hal was making at Copperas Cove, Hal would not be able to fire any of the existing coaches, which included Prins's son, Eric.

Hal turned the job down flat.

A month later Prins called back, this time with a better deal. He could offer Hal $30,000, he said, and—underscoring what this hire was really all about—would pay an additional $500 per player Hal recruited over a minimum of 25. Which made Hal a sort of bounty hunter. He would let Hal raise money through a booster club and have his own radio show. And he could have his own assistants. (Hal had no problem retaining Eric Prins.) Prins would pay for the Mumme family's move. And Hal's wife, June, could go to school at IWC for free. On January 2, 1989, Hal accepted the job. He figured that, as bad as things were, he would probably have a clean slate to do what he wanted. He had no idea of just how clean the slate would be.

It is one thing for a Texan to see photographs of wintry northern places, or to watch a snowstorm hit Des Moines on the evening news. It is quite another to actually experience it, to *feel* the winter. When the Mumme family—Hal, June, and their children, Matt, 13, Karen, 11, and Leslie, 5—arrived in Mount Pleasant in late January 1989, Iowa was enduring a typical winter. Temperatures ranged from below freezing to down near zero and were accompanied by incessant, biting winds and several feet of snow. Hal and June agreed that this part of southeastern Iowa—about 250 miles southwest of Chicago—was the bleakest country they had ever seen. And these were people who had lived in the Texas Panhandle and El Paso.

Mount Pleasant itself wasn't so bad. A prosperous small city of 11,000, it managed to be both an agricultural center and a small manufacturing hub. The Bluebird Bus Corporation was there, as were small Goodyear and Motorola factories, which did good business employing displaced farmers and out-of-work farm labor. The town's center was postcard-pretty. Once a year, Mount Pleasant held an agricultural festival called the Old Threshers Reunion. It featured antique farm equipment and drew 100,000 people. June thought the town square looked like something out of a Norman Rockwell painting.

Hal's first official duty was to attend a press conference that was meant to introduce him to the community. He wore a coat and tie and had prepared a few remarks. But the audience consisted of a single reporter, Jim Rose, from the *Mt. Pleasant News*. (Hal learned later that local reporters would compete to avoid the IWC football beat.) Rose asked a few polite questions, and the press conference ended. Hal and Rose then walked across the snow-covered ground to the old gym, where a second meeting was taking place, this time to introduce Hal to his fighting Iowa Wesleyan Tigers football team.

If the press conference was a mild surprise, the team meeting came as a full-scale shock.

Waiting for them when they arrived were five players and one coach. They were assembled in an old classroom on the gym's third floor. Three of the five players had come with Hal from Texas. The coach was Mike Major, Hal's defensive coach. Hal and Major had coached together for 10 years, at Moody High, in Corpus Christi; at UTEP; and for all three years at Copperas Cove. The other two players were holdovers from the previous year's IWC team. One was a skinny guy who looked as though he did not play football; the other looked as though he might conceivably be able to hit somebody.

The meeting had been scheduled for 3:00 p.m. Hal waited. No one else showed up. The clock hit 3:10, and the skinny guy raised his hand.

"Are you the new coach?" he asked.

"Yeah," Hal replied. "Who are you?"

"I'm Bill Link, the punter."

"Well, where is everybody else?"

Link replied, in the dead silence: "This is all that came back."

Hal went ahead anyway with his upbeat, we're-gonna-win-some-football-games speech to the remaining players. He then explained that, in order to accomplish that, the team was going to be lifting weights all winter. At that point, the bigger guy from the '88 squad got up and walked out.

When Hal went downstairs to his office—a cramped, low-ceilinged affair in a dingy basement that looked more like a broom closet—he found several dozen phone message slips. He assumed that most of them were from coaches eager to apply for jobs. All but two of them, he quickly discovered, were from athletics directors looking for an inferior team—a patsy—to pad out their football schedules. It was a long-standing tradition to schedule homecoming games against patsies, and IWC was the perfect choice, an old-line, respectable name that you could beat the snot out of before your Homecoming Royal Court. One of the messages was from a man in Los Angeles who Hal thought sounded like a gang leader, offering to bring "his guys" to play in Iowa. The other was from someone who was actually interested in a coaching job. His name was Mike Leach.

Hal quickly found Leach's résumé, which was one of the most bizarre he had ever seen from someone who wanted to coach football. As the full story later became known, Leach had grown up in a Mormon family in Cody, Wyoming. He had been a scrawny kid and, as his high school football coach put it, "not a great athlete." As a teenager, however, he had excelled at coaching. When he was 15, he had done much of the management of his father's Little League baseball team. At 17 he had taken the team over and guided it deep into a state tournament. He had attended Brigham Young University, where he did not play football but earned top grades and had a number of run-ins with the honor code police about the length of his hair. He thought of himself, as he would say later, "as a basically religious person with some clear obedience and discipline issues." He graduated in 1983 with a degree in American studies. He went on to law school at Pepperdine University, in Malibu, California, where he received a degree in 1986, finishing in the top third of his class. He compared his time there to "an episode of *Baywatch*."

Here the narrative became more complicated. Instead of taking a job as a lawyer—which would have helped him pay off $45,000 in school loans—Leach did what no sane Pepperdine Law graduate would ever do: He decided to get a degree in sports science from the United States Sports Academy, in Daphne, Alabama, a school that had been accredited only three years earlier. For no particular reason that anyone could discern, he wanted to be a football coach. He took out more loans. His wife Sharon's parents thought he was crazy. A year later he somehow talked his way into a job coaching the offensive line at Cal Poly San Luis Obispo, a Division II school in California, where his salary was $3,000. (When he told Sharon that he would be paid $3,000, she said: "Well, $3,000 a month sounds like good money." "No," he told her, "it's $3,000, total.") Both Mike and Sharon worked odd jobs. His next full-time job was at College of the Desert, in Palm Springs, California, where he coached safeties and linebackers. His salary jumped to $12,000, and Sharon took a campus job to make ends meet.

That was where Leach was when he had called Hal.

As Hal would soon learn, Mike Leach was every bit as brilliantly peculiar as his résumé. When Hal called him back, he found himself instantly entangled in what he would quickly learn was a Leach trademark—a long, rambling, eclectic conversation that dipped and swirled and sometimes came back to the subject of football and sometimes did not. Leach was like a balloon: You tapped him and he drifted. He had a dry, cerebral sense of humor that sometimes left listeners wondering what he was talking about. There was something of the absentminded professor about him. He was obviously very smart, and he was totally consumed by the idea of coaching football.

Hal wasn't entirely unwilling to drift with this odd job applicant. He discovered that both men were intensely interested in subjects far beyond football. History, for one. Both men read a good deal of it. They also shared a key interest in one exotic corner of the football world. Though Leach was a rank novice, he had attended BYU during the ascendancy of its football program and had been an avid fan and student of quarterback Jim McMahon. He had actually drawn up plays, trying to figure out how the offense worked. Leach, like Hal, wanted to be like LaVell Edwards. He wanted to throw the ball around, destroy defenses, shake up the entrenched order. For him, as for Hal, running grew out of the passing game and was set up by the passing game, which was, of course, pure heresy among most American football coaches. Leach, too, was fascinated by Mouse Davis's run-and-shoot.

Leach was also interested in another coach, with whom Hal was less familiar: Dennis Erickson, who was then at Washington State. Erickson was one of the few sophisticated passing coaches in the NFL or college. He had branched off the coaching tree of Jack Neumeier, the California high school coach whose spread offense had featured John Elway. When Elway's father, Jack, had started running the Neumeier offense at San Jose State, his assistant was Erickson. Erickson, in turn, took the offense to Idaho, Wyoming, and then Washington State, putting up impressive yardage through the air along the way. While it was one of the first true spread offenses (Hal did not consider his offense to be a spread except in the sense of spread-out linemen), it was not a pass-first offense. Erickson was still run-heavy, as both Jack Elway and Neumeier had been. In 1987, as head coach at Washington State, his team had thrown the ball 37 times a game and rushed 41 times. In 1988, with star quarterback Timm Rosenbach, Erickson called 28 passes a game and 50 rushes. Still, Rosenbach passed for more than 3,000 yards and led the nation that year in passing efficiency.

Hal learned something else about Leach: The 27-year-old was very focused and very persistent when he wanted something. In this case it was a job coaching under Hal Mumme. Hal endured constant phone calls that often rambled long into the night. But Hal was already convinced that he needed him. His other choice for the job had dropped out because of the low salary. Hal was looking for someone smart to do what he told him to do. This included putting wide spaces between linemen, something most self-respecting O-line professionals would refuse to teach on principle. Leach had no such standards. The two agreed to meet in Provo in April at BYU's spring practice, where Hal made his now-annual pilgrimage to see his friends LaVell Edwards, Roger French, Norm Chow, Claude Bassett, and Robbie Bosco and to study film and watch practice.

The two men spent a few days together in Provo and liked each other immediately. Before the trip was over, Leach was hired. There was just one thing, Hal said, that Leach had to do.

"You're going to be my guy, and so you have to come out to Mount Pleasant and do a little dog and pony show on campus with the admissions people and the vice presidents," Hal said

"Okay, I'll do that," Leach said.

"Great."

"There is just one thing," Leach said. "Is it okay if I don't show up for the actual job until August?"

He then explained that he had managed to land a head coaching job for the next few months—in *Finland*.

Leach soon traveled to Mount Pleasant and spent a day meeting with the president and various school officials. He also met David Johnsen, the school's young athletics director. Leach told Johnsen a little about his brief coaching career, and that he would soon be coaching in Finland. But he seemed most interested in talking about scuba diving in California, a sport he had taken up while in college. It seemed that was all he wanted to talk about. Johnsen had an immediate, uncomplicated reaction: This is not a football coach.

Later Johnsen walked into Hal's office.

"What did you think?" Hal asked, grinning broadly.

"You have got to be crazy," Johnsen said. "There's nothing about him that seems like a coach. He is anything but. He wants to be out at the beach."

"What did everybody else think?" Hal asked.

"No one liked him," Johnsen said. "At all."

Fortunately for Leach, Prins had told Hal he could hire whomever he wanted, and Hal didn't care what the rest of them thought. If they couldn't see the great potential in Mike Leach, the hell with them.

8

The Future Does Not Exist

The starkest of all the problems Hal faced was his immediate and nonnegotiable need to find 50 football players. So one of the first things he did was to pack up his car and head out on a recruiting trip in Iowa. He spent nearly a month on the road, making big swings north of Ames into what should have been fertile recruiting country. He called on junior colleges and high schools. What he found, in place of interest or enthusiasm, was a staggering level of apathy. Everyone within a wide radius saw his little college as a place for losers. Coaches and players would look at him with dead eyes or sometimes vaguely sympathetic eyes, but the message was always the same: no way. At local Mount Pleasant High, where the players suspected they could beat the college team, the reception was even frostier. At one point Hal sent a message into an English class, announcing that the new head coach of the Iowa Wesleyan Tigers would like to speak with Dana Holgorsen, a talented young receiver who had supposedly committed to another school. Holgorsen sent a message back, saying that, all things considered, he would rather finish his English class. His response was typical.

Part of the problem was that, by the time Hal got up and running, he was already late in the recruiting game. He was left, in effect, with the dregs of the year's recruiting class, the players nobody wanted. Which meant that he was going to have to gaze out across America from his dank little basement and somehow find, within a few months, the ones with actual talent who had been overlooked, or had lost their academic eligibility, or had washed out somewhere and needed another chance. Then, if he could possibly pick such people out from among the true losers and people who ran six-second 40-yard dashes, he had to convince them to enroll at this perennial failure in the middle of nowhere.

So Hal set up a WATS line—a fixed-rate long-distance service—and a version of a boiler-room operation in the old gym with a couple of underpaid secretaries and some big, empty marker boards to keep track of prospects. He dispatched assistant coach Mike Major on a long recruiting trip that would take him through Chicago and its suburbs, down through Mississippi, across into Texas, where both Hal and Major knew many coaches and players. Major wanted to take a college car but was told instead he would have to use his own and expense the mileage—a decision Dr. Prins would soon come to regret.

Underlying all of the other obstacles was the money problem. As a member of the National Association of Intercollegiate Athletics (NAIA), Iowa Wesleyan was allowed to offer scholarships to players as incentive to enroll. That was the good news. The bad news was that the school had a total scholarship fund of $12,000. To make any real changes in IWC's program, Hal was going to need money for everything from facilities to equipment, team travel, and, of course, scholarships. By IWC's bare-bones standards, he would need a lot of it. There was no known source for such money. When Hal went down to his desk in the old gym, he was entering a strangely inert, silent little world with no coaches, no money, no players. The phone rarely rang. When it did, the call was from yet another coach in western Illinois or somewhere looking for a homecoming patsy. It was as though the future did not exist.

Mount Pleasant had never seen anyone quite like Hal Mumme. This was apparent to many of its citizens the moment they met the rangy Texan with his long blond hair, big grin, and big ideas. Kalen Henderson, the football reporter for the nearby *Burlington Hawk Eye*, met him and thought immediately that he was so completely different, so unlike her fellow small-town Iowans, and so implausibly sure of himself, that she was convinced that people were either going to hate him or love him. She could not tell which. "He's either going to make huge things happen," she told her husband, "or they are going to run him out of town."

She was right. On all counts, actually. Hal was, from the start, a transformative figure. Though he was very much the product of modern, urban Texas, there was a strong pulse of the frontier in him, and those who met him could feel it right away: an openness, a refusal to play by existing rules, a deep distrust of entrenched authority, and a sense of boundless optimism. He reminded some people of those Old West town promoters who invited their greenhorn clients to visualize what some dusty crossroads at the edge of Comanche country was going to look like some day. Imagine the town hall there! And the theater there! And a fancy hotel by the station! With his resonating Texas drawl, Hal even sounded like the frontier.

Most of the people he dealt with had no real comprehension of what "throwing the ball" might mean. If he told them that the team was going to look like BYU, they replied, "BY-who?" All they saw was the hustler, the entrepreneur, the man with an agenda and not enough time who was constantly pushing and always asking for money. Hal reminded Henderson a bit of Professor Harold Hill, the con man who arrives in River City, Iowa, in the musical *The Music Man,* posing as a boys' band organizer who ends up, against his better instincts, changing the town forever. Henderson didn't see Hal as a con man—not at all. But she knew other people who absolutely did. He was, after all, spinning an elaborate fantasy of a *winning* football team.

He certainly made things happen. There was the disaster of a weight room, for example, which was really just a large storage space in the basement of the men's dormitory. It had a moist sand floor, raw sewage dripping from the ceiling, and piles of junk everywhere. Hal persuaded Prins to personally raise money to refurbish the room. He convinced a graduate assistant at the University of Iowa coaching staff named Dan Wirth to be his strength coach for $10,000 a year.

He managed to rehabilitate a part of the old gym, as it was known, where the football offices were. The building, which had been built in 1922, was an ancient, stained, redbrick relic of another era with wooden rafters, a rickety wooden track above the basketball court, a swimming pool full of evil-looking greenish water, and a beat-up locker room that smelled of sweat from the early 20th century. In its cramped basement—with its low, exposed steam pipes and dingy snow wells that served as the only source of light—Hal carved out three small team offices. He bought lettering for an "Iowa Wesleyan Tigers" sign from Walmart, painted it purple, and stuck it to the wall above the desk. Then he installed some cheap track lighting, which he paid for himself. The office looked so appealing that some of the faculty complained that the football team seemed to be getting all the money.

At the team's practice field, which consisted of a pasture with clumpy grass and no boundaries, Hal put up a makeshift fence using poles and a windscreen. When he discovered the sorry state of the team's equipment—it was in such poor condition that the high school team had been giving the college team its throwaways—he persuaded a Burlington sports equipment dealer to give him a new set of uniforms and pads on a vague promise of future payment.

Hal's main problem was where to find some actual money. Since fund-raising for the football team is usually the province of the booster club, Hal went to see the president. The man explained politely that, while the booster club did not actually raise any money, at homecoming his wife and her friends did make cookies for the players. They put them in nice little bags that they placed in the lockers.

"We are going to have to do a little more than that," Hal said.

"Well, what did you have in mind?" the man asked.

"I was thinking about $50,000."

The man looked at Hal as though he had misunderstood something fundamental about the nature of reality. The meeting ended cordially, and Hal got up and left.

He quickly appointed a new head of the booster club, John Lance, part of a gaggle of middle-aged sports fanatics who breakfasted every day at a combination gas station, convenience store, and restaurant known as Dicky's Maid-Rite. Hal had been hanging out there because, while the Dicky's gang were not power brokers in the traditional sense, they were the informal center of the sports world in Mount Pleasant. They were also successful businessmen and professionals who had money. One of the semi-regulars was a man named John Wright, who owned a company that cleaned meatpacking plants and was one of the largest private employers in the state. Hal persuaded Wright to lend him his six-seat Beechcraft A36 to use on recruiting trips; Wright was happy to do it. It meant that Hal could travel to St. Louis and back in a few hours. Or go to Texas on short notice. When it came to impressing recruits, Hal in a sleek private aircraft was a very different creature than Hal in a beat-up car. The Dicky's gang also provided Hal's first outside funding: He convinced 10 of them to give him $2,500 each—a total of $25,000. Hal never had any problem asking for money. He was so good-natured and forthright about it that it just seemed to Lance and Wright and the others that giving him a $2,500 check was the right thing to do. He would need a lot more than that, but it was a start.

The main act in Hal's three-ring circus that spring and summer was still the recruitment of new players. There was little time and little room for error. Failure meant that there would be no football team to take the field for the first game of the season against Dubuque College on September 9. The work he and Major did was extraordinary. Once outside the state of Iowa, they had much better luck. There was, in fact, a world of players who had somehow just missed out on a scholarship to some small state school somewhere. Hal and Major found them everywhere from Michigan and Kansas to Texas, from urban junior colleges to rural high schools. In some places the gracious meal that Hal and Major were served in prospects' homes was fried squirrel. Texas was the richest vein of all. The two coaches also discovered that even the offer of a small amount of money to a player—like $500—meant that the player, who had seen his friends sign college deals, could get his picture in the paper with a caption saying that he, too, had received a scholarship.

Hal split his time between the road and his boiler room in the old gym. When he was in Mount Pleasant, he spent long days on the phone, running through the fat Rolodex of coaches he knew or battling with the admissions department to get students in who did not fit the model of white people from rural Iowa. Major was endlessly on the road, pulling up to high school athletics departments and private homes and musty old gyms. He traveled and worked so hard that he endangered his health. In May, he checked into a hospital to have nearly a third of his stomach removed because of ulcers. A few weeks later, when Hal joined him on a trip through Texas, Hal had to pull the car over every 100 miles so that Major could get out and vomit. Major ran up $3,500 in mileage expenses. By the beginning of summer, the player boards in Hal's boiler room in those cramped old basement offices were beginning to fill up. With what, or whom, no one was quite sure.

9

A Convocation of Rejects

By early August, when football camp began, Hal Mumme and Mike Major had been working furiously for six months. They had logged thousands of miles on the road and made countless telephone calls. They had cast a wide net. They had been desperate. They had extended offers to players they had not even met, on the word of their former coaches alone. While Leach had coached in Finland, they had scoured the back roads of East Texas and the junior colleges of Chicago's West Side, and now the recruits were standing in that converted cow pasture in the humid Iowa sunlight waiting to see what was going to happen next.

Such a group had never been assembled in the history of the town of Mount Pleasant. They were, to begin with, very black—40 percent—in a state with an African American population of less than 3 percent. The current senior class at Mount Pleasant High School did not have a single black student, and the previous year's Iowa Wesleyan football team had fielded only one. Now there were big-city black kids and black kids from small towns far from Iowa. They wore high-top fade haircuts and played Public Enemy way up on their boom boxes and were from cultures as different from rural Iowa's as hip-hop was from country swing.

A large number were Texan, too, which turned out to be a sort of foreign nationality with its own language, codes, and secret handshakes. White, black, and Latino, the Texans swaggered around high-fiving one another and talking about high school football games in places like Killeen and Marshall and Converse and Katy, that nobody else had ever heard of. Texans who had lived 300 miles apart back home would now greet one another like brothers. They automatically questioned the skill level of all non-Texans until they saw them play. There were other players, too, from Illinois, Kansas, Florida, and Missouri, and even four from Iowa, who had somehow drifted in with the rest of the flotsam. Standing in that pasture they looked as though they didn't belong together: There were undersized backs who looked too small even for high school standing next to immense O-line types who looked big enough to play for Green Bay. Most did not look like exquisitely toned athletes.

It would soon be apparent that Hal's wide net had caught an astounding variety of young men. Many were serious football players. There was Chris Edwards, for example, an academic washout from Division I-AA Stephen F. Austin State University, in Texas, who played wide receiver and who could run a bona fide 4.4 40. He was D-I material, one of the few players that Hal had absolutely no business getting. He had just flunked a couple of courses he needed to pass and wanted to play somewhere his senior year. Hal's orders to Robert Draper and Dennis Gatewood, his former offensive linemen from Copperas Cove who had come north with him, were to make sure that Edwards didn't get away. Edwards hated Iowa. At one point he burst into Hal's office demanding to be taken to the bus station and given a ticket home. Hal refused.

Then there were the recruits who seemed more like pure outlaws. Some of their deficiencies were immediately visible; others took a few weeks to come out. A certain number of the kids were just, well, kids, looking for love and fun and who just wanted to drink beer and party endlessly in McKibbin Hall, the only men's dorm. Others had more specific visions of what college life was supposed to be. Two of the Texans arrived in a mud-stained four-wheel-drive pickup with intentions of doing more than playing football. It was soon obvious to everyone that they were poachers—*road hunters*, as the other Texans called them. When they weren't practicing, they would cruise Iowa's farm roads, make their illegal kills, haul them back to a remote spot off campus to clean them, and then store the meat in their room, which was soon full of venison and squirrel and possum and anything else they managed to shoot. One night they were caught in the act, and later prosecuted. Soon they were heading back home. Another recruit stole the team manager's phone credit card, ran up a large bill, and then threatened the manager's life when he turned him in. Hal kicked him off the team, deeply sorry to lose his 4.6 speed. Some of the new teammates had spent time in jail. Some had been kicked off teams. Many had been given second chances.

Perhaps the most visible of the outliers was a huge, handsome defensive tackle named Curtis McDorman. He was 6-feet-8, 290 pounds of pure meanness from Triton Junior College, in River Grove, Illinois. You could see why Hal and Major could not resist him. Unfortunately he was a little *too* mean. McDorman was a fighter. He fought with everybody from the first moment, coaches, teammates, opposing players, friends, people he didn't know. At one party, he was in the middle of a fight when he put his fist through the side of a farmer's house and could not get it back out. Hal was called in the middle of the night to extricate him. At another party, he threw someone through a plate-glass window.

Hal had known something about McDorman. He had visited him at Triton, outside Chicago. At one point he was in the athletics office along with McDorman and his coach, who said to Hal, "Now, coach, you need to know one thing. This big son of a bitch right here, if he had any brains he would stop fighting everybody. He would probably be in the Big Ten. You need to know that he will fight in a heartbeat. Won't you, Curtis?"

Curtis nodded his head without looking up.

"But you don't have to worry about him much, because he never wins. Do you, Curtis?"

Curtis just shook his head.

The recruitment process had been, of necessity, a slapdash affair.

But there were also certain players that Hal had to get. There was the speedy wideout Edwards, who had been sat on and fought with and somehow prevailed upon to stay. Then there were the O-line heavies, including Gatewood and Draper, who were absolutely critical. Hal's dreams would die very quickly if he could not give his quarterback three or more seconds to throw the ball. Major had managed to locate an unsigned center at Joliet Junior College, in Illinois, who fit the model they were looking for: talented but flawed. His name was John Coneset. He was a tough, quick Italian kid who weighed 272. According to his coach, if he had been 6-foot-4 instead of 6-foot-1, "everybody in the Big Ten would have wanted him." That was the flaw. There was another complication: Coneset wanted to go to college with his buddy Andy Pryzbylski, a 5-foot-11, 230-pound guard who was not as highly rated. A couple of D-I schools were circling; Major figured that Coneset would soon be swept up by somebody like Western Illinois.

But Hal saw a sliver of opportunity. He could agree to take both players, which other schools might not do. He could also carve out a few thousand dollars from the small scholarship fund. The real problem was the campus visit, which would mean showing Coneset and Pryzbylski the minimalist high school stadium where they would play, the cow pasture where they would practice, and the dank, medieval gym where their lockers would be. What could possibly make IWC seem like a great place to play football? The answer arose like a shimmering vision before him: John Wright's six-seat Beechcraft A36 Bonanza. Hal had already used it to travel to Texas to visit recruits. Why not use the plane to fly recruits to campus? Thus Iowa Wesleyan dispatched a *private aircraft* to Joliet, Illinois, where it picked up the two awestruck young men and flew them to the airstrip at Mount Pleasant, where they were met by Hal and whooshed off to lunch and a tour. Five days later Coneset was back at IWC with his mother, who had cooked Italian food for the coaches. Both players signed.

Hal did a similar two-for-one deal to secure a receiver he had been trying to land out of Triton named Dereck Hall. Hall was talented but not quite good enough to play for the bigger schools. He was, in other words, perfect for IWC. He had a buddy, too, as it turned out, a tight end named Marcus Washington, who, in two seasons at Triton, hadn't caught a single pass. Washington was a nice kid, a "yes, sir," "no, sir" kind of kid, who had refused to quit in spite of riding the bench because he thought of the team as his "comfort" in the hard world of his upbringing and was convinced that football was going to be his ticket out of Chicago. Everybody liked him. Both young men had seen football and college as a way out of the dangerous neighborhoods where they lived.

Hal had assembled a team from scratch in a few months. Now he had to teach them a type of football they had never seen.

Earlier that summer, Hall and Washington had experienced exactly the sort of neighborhood violence they were trying to escape. They had been standing on a street corner next to one of their Triton teammates, who was headed to Illinois State to play football. He was also dealing drugs. As the three of them stood talking, several men approached their teammate. A fight broke out, Hall and Washington stepped back, and one of the men shot their friend in the head. He would survive, but in a vegetative state.

Like Coneset and Pryzbylski, Hall and Washington wanted to go to school together. But this time the deal was nonnegotiable. "If I am coming to Iowa Wesleyan," Hall told Hal, "Marcus has got to come, too."

Hal thought about it for a few seconds and said, "Sure."

The two young men soon committed to Iowa Wesleyan. The problem was that the admissions committee then rejected Washington. His grades weren't good enough. "He's not college material," one member of the admissions board told Hal. "We're not going to let him in."

Hal was furious. He believed that other applicants—from Iowa—had gotten in with similar grades. So he did what he had done before and would do again, many times: He went to Dr. Robert Prins to protest. Though Hal stopped short of suggesting that race had something to do with the decision, he was convinced that the committee was setting the standards higher for out-of-state black kids than for in-state white kids. Prins intervened. Washington was in.

Standing on the practice field in August, Washington felt nothing but lightness and happiness. He liked the polite, friendly people of the town. He immediately liked the swaggering, confident Texans, and he was already impressed with Hal as a teacher. Above all he saw IWC as a refuge, a place surrounded by cornfields and far away from the danger and chaos of his old neighborhood. He was ready to play football.

The critical part of Hal's equation, of course, was the quarterback. To run his offense, he needed someone who was smart, accurate, and in possession of a quick release. As it happened, those qualities were not what 99 percent of all other football coaches wanted. They were after what Hal thought of as the quarterback cliché: a big, strong, fast kid with a rocket arm who could deliver 50-yard frozen ropes downfield. If that player had been somewhat less than accurate in high school, so what? They would teach him accuracy. They would teach him to read the field and get rid of the ball fast. Hal believed that such players were extremely rare. Either you threw accurate passes or you didn't, and if you didn't, then there was little chance you could be taught to. And that talent was visible at the high school level. An inaccurate quarterback was like a one-legged man: He would always be that way.

What did matter was that Hal's quarterback could learn what Hal wanted to teach him. The teaching was going to be everything. Though Hal had never played quarterback himself, his experience at Copperas Cove had convinced him that he could teach a quarterback to decode the football field in a way that had not been done before, to see truth and simplicity in a world of deception and complexity.

In the late spring of 1989, Dustin Dewald was largely innocent of all such notions. He was a quiet, serious, 175-pounder who stood 6 feet tall in cleats. He wore a thin mustache and a shaggy blond mullet and looked perhaps just a bit too slender to be a football player. Dewald had been Hal's quarterback at Copperas Cove in 1986, Hal's first year. He came from a family of Cove quarterbacks: His grandfather had played quarterback there, as had his father and his older brother. He had quickly picked up the modified run-and-shoot system that Hal ran that year, starting each play under center and rolling either right or left on every play, then either passing the ball, sprinting around into the flat, or handing the ball off. He had learned a couple of the BYU plays. He got the concepts of receivers reading defenses, and of a quarterback understanding how and why they were making those reads. He had a natural ability to keep his eyes downfield and to instantly tell a zone from a man defense. He also had a release that was so fast that he seemed to launch the ball from the top of his shoulder pads. That season he had done what few high school quarterbacks in Texas would do: throw for more than 200 yards in five successive games.

All of this grew out of his close relationship with Hal. Dewald had always played sports in the shadow of his older brother, who had been the quarterback on the previous year's team and the reason Dewald did not start at that position until he was a senior. He had spent his life hearing how great his older brother was. Under Hal's tutelage he had defied all expectations; he had not only emerged from his brother's shadow but had outperformed him.

There was something else about Dewald, too. Though he was not outspoken by nature, the other players on the team clearly looked up to him. When a question came up, they invariably cut their eyes toward him to see what he thought. He was also willing to assume what amounted to coaching duties. Part of this involved babysitting one of the team's best players, who had a habit of missing school and practice and getting into trouble. Dewald took full responsibility for him, looked after him, made sure he showed up, and got him through what turned out to be a superb senior season. Though he was low-key and well-liked, Dewald was also quick to let his buddies know when they made mistakes. Hal saw him as a true leader; Dewald saw Hal as a brilliant coach who had made the game of football—which used to seem like drudgery on a terrible team—fun.

Dewald finished fifth in the state in passing that year and won a full scholarship to play at Stephen F. Austin State University, a highly rated Division 1-AA school in East Texas. Though he got some playing time as a freshman, what he mostly experienced was misery in the form of screaming, red-faced, hard-ass assistant coaches. They were the opposite of Hal, and a bitter disappointment. He hated them. He burned out. At the end of his first year, he decided to walk away from his scholarship and play golf instead as a walk-on at Tarleton State University. He was happy enough there, but he had not forgotten his days under Hal at Copperas Cove. And so it did not take a great deal of persuading for Hal to convince him to move to Mount Pleasant and play for him. He had three years of eligibility left; and now he had Hal, too.

In June Dewald, his parents, and Tiffany were loading a horse trailer for the trip north when a .22 Magnum single-action revolver Dewald owned fell to the ground and went off. He was angry at himself for letting that happen, but when he went to pick the gun up, his father noticed he was limping. A moment later they were all staring at a hole in his shin just below the knee that was pumping blood into his boots. He went to the emergency room, where the doctor removed the deformed slug with needle-nose pliers, an action that produced a loud popping sound. After the wound was bandaged, Dewald called Hal to tell him that his prized quarterback had accidentally shot himself and was going to be a little late in arriving.

Approximately 90 young men showed up for Iowa Wesleyan's fall camp. That was more than Hal had figured on and fewer than Prins had dreamed about, but in any case the number could not possibly hold. From the moment they arrived, players started dropping out. They had many reasons. Some had recoiled at the unalloyed horror of landing in rural Iowa. The Texans, in particular, felt that culture shock. There was the sudden reality of grueling two-a-days in hot weather. There were the usual student-conduct violations—drinking and getting caught during off-hours in the girls' dorm—and then there were actual misdemeanors and felonies. It was quickly apparent, too, that the academics were going to be demanding. Studying was serious business at IWC, and many of the professors had already targeted the "football guys" for special scrutiny. Most of all, there was Hal, who, in spite of what sometimes looked like *Dirty Dozen* recruitment strategies, had certain inflexible rules when it came to student conduct. Football players who only wanted to drink beer, smoke a little dope, cruise to parties in Iowa City, and blow off class were soon told to move on. By the end of fall camp there would be 58 surviving Iowa Wesleyan Tigers: 34 white and 24 black. Twenty-nine were from Texas. Half had come directly from high school. Half had played at some sort of college. For them—and for the small town they had descended on—it was already a whole new world.

This was the raw material from which Hal was going to build his football machine. He had, of course, recruited defensive players, too. They would be Mike Major's worry. Hal personally had little time for defenses, which he saw as inherently flawed and ultimately futile enterprises. He specifically hated defensive coordinators, who he thought were like offensive coordinators, only with 50 IQ points removed. "Maj," as Hal called him, was an exception to this rule; in any case, tackling the other team was going to be his lookout. Major was joined by the rest of a hastily assembled staff, a combination of full-time coaches (five, including Hal), part-timers, and volunteers: Mike Leach, David Johnsen, Eric Prins, Marshall Cotton, Dean Hamilton, Dan Wirth, and Kirk Soukup. This was half of what most colleges had.

Hal was going to think about nothing but that offense: his custom-tweaked, jerry-rigged synthesis of the systems of LaVell Edwards, Bill Walsh, and Mouse Davis that was going to put more balls in the air and score more points than anyone ever had before. It was strange to think, as he surveyed the remnants of his recruiting efforts, that these shaggy-haired rejects with their shirts untucked were the guys who were going to get him there. But he reminded himself that this was part of the idea: If he could design a system that featured passing and could be run by average or sub-average football players who could not throw like Dan Fouts or Jim McMahon or catch like Charlie Joiner or Jerry Rice, he could truly change the game of football.

10

Hal's Theory of Relativity

What Hal Mumme was proposing was an almost nonexistent phenomenon in the late 1980s in American football: to make a full commitment to the forward pass. That meant 50 passes a game, and eventually more than that. That meant throwing on first down and second down and fourth down. It meant throwing 70 percent of the time, or more. It meant violating that time-tested rule of football, which held that the run sets up the pass. Sacred tradition dictated that, by running the ball over and over, you persuaded those linebackers and safeties to stay close to home. You coaxed them closer to the crowded middle. Then, just as they were leaning the wrong way, you burned them with a play-action pass for 30 yards. That was latter-20th-century football at its best, smashmouth with a layer of aerial finesse. Anyone doubting that model needed only to look at the Pittsburgh Steelers during their first two Super Bowl campaigns. In their brilliant 1975 season, the Steelers ran the ball an average of 42 times per game and completed 14 out of 20 passes. We all remember Terry Bradshaw hitting Lynn Swann on those artistically perfect post patterns. But the typical Steelers play was Franco Harris breaking off tackle for 4 gritty yards, again and again. Hal's system would be the antithesis of all that. Defenders, strung out all over the field and punch-drunk from a relentless barrage of vertical and horizontal passes, would be shocked by a sudden blast into the middle of the line. BYU's magnificently simple draw trap, which often produced 50-yard-plus runs, was Hal's model. That was the theory, anyway. It worked well on the back of restaurant receipts.

Hal's ambition went against football's fundamental concepts of risk, too. Most of the football world fondly embraced the notion that passing was dangerous, both to a team's success and to a coach's career, with emphasis on the latter. It was difficult to teach, harder to practice, and depended largely on the abilities of a few players. If you threw the ball most of the time, that meant the defenders were expecting that you were going to do just that—they were *waiting for it*, for heaven's sake—which made passing even more risky than it already was. These were articles of faith among football's cognoscenti.

They were not just imagining things. In 1933 the average pass-completion rate in the NFL was 35.7 percent. The interception rate—interceptions as a percentage of passes attempted—was a shocking *15.4 percent.* This idea took root in the first half of the century and stayed in fashion for a long time. As usual, this was in spite of intermittent evidence that passing could be just as safe as running.

In three years at TCU (1934–1936), Sammy Baugh's completion rate went from 40.4 percent to 50.5 percent, far above contemporary averages. That was largely because his coach Dutch Meyer's game was built on "short, sure" passes, delivered from a rifle-armed quarterback sitting in what amounted to a shotgun. His completion rate went up yet again in the NFL, where his career average was 56.5 percent. (In 1945 with the Washington Redskins it was a blistering 70 percent, with only 4 interceptions, so far outside the statistical norms that it needs its own category.) But Baugh—like every other passing innovator of the first part of the 20th century—turned out to be the exception that proved the rule. The Meyer spread was considered a gimmick, placed in a box with the flying wedge, and shelved. Most people assumed that a talent like Baugh's, whether at the college or the NFL level, was so rare that it couldn't be duplicated anyway.

But the concept of risk was shifting. The game was slowly—in a long, wobbly line graph that started in 1906 and inched upward—improving in its execution of the forward pass. By 1943 the NFL's average interception rate had dropped to 10.6 percent. In the 1960s, the greatest downfield passing team of the era, Sid Gillman's San Diego Chargers, threw interceptions at a rate of around 6.5 percent, just above the NFL's rate of 6 percent. Completion percentages went up, too. Supporters of the pass liked to point out the rather obvious fact that, while a receiver knew exactly where he was going, his defender did not, which should offer natural advantages to the offense.

Still, there were a few sharp reminders of the lingering danger: In 1964 and 1965 Gillman's quarterbacks threw more interceptions than touchdowns (30 to 28 and 26 to 23, respectively). And in the 1960s the fumble rate for running backs was 3 percent—half of the interception rate—which suggested to some skeptics that by passing you were still twice as likely to give the ball away.

But the upward trend persisted. By the early 1980s the interception rate had fallen to around 4 percent, which meant that on average an NFL team would be intercepted 1.2 times a game. And completion rates finally hit 50 percent and climbed steadily upward, hitting 55 percent. Major colleges lagged but not by much. The clear message was that by throwing more passes, quarterbacks and receivers were actually getting better at it. Though this was statistically obvious, it swam upstream against the oldest prejudices in the game. Coaches could see it happening and still not believe it. The reason was that, for the first time in history, teams were devoting significant time to *practicing* the pass.

That idea might seem self-evident. But what struck Hal even more was its corollary. Though passing efficiency was on the rise as measured by completion percentage, interception rates, touchdowns, and yards, these were only *incremental* changes. Only a handful of teams at any level had ever committed to being true pass-first offenses. That meant that most teams' priorities, especially during practice and drill time, still tilted heavily toward the run. Hal's insight was that if you practiced the pass all the time, made it the focus of everything you did, you would see truly huge gains in efficiency at all levels. You would see completion rates in the 70s; you would see interception rates in the sub-2 percent range; you would see an explosion of passing touchdowns. In Dutch Meyer's 1952 book, *Spread Formation Football,* he wrote, "Through long years of experimentation, I have come to the conclusion that the pass is no more 'dangerous' than the run play provided the same amount of work and preparation has been given to the maneuver." That was the key: *provided that the same amount of preparation has been given to the maneuver.* Meyer wasn't some cockeyed dreamer. And he was, as history would show, right. Following that logic, if you practiced throwing passes all the time, and increased your number of passing attempts by, say, 60 percent or more—from 30 to 50 per game—you would unleash a staggering statistical shift.*

Thus the revolution that Hal was proposing would come about in the way his team practiced. To paraphrase Gandhi, the path itself would be the goal. Practice was, of course, a set of drills. But in Hal's conception it was also a mode of thought, one that happened to contradict much of the coaching dogma that had existed since Princeton played Rutgers in 1869.

Imagine you are in a jet plane, traveling at 500 miles per hour. You and a friend are sitting close to each other, tossing a tennis ball back and forth. From your point of view you see the ball coming toward you at a very slow speed, with a gentle arc. The ball's path covers a few feet. It's just a game of toss.

Now imagine that there is a person in a hot-air balloon who, thanks to a large window in the plane, is observing your little game

---

* Thirty attempts is just a rough running average of college and NFL passing attempt rates over the early 1980s. The NFL is consistently higher than college.

through binoculars. What he sees is something radically different. To him, every time the ball is tossed, it travels an enormous distance in a huge arc at 500 miles per hour (or slightly less or more depending on which direction the ball is traveling).

This scenario is often used to illustrate a basic idea of the theory of relativity. It shows how a single event can be experienced in two entirely different ways, depending on the point of view of the observer.

Hal did not sit around doing Einsteinian thought experiments. But the system he planned to build would operate on a similar principle: that his players and the opposing players would see and experience different games on the field. This meant first creating an offense that from his players' points of view was dead simple. Easy to understand, easy to teach, easy to operate. His offense, measured by the number of plays and formations, would be simpler than anything that was being done. Meanwhile, the opposing defense, like the observer in the balloon, would see the other side of that reality, a whirring, high-speed, multidimensional machine that looked so intricate and complex that even though they watched it on film over and over, defensive coaches still could not devise a way to stop it. The more complex and multilayered the defense that was built to stop Hal's offense, the better.

Simplicity against complexity was just the beginning of Hal's experiment in gridiron relativity. While the opposing team played on a small field, circumscribed by its traditional ideas of offense and defense, Hal's team would play simultaneously on a much larger pitch, stretched both vertically and horizontally. The dimensions of Hal's playing field were 35 yards (vertical) by 53 yards (horizontal). The enemy might practice on half that square yardage.

Hal's teams, moreover, played with entirely different assumptions about one of the game's fundamental rules: the number of plays a team gets to make a first down. If his opponent played a three-down game, his team would play a four-down game, a shift determined by the frequency of punts on fourth down. Hal instinctively hated to punt. He saw it as a wasted opportunity. To him his own 40-yard line was often not a punting situation. Sometimes his 30-yard line was not a punting situation. In a four-down set with no punt, *his opponent's third down became his second down,* which meant that the defense had entirely inappropriate and unrealistic expectations of which plays their opponents might be calling. This was a staggering offset, as though the two teams were not playing the same game.

If the other team was convinced that the main goal of football—other than winning itself—was to dominate time of possession, Hal's team would play as though that statistic was irrelevant. Hal wanted to score a lot of points, quickly. That was the idea. Holding the ball for long periods of time was not.

And so on. Two teams, two realities. They would diverge even more sharply as the new offense evolved.

Though his players at IWC understood that Hal planned to throw an unusually high number of passes, none of them except the Copperas Cove kids had any idea of what lay in store for them. Certainly not Marcus Washington, the earnest, hardworking kid with average speed from Chicago's mean streets who had not caught a pass in two years at junior college. As he went through August practices on the weed-choked field in Mount Pleasant, he began to think that something was terribly wrong. He had been excited to come to Iowa Wesleyan with his friend Dereck Hall, but now he wondered if they had not made a big mistake. What he was doing resembled no football he had ever experienced. His reaction to the first week of practice was, we will never be any good.

There were so many things *missing* from these practices. Most teams start with highly structured stretching drills. Normally they are like stationary military drills, tightly orchestrated. They allow the players to gather as a team, to look and feel like a team. Hal wanted nothing to do with any of it. Nor did his new coach Mike Leach. They believed that flexibility had nothing to do with speed or with preventing injury. There were flexible people and inflexible people, as they saw it, and no amount of stretching was going to change that. Panthers and antelopes and other wild animals did not stretch. Coincidentally, Hal was putting this theory in play just as the idea of stretching was becoming fashionable. On every corner joggers were limbering up. Yoga was enjoying a comeback. There were even people who believed that stretching was better for athletes than weight lifting. Iowa Wesleyan football players never spent a minute on it.

Nor did the team run wind sprints at the end of practice. Sprints had been part of football since its origins. They were the stripped-down essence of the game, meant to increase endurance, toughness, and will and to weed out the mentally weak and the spiritually suspect. There were variations that involved squat thrusts, burpees, sit-ups, and push-ups in between runs, but in the simplest version the coaches marked off 40 yards on the field, and then the team, already exhausted from practice, ran 40-yard sprints with one minute rest between them, preferably until they vomited, which many of them did. Some passed out from heat exhaustion. Kids hated it. Coaches, especially sadistic ones, loved it, particularly in high summer temperatures. (Legendary coach Bear Bryant was famous for running his players hard in 100-plus-degree heat and deliberately depriving them of water. At one of his camps in Junction, Texas, when he was head coach at Texas A&M, 60 players out of an initial 95 to 100 dropped out. The remaining "Junction Boys" were considered the gold standard for toughness.) To the delight of the offensive linemen, who harbored a special hatred for these drills, they never had to run sprints.

The players were even happier when they learned that practice would involve only light hitting. This was perhaps the most heretical of all of Hal's practice heresies. Most coaches considered hard, physical contact to be a key part of the Darwinian selection process that lay at the core of the game. Hitting and taking hits all week long hardened players for games and allowed coaches to see who their meanest and toughest players were. A spectacular hit in practice that resulted in a teammate's temporarily forgetting his name and country of residence might guarantee a player a place in the starting lineup. Players were encouraged to knock the crap out of their buddies, which meant that they were, de facto, encouraged to injure them. Many coaches refused to use tackling dummies, taking pride that their boys hit nothing but human flesh.

Hal saw things differently. Though he loved the game's bone-rattling brutality, he also understood the impracticality of encouraging full-scale violence at practice. He had watched NFL practices, which during the season were very light on hitting. That was a purely practical matter. NFL teams carried only 45 players on their rosters, compared with the 100 or more found on many high school and college teams. Their better players were paid millions of dollars. Coaches couldn't afford to beat them up in practice. When Hal first implemented his light-contact practices during the season at Copperas Cove, he was amazed at how much the players' parents loved them. "If your kid gets hurt," he would tell them, "he's going to get hurt in the game," thereby reducing by an enormous percentage the overall chances of injury. The offensive and defensive lines would have one-on-one pass-rush drills for 10 to 15 minutes, then they would work on the running game for another 10 minutes, and that was most of the hitting. Like NFL teams, they practiced a lot in shorts, shoulder pads, and helmets.

Finally, Hal's practices at IWC were *short*. Very short. Usually only an hour and 45 minutes. There was no large theory behind this. Like everything else it was a result of his deliberately uncomplicated system. He didn't need any more time. That in itself was a seemingly counter-rational idea. Why wouldn't more time be that much better? Wasn't practicing till you dropped the way to build great football teams? Time didn't actually matter to Hal. *Focus and purpose* did.

To the overwhelming majority of coaches in American football in the 1980s, what Hal was doing was purely for sissies.* You could

---

* By 2015, when this book was being written, football coaches on all levels had adopted this style of practice, but it was extremely rare outside the NFL in the 1980s.

almost hear Walter Camp protesting from beyond the grave. Football had finally been completely feminized. Passing had finally done to the game what its critics said it would do. Both at Cove and at IWC the reactions from outsiders had been consistent: Your players will never be tough enough to compete on game day. It won't work. Pittsburgh's Terry Bradshaw once suggested, apropos of a rule change to protect quarterbacks, that they should all wear dresses. Sentiments of that sort were widely shared by fans, coaches, and players alike. Taking sprinting, hitting, and stretching out of practice suggested a breathtaking apostasy.

While he was recruiting, Hal had told his players that football at Iowa Wesleyan was going to be fun. Yes, the facilities were terrible, the school was so-so, the girls were not as pretty as the University of Iowa coeds, the town was not exactly exciting, but they were going to throw the ball all over the field, and that was going to be fun. Practice was going to be fun. The recruits had heard from coaches all their lives only how hard they were going to work, how tough it was going to be, how much sweat and blood and dedication it was going to take, and how all that would pay off in the end. Hal did not talk about those things. He sometimes thought he was the only one in all of football talking about the joy of playing the game. He believed that football had somehow forgotten that. One of the things that made Marcus Washington so uneasy was that, in the heat of August two-a-days, he was actually enjoying himself. The coaches played Jimmy Buffett's "Cheeseburger in Paradise" through the loudspeakers and joked with the players about their girlfriends and hardly yelled at all. Nobody was screaming in anyone's face. If Washington and Hall were having such a good time, and there was no bug-eyed drillmaster pounding on them, *something* must be wrong. Hall thought they were being treated "like pros," which was interesting, since there was nothing about any of them that suggested "professional." Hall was not sure that they *should* be treated like pros.

Part of the fun was the simplicity itself, which was the radical innovation that underlay all the other more visible innovations. By the late 1980s the hundred-year-old war between defenses and offenses had produced a high level of complexity in game tactics. This trend was accelerated by the expansion of the passing game. With 22 players in motion on both sides of the ball, the permutations seemed to grow logarithmically. In addition to plays, the game had produced a dizzying array of formations and counterformations.

This shift eventually produced that masterpiece of diagrammatic intricacy, the modern football playbook. By the early 1960s George Halas of the Chicago Bears was already boasting that his players had to learn 500 plays. That number only went up. It became the norm for players, especially rookies, to lug around their coaches' phone-directory-sized playbooks, trying to commit to memory the contingencies that multiplied on every page. They were quizzed on it. Size and difficulty of the playbooks were seen as signs of coaching genius. There was something wondrous and impressive about a mind that could produce so many tiny variations of so many different plays. Observers of the sport spoke of such coaches with a sort of hushed reverence, as though sheer volume was a mark of excellence. To read one of these monsters is to not have a clue, much of the time, what you are looking at. In one NFL playbook, for example, blocking instructions for the center position alone on a single play read like this: "Block 50 (40) Punch vs. Time Look weak block back let defender cross your face leak out weak. Vs. Bubble weak block back. Be alert for DE on the pinch." This way of thinking was creeping into college playbooks, too, though in general they were less complex.

But the movement toward ever greater complexity had become an integral part of the game. The process was almost never reductive: If a coach found a new play or formation or a new twist, he simply added it to the pile. Play calls in the huddle began to sound like a new form of language. From an actual NFL huddle came this: "B reset I left wing U flex FB right HB Q8 crunch right flex y counter bone dq f boundary I right west squeeze new left toss 99 bust 6 check frisco halfback check slow screen right dynamite FB follow on ducks." Though this language is impossible for an outsider to parse, it seems evident that the play is so complex that the quarterback must tell players at each position precisely what to do in this weird, codified football shorthand.

Hal's offense did not have a playbook. Of any kind.

That was partly because he had so few plays, but also because he did not want to clutter his players' minds with a lot of unnecessary ideas. He had 15 pass plays and 6 rushing plays and various formations that these could be run out of. There was nothing to take home, no sheets of play diagrams to memorize. He did not actually want his players thinking about it. He did not even want them watching much film. The teaching was all live, all in practice. Where many teams had page after page of pass protections for the offensive linemen, for example—UTEP had had dozens of ways to attack various defensive formations, stunts, twists, etc.—IWC's man-blocking approach would have exactly *two protections*. Many teams had dozens of ways for the O-lines to account for linebackers. Hal had learned—in one of those shockingly elemental lessons from Roger French at BYU—to mostly ignore them. What an observer at one of IWC's practices would see was offensive linemen spending almost no time at all doing what football coaches call "scheme," the Xs and Os of football strategy. The idea itself was simple: "We don't practice mediocrity." Hal and Leach had come up with a list of training fundamentals for each offensive position. Practices would be devoted only to what was absolutely necessary to playing and winning. Thus they devoted all of their time to *technique*, even to the point of tedium, preparing themselves for the street fight that occurs when one man tries to stop another man from getting to his quarterback. At IWC practices it was all about "hands up, head back, stay square, punch the guy's numbers and don't let him hit you in your numbers, keep your feet moving." Over and over.

The running plays were the least complex of all. They were

drawn from the early 20th century: trap, counter, iso, sweep. They were so basic that most high schools ran them. Junior high schools ran them. Hal's stated policy was to assume that the players' high school coaches had taught them how to run-block. IWC wasn't going to waste time on it. In practice, the backs quickly ran through the running play drills but spent most of their time on the pass. With so little attention to the running game, one might have thought that Hal had no particular running ambitions. The reverse was true. He believed that he could produce a 1,000-yard rusher every year against shell-shocked defenses that were forced to account for receivers all over the field on every play. He didn't believe he would need 35 variants of a draw play to do that.

The rudimentary nature of the offense lent itself to rudimentary calls, too. In fact, Hal believed that if you could not call the play in fewer than five words, preferably fewer than four, you shouldn't be running the play. He had experimented with this at Copperas Cove and perfected it at Iowa Wesleyan. Thus play calls in the huddle were the opposite of everyone else's: brief and unadorned.

The snap count, called out by the quarterback to start plays (and taken from Mouse Davis, one of the few believers in ultra-simple play-calling), consisted of two words, every time. "Go. Hit." Hardly anyone else but Mouse Davis did this. Most teams went on "three" or "two" or something with at least some randomness in it. Hal believed that such extended snap counts were more useless clutter.

For those who thought that Iowa Wesleyan Tiger practices were just afternoon tea parties for a bunch of pansies, watching the sessions themselves would have quickly changed their minds. There was no wasted time. The moment the players arrived, the entire field spun up into constant motion, all of it involving specific passing drills and techniques. Balls were in the air at all times, arcing across the field. It was all throwing and catching and running routes and protecting the passer. Everything was done to a purpose. Instead of stretching or sprinting—or standing around watching others do drills—they were working on every phase of their offense every day, doing in effect what they did in games, over and over. It was like watching a group of people from an exotic island who only knew how to throw and catch balls.

The team's quintessential warm-up drill, the one that Hal considered as important as anything they did, illustrated his priorities. It was called "settle and noose." It was so simple that, as Leach put it, "it would insult the intelligence of a four-year-old." That was the point. In it, the quarterback dropped back and threw to a receiver who had "settled" on open grass between barrels. The quarterback threw to the shoulder away from the defense, whereupon the receiver, making the technically correct "noose" shape with his thumbs and forefingers, caught the ball and turned upfield. The catch and spin was everything and depended on the quarterback throwing the ball to the correct shoulder. Most coaches assumed that such throw-and-catch drills were a waste of time. For Hal it was the essence of his offense, the very method by which his players were going to out-execute yours. He would beat you at it because his players had spent more time, more actual minutes practicing it than your defenders would ever spend figuring out how to stop it. It would have sounded ridiculous to most coaches, but "settle and noose" was actually a touchdown machine.

Next came "pat and go" drills, slightly faster, where, at a slightly faster pace, quarterbacks dropped back and threw balls to receivers running routes with no defenders. Two lines formed opposite each other so that when the receivers caught balls, they could just go to the end of the other line. Very few minutes had elapsed, and though no stretching or wind sprints had been done, the quarterbacks and receivers had already logged many repetitions. It was all constant motion, constant throwing, catching, running. This was followed by "routes on air," an ingenious drill Hal invented at Copperas Cove in which five quarterbacks threw to five receivers simultaneously, representing the five "reads" each quarterback needs to know on each passing play.* The drill moved extremely quickly, as quarterbacks rotated positions so that they threw to each of their receivers as they ran their routes (which meant that even second- and third-stringers were getting reps, something no other teams did). Then they played with live defenders. The whole thing was a passing circus, with great emphasis on the precision of each route and the way receivers reacted to the defense. When a receiver caught a ball in routes on air he would always run and score a touchdown, just to get him used to the idea, accustomed to the real reason he was running that route. In every practice quarterbacks threw 250 or more passes—well beyond what any other team was doing anywhere or had ever done. There were oddball new drills, too: Coaches fired tennis balls at receivers and gave them Silly Putty to work their fingertips in meetings and had quarterbacks throwing into garbage cans to perfect fade routes; offensive linemen jumped rope and shuffled along long planks of plywood.

They practiced new ways of thinking about passing, too. One play, which they worked on every week, was designed for the moment they were trapped on their own 1-yard line. Its purpose: to score a touchdown. They had a specific drill that told players what to do when a play broke down, and the quarterback broke out of the pocket. The rule was easy to remember, and always the same: The deepest receiver on the side of the field where the quarterback is heads toward the end zone corner on that side. The deepest receiver on the backside runs toward the goal post, and everyone else scrambles like mad to get outside the quarterback's throwing arm so the only cross-field throw he has to make is to the post receiver. Even under fire, the field was being fully spread, the defense fully stretched.

Some of the magic was not immediately apparent. Because there were so few plays, the players focused in great detail on executing the

* Hal had invented it to comply with rules for athletic periods at Copperas Cove High, which in the off-season limited him to five players plus a ball. He improvised by using folding chairs instead of real boys to act as defenders.

ones they did know. Most teams, with their voluminous playbooks, could practice only a fraction of their plays during the week before a game. But Iowa Wesleyan could run through its entire repertoire in three days, with plenty of repetitions. Which meant that it was always giving priority to technique over scheme. Almost everyone else was knee-deep in Xs and Os. They were forced by time constraints to run a play once, then move on to the next one, which of course violated the basic cliché of learning: that practice, repeated practice, makes perfect. (Joe Gibbs, one of the great tacticians of the game and former coach of the Washington Redskins, once suggested that coaches should get rid of all but two of their run plays, and practice them all the time until they were very good at them and then run them against every defense they faced.)

The huge majority of these plays were passes, of course, which meant the team was practicing passing most of the time. As always, the emphasis was on what many players and most coaches might have considered mind-numbing repetition. Another point of relativity. They were playing a game in which practice consisted of few plays and high reps while their opponents were playing a game with hundreds of plays and few reps. Hal's dark secret was that he was going to beat them just the way those Pop Warner and Red Blaik teams won: by out-doing their opponents at fundamental football. There was no voodoo. Reps and execution were all that mattered, he told his players, repeating the mantra all season long. What mattered was the system that allowed them to do that. You could have said the same things about Vince Lombardi's terrifying ground offenses of the 1950s and 1960s.

11

The Air Show Comes to Town

Mike Leach was on a roll. He had spent the summer as a head coach—a head coach!—in Finland, a place where teams had names like the Porvoon Butchers and the Helsinki 69ers and where the players smoked cigarettes on the bench. And now he'd arrived in Mount Pleasant in August to work for a man he admired in a job that seemed to offer nothing but boundless opportunity.

There were just a few little problems. There was his $12,000 salary, for one, which was more than he had made coaching in the California desert but starvation wages for a 28-year-old with a wife, a child, and a baby on the way. There was the moldy one-bedroom trailer on the outskirts of town where they lived. Located in a junk-strewn trailer park, it was engulfed by three-foot-high weeds. The bedroom was carpeted with grubby, two-inch-deep, blood-red shag. The ceiling fan was mounted so low that the blades would sometimes hit Leach in the face when he crossed the room. The only good thing about the trailer was that it was free; somehow Iowa Wesleyan was picking up the tab for the hideous thing. The Leaches were so poor that the wife of one of the Dicky's Maid-Rite regulars had taken Mike's wife, Sharon, out and bought her a mattress.

To help support themselves, the Leaches took other jobs. Sharon became one of the football team's secretaries (the other was Tiffany Dewald, Dustin's wife), working for minimum wage in the basement of the old gym. Mike taught two courses at Iowa Wesleyan, criminal law and history, which he encouraged some of his offensive linemen to enroll in so that the course would have enough students. (Their goal was to send the young professor off on discourses about Apaches, pirates, scuba diving, or other unrelated subjects, and they often succeeded.) This was in addition to Leach's duties as offensive line coach, recruiting coordinator, equipment manager, video coordinator, and sports information director.

In spite of the hardship, all Leach could think about was how interesting this new job was, how remarkable it was to sit down with Hal and swap Xs and Os and dream up plays on paper napkins. It did not seem to matter to him that while he had coached the offensive line at the college level, he did not yet know Hal's blocking techniques as well as Hal's former Copperas Cove players Robert Draper and Dennis Gatewood did, or that he had never seen Hal's offense in action on an actual football field. He would learn all of that soon enough. Leach learned everything five times faster than anyone else, anyway. Most of all, he had a deep and abiding belief in Hal. No one believed in Hal Mumme more than Mike Leach.

As the August practices came to an end, other members of the team were starting to believe, too. Part of it was Hal's own industry. There had been no weight room; he had gotten them a decent one. There had been no football office; he had improvised one. There had been very little scholarship money; he had scavenged and begged and somehow had gotten more. He had procured new uniforms and equipment. For the first time, thanks to Hal's efforts, the field that belonged to Mount Pleasant High where they played finally had a banner that said "Home of the Iowa Wesleyan Tigers." To Tim Smith, the backup quarterback whose main focus was baseball but who had agreed to show up at the games in case Dustin Dewald got hurt, there was a sense that things were being done right, that someone cared about the team, and that, as some corollary of all this, there was very likely a method behind such carefully calibrated madness.

For many players, however, the new offense seemed either too simple or too abstract—or a combination of both—to work in an actual football game. The abstraction was enhanced by the fact that they did not practice in any conventional way and did not even have a playbook to keep track of things. There was a fluidity to everything, especially in the way routes were run. And nobody was certain that running just a few plays over and over until everybody got bored with them was a good idea. Nobody else did that, right? No sane person used "Go. Hit" for every snap count, right? Using just a few absurdly simple running plays was going to make it easy on the defense, wasn't it? By the time the season started, the Tigers had been working on their supposedly high-flying offense for less than three weeks. To many of those who had never played on a Mumme team—which was all but four of them—none of it seemed quite real.

The Illini-Badger-Hawkeye Conference, to which IWC belonged, was a purist's dream of how football ought to be played: on natural grass, at picture-perfect, brick-and-ivy campuses of small private colleges with names like Lakeland, Greenville, and Blackburn. Here, in the old Protestant heart of the Midwest—most schools had been founded in the 19th century and had Christian affiliations—scholarships were rare, corporate sponsorships were unknown, and stadiums were small and austere. For most of the players at these schools this would be the end of the line: The NFL did not await them. Nor did the Canadian Football League. This was football from some remote mythical past: young men outlined against a blue-gray October sky, playing for the sake of the game, for the untainted glory of victory.

The conference was not, of course, perfectly pure. Its member colleges were either, like IWC, part of the NAIA, which gave limited scholarships, or part of the NCAA's Division III, which gave no scholarships at all. But in practice there was not that much difference between the two. Neither had many recruiting rules. Members of both wielded a variety of financial tools other than straight athletic scholarships—state grant money, federal Pell grants, tuition discounts, academic grants based on test scores, loans—that could help an athlete pay for school. (Hal had his $12,000 in scholarships to divvy up among 50 or more players.) Most of the colleges had at least a handful of really good athletes who had unaccountably been passed over by D-I and D-II schools. There was the odd receiver who could run a 4.5 40, or the quick, agile 290-pound lineman who had not found a college home anywhere else.

The Iowa Wesleyan Tigers made their debut in the Illini-Badger-Hawkeye Conference on September 9, 1989. That day they made the three-hour bus trip to Dubuque, Iowa, to play the Spartans of Dubuque College. This was a nonconference game, but Dubuque fit the model perfectly: a Presbyterian school, founded in 1852, with an immaculate campus of stately redbrick buildings. The school was more than twice the size of IWC.

From the moment they took the field, the purple-and-white-clad Wesleyan Tigers were like nothing Dubuque's players and coaches had ever seen. If the latter had consulted film from the previous year's games—which they most likely had—they would have seen a single wing formation with an unbalanced line from out of the primordial ooze of the early 20th century. But, in person, what IWC actually did was even more bizarre. Its offensive linemen came to the line of scrimmage in *two-point stances*. Which meant that they were essentially standing up with their hands on their knees to face the defensive line, which was coiled down low in three- or four-point stances. IWC's linemen were not, moreover, actually on the line of scrimmage. Taking advantage of a technicality in the rulebook, Hal had instructed them to set up several feet behind the actual point of scrimmage, so that the helmets of the guards, tackles, and tight end were even with the center's belt.* It was as though they were

---

* NCAA rules technically allowed the linemen to have the tops of their helmets touching an imaginary line through the bottom of the center's jersey numbers. IWC's O-linemen were in this stance at least 80 percent of the time, as were its running backs, also a rare practice.

already retreating in fear of the defensive attack. In fact, it was one of the signature features of Hal's pass-first, pass-all-the-time offense.

Finally, and weirdest of all, there was a full yard or more between the feet of the offensive linemen. (Both the two-point stance and the wide splits were inspired by BYU's Roger French.) This meant that, instead of forming a solid wall, the men looked more like lonely islands on a sea of grass. It also meant that the line of scrimmage itself was a full 10 feet or more longer than usual, dictating, in turn, that the defensive ends, positioned as they usually were outside the offensive tackles, were the equivalent of a short bus ride from the center of the action. This was Hal, again, messing with the two teams' relative perceptions of the game. You want to play with a cramped, fortresslike line of scrimmage? Fine, we'll play with something strung out across the field that resembles a popcorn necklace. The clear message to the opposition: *We are not playing the same game you are.*

And then the whole odd contraption—all those Texans and rejects and juco kids and reclamation projects—whirred into action. Actually it sort of clanged and bumped and wheezed and shuddered. Though Hal had been teaching a full-field attack, long passes and short passes to streaking receivers who were often given freedom to adjust their routes on the fly, those lessons had not fully sunk in. There was no precedent, no model for such an offense. The players had zero institutional memory of anything at IWC. Most had practiced for only three weeks together. Dewald and his receivers—with the exception of Chris Edwards, who had played with him at Stephen F. Austin but who did not know this offense—were still on different pages of the nonexistent playbook. Run-blocking from two-point stances was a concept most of the linemen had never heard of. It seemed to some of them to be a ridiculously impractical idea. The defense—yes, there was a defense here, too, under the tireless Mike Major—had not yet fully sorted itself out.

The result: a big, sustained yawn. The Tigers lost, 22–19. They played sloppily. They were intercepted twice and penalized for 77 yards. The ride back home was long and quiet. Hal had gotten his players pumped up about how great they were going to be running this new offense, and they, and it, had let him down.

To anyone watching closely, however, the game represented something more than just Wesleyan's 11th straight defeat. For one thing, the Tigers had not lost 50–0 or 40–0. They had actually scored touchdowns. They were competitive. And though Hal's offense was not fully functional, Dewald had still managed to complete 22 of 36 passes for 283 yards and 2 touchdowns—by the standards of the era, a strong performance. He had even put the Tigers ahead in the third quarter with a touchdown pass. But the defense had been unable to hold on. The Spartans, running their traditional I formation, scored the game-winning touchdown with a minute to go.

Bob Prins was among those who were paying close attention. He had driven up for the game to witness what he had wrought, and he was thrilled by what he saw. Here was hope. After the game he approached Hal, shook his hand, and told him what an exciting game it had been and what a good job he was doing with the team. The next day the local paper added its verdict, noting in its headline, as though with some amazement, that the team had somehow "played well."

The following week Iowa Wesleyan went on the road again and lost again in the last minute of the game, this time to Culver-Stockton College, in Canton, Missouri, a team that had beaten them 41–2 the previous year. The Tigers had mounted a 92-yard drive late in the fourth quarter to take the lead, 28–24, on a pass from Dewald to Dereck Hall. With 100 fans cheering lustily in the stands, Iowa Wesleyan watched its opponents once again blow through the defense and score the winning touchdown, this time with 21 seconds remaining. Final score: 31–28. Though IWC had shown some improvement—the running backs had performed well—it was a disappointing showing. Dewald had completed just 15 passes on 29 attempts, stats that were not even close to fulfilling Hal's lofty ambitions. The loss was disheartening. With its big splits and two-point stances and receivers crisscrossing the field, IWC might have looked like a passing team. The statistics said otherwise.

But something had happened in that game that was not visible to anyone in the stadium. The final minutes against Culver-Stockton actually represented the season's pivotal turn, the moment everything changed. No one on the team could quite explain it at the time. After the game Dewald, who was more angry than anything else about the loss, decided that if the Tigers had replayed the two games, they would have easily beaten both teams. He had experienced a particular, exhilarating feeling on that late scoring drive that he put into words for one of his receivers: "They can't stop us."

The rest of the season had a completely different feel, as though some invisible burden had been lifted.

On September 23, the Tigers played their first home game, against the Grinnell College Pioneers, an undefeated team that had beaten them the year before. Grinnell's coaches apparently thought so little of IWC that when they sent over film of their previous game, the on-field action was intercut with shots of coed nude volleyball. The Pioneers played traditional football: lots of running, a little passing, and hard-nosed defense.

Iowa Wesleyan destroyed them, 49–7, completing 30 of 50 pass attempts for 408 yards and 6 touchdowns. To put those numbers into perspective, that same year NFL teams averaged 18 passes per game out of 32 attempts for 211 yards. And the NFL as a whole passed far more than the various levels of college football. Dewald spread his passes all over the field, too, hitting five different receivers for touchdowns. In what might have been an Iowa Wesleyan first—certainly in recent history—Hal was even accused of running up the score. Though he had taken Dewald out after his fifth touchdown and put Tim Smith in, Smith had continued to drive and score. "I can't tell Tim Smith to sit on the ball when he's in there getting a chance to play," Hal told the *Burlington Hawk Eye*. "So yeah it probably looked like we were trying to run it up a bit." Now that the machine had started to work, it was hard to turn it off.

The next week the Tigers rolled into Sheboygan, Wisconsin, and beat Lakeland College, the favorite to win the Illini-Badger-Hawkeye Conference, 21–7. Dewald was 28 of 42, and the team rushed for 167 yards. The following week IWC ripped through MacMurray College, 38–0, in Jacksonville, Illinois, piling up 679 yards of total offense and setting 12 school records in the process. Dewald completed an astounding 32 passes out of 58 attempts for 4 touchdowns and 436 yards. When backup quarterback Smith's stats were added to Dewald's, IWC had thrown 65 passes and completed 34 of them. No other team in America was throwing and completing that many passes. Only a few were even close.

Five games into his career at IWC, Hal had produced a team that was suddenly fourth in the NAIA in passing and fifth in total offense. And suddenly, too, this unexpected prodigy of passing found itself in what was being billed as a great game. IWC was matched against Greenville College, a Methodist school 40 miles east of St. Louis that had one of the best ground attacks in the country. A month earlier, a Greenville–Iowa Wesleyan game might have suggested the need for a mercy killing. Now it was the most exciting NAIA matchup in the nation, pitting the Panthers' devastating running attack against Hal's pass-crazy offense.

The game, which would be played at Iowa Wesleyan's home stadium, Maple Leaf Field, also matched Hal against a former colleague: Max Bowman.

Bowman had been the assistant head coach and offensive line coach at UTEP while Hal was offensive coordinator. Even then they had completely different theories of offense, and they had clashed repeatedly. Sometimes before games they were not even on speaking terms. It would be hard to find two more opposite people. Four years later, nothing had changed.

Greenville was one of the purest examples of the running game in the country. The team barely passed at all. Bowman distrusted the whole concept. Greenville instead deployed Bowman's unique, quadruple-option triple-I offense with three backs stacked behind the quarterback. With its layers of reads and options, it was like a ground version of Hal's offense. It favored finesse over pure power and was devastatingly effective. Greenville had beaten Iowa Wesleyan, 52–0, the previous year and was now undefeated and first in the NAIA in rushing. (Bowman was on his way to a four-year record at Greenville of 34-3-1 and would go on to be tight ends coach and assistant to the head coach of the Buffalo Bills.)

In the first half Hal offered an object lesson—for anyone who might be watching—in how to beat the blitz. An invention of the late 1940s, the blitz rested on the simple principle of sending additional players to rush the quarterback. It had been the death of many a passing team.

Bowman's strategy was to drive right at Iowa Wesleyan's strength: He called blitzes on almost every play. Hal's response was so unconventional that it seemed irrational. Instead of keeping two backs near the quarterback to pick up the onrushing linebackers, he emptied the backfield (with Dewald's eager encouragement), putting the halfback and fullback into slot positions outside the tackles. The idea: Bowman could blitz his linebackers, but Hal could send receivers to those open spaces and beat him to the punch. Dewald might get hit, but the ball was away, and so was the receiver. He was happy to throw short passes, quick screens, and back-shoulder throws all day. Of course, 10-yard completions often turned into 30- or 40-yard plays, especially with a depleted defensive backfield.

The Tigers shocked everybody, exploding to a 17-point lead at halftime.

In the locker room at the half, a furious Bowman told his players, "Get dressed. We're going home." The players, especially the coaches, looked at him in disbelief. "You heard me," he went on. "They're gonna beat our ass by fifty points because you're not playing. I'd rather lose a forfeit. Hurry up, I want to be on the bus before halftime is over." Bowman wasn't exactly sure what a forfeit was, but he left the locker room, dragging his furious, incredulous coaches with him. Several minutes later the team captains appeared at the locker room door.

"We're not going home," they said.

In response, Bowman laid a line of tape on the floor and told them that if they crossed it, it meant that they were going to score 18 more points than IWC in the second half. If they did not, Bowman said, he would take his two buses home empty and how they got home was up to them. "By the time I get home, I'll be fired," he said. They all crossed the line.

The crowd at the start of the game had been typically sparse. A few hundred hardy souls. Greenville had beaten IWC so badly the year before that no one expected much this time around. But as the local radio broadcast of the game crackled out into the county—in a place where not much happened on a Saturday other than the broadcast of the Iowa game—a line of cars began to stream into the parking lot at Maple Leaf Stadium. What the rapidly expanding crowd saw was an offensive explosion by both teams. Greenville's big option quarterback pitched and slashed through IWC's defense. Greenville closed the gap. With 2:30 remaining in the fourth quarter, Iowa Wesleyan drove for a touchdown, making the score 46–39. With less than a minute remaining, Greenville answered with its own touchdown. The score was now 46–45, Iowa Wesleyan. A tie would likely guarantee that Greenville would go to the NCAA Division III national playoff. To the delight of his team, Bowman decided to try a two-point conversion. Winning the game, they all realized, meant more to them than going to the playoffs. His team converted. Greenville won, 47–46.

When the game was over, Hal crossed the field to congratulate his adversary. "Bowman! Why would you go for two?"

"Because tying you would be like kissing your sister," Bowman replied. He put his arm around Hal, and the two walked off the field together. (Hal and Bowman have since become friends.)

The statistics showed what had happened on the field. The Greenville Panthers had rolled to 585 yards of total offense, 449 of that on the ground. They had completed only 5 passes. IWC registered 542 yards of offense. Dewald completed 26 of 46 passes for 436 yards. He threw touchdown passes of 44, 25, 60, and 35 yards, including key strikes to Marcus Washington and Dereck Hall in the second half. IWC's ground game had been strong, too—106 yards, including touchdowns by running backs Derrek Callis and Derrick Wagoner.

Most of the people at the game thought it was one of the best they had ever seen. The *Burlington Hawk Eye* gushed, calling it a "gunfight." And the meaning was clear to everyone who was paying attention: Hal's Tigers had taken on one of the best teams in the country and had nearly beaten it. (Except for a bad snap on a field goal attempt in the last quarter, they would have.) At this point in his first season he had rewritten most of the school record book, had a nationally ranked offense, and had lost three games by a total of seven points. Dewald was among the national passing leaders, Edwards was ranked number one in the NAIA in receiving, and even Hal's running backs, Wagoner and Callis, were ranked, number 6 and number 10, respectively.

The Greenville game had given the Tigers the feeling, too, that, while they could be beaten, their offense could not be stopped. The rest of the season proved they were right. They won their final four regular-season games. Most were blowouts: They beat the University of Chicago, 34–9. Central Methodist fell, 54–23, in a bizarre game that featured a bench-clearing brawl when Methodist accused Hal of running up the score. It was also the game that Hal, tired of watching his giant, violent nose tackle Curtis McDorman take cheap shots at the other team's players, kicked him off the team. McDorman retaliated by removing his uniform and padding in stages as he walked off the field during the game, finishing his striptease as he left the stadium.

IWC demolished Blackburn, 47–10, and finished the season by

beating Trinity College (Illinois), 28–18. Only Trinity, coached by future Minnesota Vikings head coach Leslie Frazier, gave the Tigers any trouble, roughing Dewald up and intercepting four passes. IWC played a post-season game—the Steamboat Classic in Burlington—against a nationally ranked Lambuth University team from Jackson, Tennessee. Though IWC lost, 55–41, the team again posted passing numbers that in 1989 looked more like they belonged to a pinball game than a college football team. Dewald threw for 425 yards and 4 touchdowns. Lambuth beat them, but couldn't stop them.

There were many lessons to be learned from the 1989 season. The first and most basic was that Hal's ideas worked. Many of them worked brilliantly, even when executed by hastily recruited players of average or sub-average ability.

The bedrock under the whole thing, the offensive line, was one of the best proofs. Hal's ultra-simple protections, which he learned from BYU, meant that his linemen never worried about the complexity of the defense or what the defense was trying to do. Leach, who had quickly mastered his job, had taught them to pick up twists and blitzes, and their two-point stances and position several feet off the line of scrimmage gave them huge advantages in the opening seconds of combat on each play. Blocking for the running plays was even easier. (Two of the plays were draws that were meant to look like passes anyway.) The handful of others involved zone blocking, the entire line moving in one direction laterally, opening holes as it went along. It all required great execution, but—and here was Hal's trademark—not a lot of thought. Against a normal, nonblitzing pass rush, Dustin Dewald usually had plenty of time to throw the ball.

But the offensive line's most striking characteristic—the wide splits—actually rearranged the geometry of the game. The oversized gaps worked in several key ways. Because they forced the defensive line to spread with the offense, they created running lanes. They made it hard for the defense to run stunts that would have lured

IWC's linemen into blocking the wrong man. They also naturally spread the field so that the quarterback could see it more easily. The middle was no longer congested and thus its hallowed resident, the middle linebacker, had lost a big part of his old game-defining power. In the early days of football in the 19th century, the middle was everything. In the era of Dick Butkus, Ray Nitschke, and Sam Huff almost a century later, the middle was still everything. The middle linebacker was usually the best player on the defense, tough enough to plug holes in the line and fast enough to cover receivers and rush the passer. Part of what coaches like Hal, Mouse Davis, LaVell Edwards, Dennis Erickson, and Bill Walsh were doing was a deliberate attempt to disarm him and render him ineffective. As the line spread wide and receivers sped to the far corners of the field, as action moved to the margins, he was increasingly isolated and purposeless, reduced to chugging back and forth after people he was unlikely to catch. There was another wonderful thing about the splits, too: Since the defensive tackles and ends were farther down the line, it took more time for them to actually get to the quarterback, thus buying him critical time.

Short passes, as it turned out, were instruments of murder. Hal held no reverence for the testosterone-infused myth of the deep pass, the romantic long bomb. This idea baffled his opponents. Though he drilled it into his quarterbacks that they "could never be wrong by throwing deep," and on all of their five-step drop pass plays they were always to read the field deep to shallow, he taught them that the most important thing was to get completions. Which meant short passes. If the cornerbacks, leery of the long pass, were playing off the outside receivers, Hal would respond instantly with a quick screen. Not just one, either. If the cornerbacks stayed back, he would call the play repeatedly, to the same receiver. In this way he would dictate the defensive formation. He would beat the defenders and annoy them to death, since this was not the game *they* wanted to play. They were all about passing on third and long; that was the game, that was the assumption. It is astonishing, in retrospect, how long it took to break football coaches of these habits. And then of course when the cornerbacks finally did come up, an eye signal from Dewald would send the receiver streaking downfield. Short, ball-control passes, perfected by Walsh with the Cincinnati Bengals in the early 1970s, spread the field horizontally. They made use of the full 53.33 yards that had hitherto been seen as pointless because they did not represent *forward* movement. Just as important, short passes made defensive coaches lose sleep, worrying about how they were going to cover that much larger box. The more they had to think about it and the more schemes they came up with, the more complex their defenses got. Which meant that their players could not play as fast as players who did not have so many things to think about. The main idea was to let the players make plays.

Other lessons: If you taught players that they could score from anywhere on the field at any time, they actually believed you. Hal went for it often on fourth down; as time went by this habit just became a part of his offense. He also believed that one of the best times to try to score was when his team was backed up against its own goal line. He had designed a play specifically for that situation—a pass that featured a deep shot down the field. There was perhaps no better example of his concept of football relativity than this. The opposing team was thinking, we're going to force a safety. Hal's players were thinking, we're going to score a touchdown. In that situation, the defenders naturally acted as though the dimensions of the playing field had dramatically shrunk. They and their coaches assumed that there was going to be a brutal collision in the cramped space at the line of scrimmage worthy of Walter Camp, a contest over a few precious yards of real estate. The enemy expected an elemental war of blood and guts and slobber at the line of scrimmage; Hal saw the better part of an acre of grass with no one in it, pure open space extending far beyond his own quarterback's throwing range. Of course this came with high risk. That was the point. No single play was more representative of the mind-set behind Hal's offense.

There were other revelations. Defenses that stuck with old-fashioned, run-stopping 4-4-3 schemes (not uncommon among D-III and NAIA teams) were defeated by four or five receivers streaking vertically down the field. Defenses that stuck to Cover 2–like zones were nickel-and-dimed to death with quick slants, crosses, and screens. Defenses that blitzed through those oh-so-inviting gaps in the O-line were destroyed outright. Different games, different rules.

The team had also learned something about its own players. Dewald was something of a shock to everybody. He had not struck his new teammates as much of anything at first. He was a quiet, serious kid who was a little older and more mature than most of them. He had been to college for a year and a half. He had married his wife, Tiffany, right out of high school and lived in a house off campus instead of in the party scrum at McKibbin Hall. He wasn't part of those mythic night trips to Iowa City looking for girls and good times. He was so reserved that it was hard to know what to think about him. Reporter Kalen Henderson, of the *Burlington Hawk Eye*, felt he had to be coaxed into saying anything at all.

On the field and in the huddle he was something else altogether: resolute, self-assured, fearless, fully in command, deferred to by everyone. Like Hal he loved the idea of danger. He loved to gamble. Going for it on fourth-and-long was exactly what he liked to do. Emptying his backfield when a blitz was coming and exposing his undersized body to the fury of linebackers seemed to him to be a decent risk-reward proposition. He may have been quiet around campus, but his eyes lit up at the idea of burning safeties and cornerbacks. Having learned Hal's new offense (it was quite different from the run-and-shoot with a few BYU plays that he had run his senior year at Copperas Cove), Dewald had now also developed the skills to run it. He also had an uncanny aptitude for reading the field and the sort of accuracy that his receivers believed "could knock a dime out of your hand at forty yards." Knowing that these were the skills this new offense needed, they were now all he worked on, night and day.

Another revelation was Marcus Washington, the kid who had

never caught a pass in two years of junior college and who had been admitted only as a favor to his friend Dereck Hall. Washington loved everything about Iowa Wesleyan. He felt liberated by the cornfields and the vast open spaces. He loved the camaraderie and the dorm life. He loved his classes. He began writing for the school newspaper, joining clubs. He was popular. He was also the tough possession receiver every passing team must have: the one catching the ball over the middle for 8 yards and taking a vicious hit from the safety or linebacker for his trouble. Because he was only 5-foot-10 and 180 pounds, he took a pounding. But he loved it. He liked to be hit. He liked what it meant. He liked popping up after a tackle, as though to say, "You barely touched me," and jogging back to the huddle. Washington wasn't fast, either. But Hal had taught him what no other coach ever had: how to read the field, how to see it scientifically, how to decode it as he streaked across the grass. Hardly anyone in American football that year was teaching receivers how to adjust their routes according to what the defenders did. Routes were routes, and receivers were supposed to run them exactly as diagrammed. Otherwise, how was the quarterback going to know where they were going? In Hal's system, Washington and the other receivers had to read "zone," or "man"; they had to spot the piece of open grass; they had to bend their routes to match the reality they were seeing in front of them—*and* they had to do it in a way that the quarterback knew exactly where they were going. Washington was one of the first brilliant students of Hal's system. In his first season at Iowa Wesleyan he became a star receiver and one of Dewald's favorite targets.

On the Monday after the Lambuth game, Prins summoned Hal to his office to tell him how happy he was with the football team. The game had been played in nearby Burlington, and Prins had attended, and he had seen firsthand what it meant to have an exciting football team. A big crowd attended the game. The two teams had put up an electric 1,112 yards of offense. Hal's offense had been magnificent in a losing cause. Prominent people from the community had come up to shake Prins's hand and tell him how exciting his team was.

Prins was so happy that he raised Hal's salary to $45,000 and gave him a three-year contract. He doubled the salaries of Mike Leach and Mike Major and allowed Hal to add two additional coaches. Just as important for the future of the team, he gave Hal de facto control of the so-called Harlan grants, which were not real money but tuition discounts and therefore almost as good. Hal had argued that the best students and best players were not getting the bigger Harlan grants, and that if he could divvy them up, superb student-athletes like Dewald and Washington would get, appropriately, more money. Hal's 7-4 season turned out to be a spectacular success. He had gotten everything he wanted. The *Burlington Hawk Eye* wrote: "Hal Mumme just might be one of the hottest commodities in the small-college coaching arena." He was, in fact, just getting started.

12

The One, Holy, Catholic,
and Apostolic Pass

In the 1989 season Dustin Dewald completed 267 of 420 passes (64 percent) for 29 touchdowns. He had thrown posts, crosses, corners, sails, shoots, curls, hitches, and seams, and the majority of them had worked as well on the field as they had on Hal's scribbled-over paper napkins. But there was one play that, for reasons the players could not quite fathom, worked better than the others. There was a magic to it that wasn't immediately apparent in its brute mechanics, a particular sort of havoc it created against defenses that the other route combinations could not match. This single play also produced more than half of all the touchdowns Iowa Wesleyan scored.

In the huddle it was called 92. The coaches often called it "mesh." Whatever name the play went by, it destroyed defenses with astounding efficiency. There is of course no such thing as a perfect pass play, just as there is no such thing as an unhittable pitch, an unblockable shot, or an unreturnable serve. Sports are built on imperfection, both of humans themselves and of the systems they design. Still, there was something about mesh, when it was working well—which was most of the time—that seemed to transcend these notions of fallibility, even with defenses that had seen the play before and had studied it and prepared meticulously for it. As the season evolved the players and coaches came to see mesh as unstoppable, which was not quite the same as perfect, perhaps, but it was awfully damn close.

Hal had first seen the play while watching BYU game film when he was offensive coordinator at UTEP. Considering the damage BYU inflicted with it, it did not look that complicated. Two receivers ran shallow crossing patterns, intersecting with each other in the middle of the field, while an outside receiver ran a corner route and the two backs flared to the outside. He had diagrammed it, and diagrammed it again, but in spite of his efforts, he did not feel he understood it well enough to try it in a game. The timing between quarterback and receivers was not right.

When he had visited BYU in Provo in 1987 and 1988, Hal had watched more film and observed the play in practice. He had asked questions about it, particularly of quarterbacks and receivers coach Norm Chow, whose answers were evasive. "It's just a backyard play," he would tell Hal dismissively and move on to something else. The other coaches were vague, too. And the more Hal felt he was being stonewalled—in a polite way—the more determined he was to understand how mesh worked. He became obsessed with it. The full-blown magic—its ability to rip the guts out of defensive formations—still eluded him.

In the spring of 1989 he had gone to Provo again to watch film and observe drills as well as to meet Mike Leach. This time he approached former BYU quarterback Robbie Bosco, who was then a lowly assistant offensive coach. Bosco had thrown many mesh passes and scored many touchdowns with them. Hal told him he had been working on the play and needed help, then sketched it out on a blackboard.

"What I am doing wrong?" Hal asked.

Bosco looked at the diagram for a moment, then said: "You're running it too deep." The "mesh" referred to the point at which two receivers intersected in the middle of the field.

Hal had mapped that critical junction 8 to 9 yards deep. "It's always six," said Bosco.

Hal's calculations were also off on the play's corner route. His receiver was making his cut too far down the field. Hal had plotted the point at 10 yards from the line of scrimmage. "It's really just four steps," Bosco said, marker in hand, "more like about seven yards."

Like a conductor reading a musician's score, Hal understood immediately what Bosco was saying. To outsiders, the few yards in question would have seemed a small adjustment, a minor twist in one segment of a multifaceted play. But in the world of pass strategy, space defined everything: the play's timing, velocity, and separations between receivers and defenders. Much of what Hal spent his idle time doing in his early years was figuring out how to hold defenders in place to create gaps, how to use a receiver to control a defensive back by pulling him this way or that, how to force safeties or linebackers to make fatal choices to defend what he called "pieces of space." In a game where time equaled distance, and all of it had to be synced to the quarterback's drop, 2 or 3 yards meant everything. When Hal returned to Mount Pleasant, he installed the changes. In IWC's first game, against Dubuque, it took him only a few 92 calls to confirm that Bosco had indeed unlocked the final door. There was the magic, right in front of him.

The original mesh play had most likely resulted from the Xs and Os that offensive coordinator Doug Scovil had dreamed up coupled with LaVell Edwards's willingness to put them into heavy rotation. But mesh, as it evolved, was far more than just a simple theft from BYU's playbook. Working from what Bosco told him, Hal soon made his own key changes in how the receivers ran their routes and how the quarterback read them, and completely altered the way the play was coached. His obsession with the play in the first place was closely linked to his admiration for Bill Walsh, who was busy reinventing the game with short passes, particularly crossing patterns, and disruptive horizontal stretches of the field. Mesh could have been something directly out of his playbook. It certainly worked according to his principles. Hal had contacted Walsh periodically over the years, and Walsh had always made time for him. In some sense mesh represented the merger of the BYU and Walsh systems.

If you were going to invent the perfect pass, one that could consistently beat any defense no matter how many times the defenders had played against it or seen it on film, it would have to have three basic characteristics: First, it would have to be plain and straightforward and easy to execute from your own players' point of view, while your opponents would have to see it as complex, verging on random. Second, it would have to be so good that the defense's tactics were rendered largely irrelevant; executing your own play correctly was all that mattered. Finally, like a good confidence operation, it would have to be pulled off in such a way that the mark did not know that he had been conned. He would be left thinking that it was the structure of the play itself that had beaten him, when in fact it was the *idea* behind it. In this way the play would beat the opponent again and again. When it worked properly, mesh was all of those things.

To understand mesh is to grasp many of the underlying concepts of Hal's offense and how they worked to defeat defenses. In its most elemental state, the play looked like this:

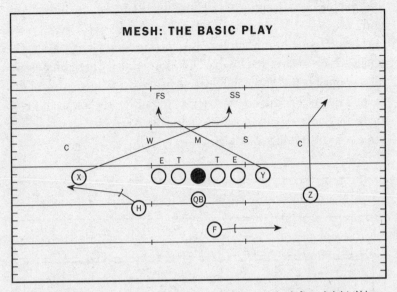

MESH: THE BASIC PLAY

The routes of five receivers. X and Z are wideouts on the left and right, Y is the tight end position, H is in the slot on the left, and F is in the backfield.

The offensive formation is called ace, with two receivers on the right and two on the left and a fullback behind the quarterback. As diagrammed above, Z runs a deep route to the corner; Y and X run shallow crossing routes; F runs a swing on the right; and H runs a shoot on the left.

The play seems straightforward. It is not.

Because what matters most is what mesh does to defenses, it is important to understand what IWC's offense was up against. The defense shown in the diagram below, known as Cover 2, was the most common one Iowa Wesleyan faced during Hal's time there. The number "2" refers to the two safeties, strong (SS) and free (FS), who are positioned deep behind the line of scrimmage. In front of them on both sides are two cornerbacks (C). The defensive line consists of two ends (E) and two tackles (T). They are backed up by three linebackers, labeled here as W, M, and S, for weakside, middle, and strongside. Football coaches call them Willie, Mike, and Sam. (The strongside is defined by the presence of the tight end, Y.)

Cover 2, one of the staples of American football, is a zone defense, which means that linebackers, cornerbacks, and safeties are all responsible for covering receivers in clearly defined areas of the field. They watch the quarterback's eyes and body language, react to the flight of the ball, and close on the receivers. Here is what their zone responsibilities look like:

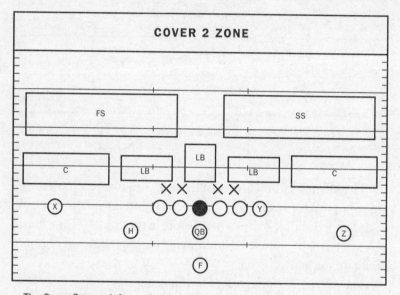

The Cover 2 zone defense that Iowa Wesleyan usually faced. The rectangles represent pass coverage responsibilities of individual players.

The other main defense Iowa Wesleyan faced was a variant of Cover 2 called Cover 2 man. In this version (below), the two safeties each play a half-field zone as they did with the Cover 2. But now the cornerbacks and linebackers take individual responsibility for the receivers, covering them man-to-man and running with them the length of their routes.

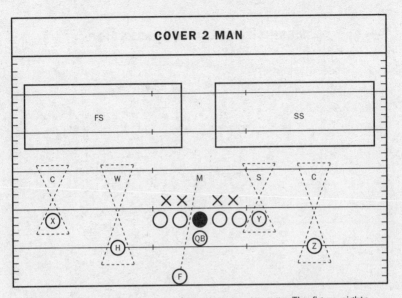

Cover 2 man combines zone and man-to-man coverage. The figure eights represent pairings of receivers and defenders. Note that M (middle linebacker) covers F (the fullback) out of the backfield and that the two safeties, FS and SS, are free to play conventional zone defense.

The best way to understand how mesh works is to follow the quarterback's eyes as they move across the field in search of an open receiver during the three to five seconds the play will last. He has a progression of sequential reads—separate looks at potentially five receivers—which was one of the basic building blocks of Hal's offense. Those sequential reads (1 through 4, since two of them are simultaneous) were as follows:

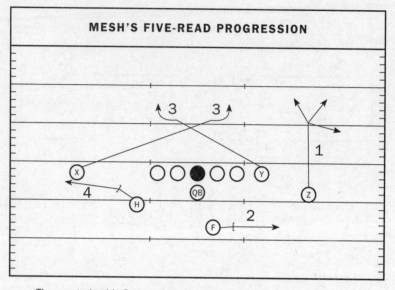

The quarterback's first read is always downfield: Z on the right runs a corner route but can also run a post or break it off. The third read—simultaneously X and Y—is the key to the play.

His first read is Z, and his reads will progress in sequence, right to left. Because Hal has taught him to read the field deep to shallow, the long vertical shot is always his first option. Before the play begins, the quarterback looks at the coverage in the area of Z's planned route downfield. He looks specifically at the strong safety and at the cornerback, whose zones of responsibility cover the route of his receiver. If he sees the safety cheating up, he touches his nose, telling Z to run a post route because he will have a step or two advantage by doing so; if the safety is deep and the cornerback shallow, he touches his chin for a corner route. If both the safety and the cornerback are staying back, he gives the baseball "out" sign to indicate an abrupt cut to the sideline. This is the only part of the play where the quarterback can adjust receivers' routes. It was something that few, if any, other coaches in the country were doing at the time.

On "Go. Hit" the play begins, and the quarterback starts his drop with his eyes on Z. Let's say the quarterback has seen the safety edging to the middle of the field and has signaled a corner route. Z runs at full speed for four steps, then angles toward the corner of the end zone. If the quarterback sees *grass* where Z is going, or if he sees the numbers on the back of the defender's jersey, he throws the ball. Hal's players have been taught to see that configuration in simple terms: This is a touchdown, or should be. The quarterback will not even get to his second read. If instead of grass the quarterback sees *color*—a uniform—he holds the ball.

In this example, the cornerback does the predictable thing and stays with Z, while the strong safety comes over and positions himself between Z and the end zone. That means the quarterback will not throw to Z. This is a binary read: color, no color. Switch on, switch off. There is not a lot of thought involved. That is the fundamental beauty of the offense: Instant reactions rule.

A little more than one second of time has elapsed since the ball was snapped.

The quarterback's eyes now flick to the far right to pick up his second potential target: F. F has checked to make sure no one is blitzing—he needs to block the blitzer if he sees one—then has taken off on a flat trajectory toward the right sideline. He takes three steps and looks for the ball. If there is no one chasing F—that chasing player would most likely be the Sam linebacker—then the defense has already made a mistake and will immediately pay for it: A short pass to the uncovered F will produce all those yards the Z has cleared out by dragging the safety and corner with him on his deep pattern. A nice gain, probably a first down.

But if someone *is* chasing F, then the quarterback's eyes shift to the middle of the field. This opens the critical second phase of the play. Because even though the first two reads are to his right, the lion's share of mesh passes *go to the middle*. The quarterback's first two reads thus constitute live feints; they are deadly if the defense ignores them but are not the play's main objective. The action on the strong side of the field amounts to a lot of elaborate theater concealing the fact that a single defender is being isolated. This is the heart of mesh. Though he does not suspect it yet, that man—the middle linebacker, the defense's best player—is being separated from the herd and targeted for destruction.

As the quarterback's eyes move to his third read, at the center of the field, he hits the last step of his drop. He steps up in the pocket. While he has been looking at his first two reads, his X and Y receivers have been running shallow crossing routes toward each other. They have to be extremely precise. Y must run under the Sam, and it is Y who sets the depth of the mesh at 6 yards from the line of scrimmage. No more, no less. X will cross under Y, so close the two players can touch hands.

At two seconds of elapsed time, X and Y intersect.

By this time several important things have happened, all with that singular goal—the destruction of Mike—in mind. On the right side, Z has drawn off the cornerback and the strong safety, and F has drawn off the Sam linebacker. On the back side of the play—the left—H has checked for a blitz then taken off on his shoot route, curving toward the sideline. He has—or should have—the full attention of both the cornerback and the Willie linebacker.* This, plus the sight of X streaking across his face toward the middle of the field, freezes Willie. In any case, in the zone defense, X is no longer his responsibility. (H is the fourth—and only occasionally used—read.)

All of which leaves Mike, the storied middle linebacker position, core of the defense and mainstay against both the run and the pass, as the only defender looking at the short middle of the field. Everyone else's eyes are occupied. He is being methodically stranded on his own island. He still does not know this. At this point, the world seems rather chaotic around him. What the meshing receivers do

---

* If the Willie linebacker is "pattern reading"—a common defensive technique—he will likely be expecting a curl route to offset the H's flat, which will further freeze him on the left side and surprise him when he sees X streaking toward the shallow middle of the field.

now is what they have been trained to do against a zone defense by the routes on air drill. Since no defenders are chasing them, their instructions are to find the first patch of unoccupied grass, stop, turn, and wait for the ball. It is entirely up to them where to go. In football terms, they "settle" in the gaps of the zone defense. They read the field on their own and move to the open spaces they see— twin options in the middle of the play.*

Which leaves the stranded Mike with an impossible choice. He can't cover both Y and X. Both are in his area of responsibility, and at least one of them is wide-open. Hal called this "playing keep-away," which is exactly how it seems to the linebacker, who has had all of his support systematically stripped away. It's two against one, and whatever choice he makes is the wrong one. A play like quick screen tires the middle linebacker out by making him chug back and forth across the field. Mesh renders him completely helpless. He makes his choice, quarterback sees it and hits the open receiver, Y or X, on the part of his jersey closest to the widest open space, and the receiver turns and runs straight downfield with no horizontal dithering. *Settle and noose* leading to *yards after catch*.

What if the defense is playing man-to-man? To see what happens, consult the diagram of the Cover 2 man defense. Assume that each defender will run as fast as he can to cover his assigned receiver. Now follow the receivers' trajectories to see the result: collisions and total chaos in the middle. Here, too, Hal added an innovation. In BYU's system, the meshers, recognizing the man-to-man defense, headed straight to the sideline. In Hal's version, they curved their routes downfield, climbing out of the chaos in the middle. They will be

---

* Option routes were still not in wide use when Hal coached at IWC. Most coaches wanted receivers to run the exact routes they had diagrammed. Exceptions to this were LaVell Edwards at BYU, whose plays included true options; Don Coryell; and Lindy Infante, who studied Coryell's offense and used similar techniques when he was offensive coordinator for the Cincinnati Bengals. Most defensive coordinators were not trained to understand how such routes worked, or how to cover them. Of course the run-and-shoot was an offense based on option routes.

either uncovered or single-covered, and the quarterback will hit one of them with a 15-yard pass thrown about eight feet off the ground. "If we catch them in man and we hit it, we will probably score," Hal would tell his quarterbacks and receivers with his usual optimism. "Even if we don't, it will be a huge play." In both cases—man and zone—the receivers themselves were allowed to read the coverage and adjust their routes accordingly.

Mesh drove defensive coordinators crazy in other ways as well. For one thing, it was almost impossible to figure out what the play actually looked like on paper. There were two main reasons for this. The first was that Hal could run it five times in a row and it would never look like the same play. This was because it was constantly shifting, adapting to the defense. In a man defense, for example, the X and Y ran routes that climbed toward the post, receiving the ball at 15 yards instead of 6 yards for long gains. Against a straight zone, they might settle in completely different places, depending on where the most open spaces were. And, of course, the Z had his own three options that were determined entirely by the defense itself. Which was the real mesh? In a conservative pass defense, Z would run an out—a completely different route than he might run against more aggressive, pressing coverage. Second, Hal could change the formations from which the play was run, doing things like moving his slot receivers to the outside and then motioning them back to their original positions. Again, which was the real mesh? How was a defensive coach to teach his players to recognize it? And even if it were recognized, how was the middle linebacker supposed to solve his fatal-choice problem? This was Hal's system: simple for his players, brutally hard for yours.

There was something more here, too. Inside mesh was a revolution, a way to decode the football field that had never existed before. The key to everything was the read progression, the binary system that allowed the quarterback to see the field in fast, easily recognizable chunks. Man or zone? Grass or uniform? The rule: Never throw to a covered receiver, never pass up an open one. In most offenses of the time the quarterback either had a clear primary and secondary receiver (or as Terry Bradshaw once conceded, often only a primary) or had to read one of the safeties or in some cases read the whole defense before deciding what to do. If you watch football on television, you will hear the commentators saying that the quarterback had "looked the safeties off" to describe an eye trick to help beat the defense. In Hal's system there was no need to look anyone off. The machine did the looking for you. The machine read the field for you. Beyond recognizing a man or a zone—a talent IWC receivers and quarterbacks quickly mastered—and looking for the blitz, there was no need to worry about what the defense was doing. You had five options in front of you. The defensive coordinator might think he was being beaten by a receiver running a clever crossing route. He was actually being beaten by a unified system of field-decoding.

The main virtue of the play was its simplicity. It could be taught, easily, to high schoolers. So could the rest of Hal's offense, and therein lay great possibilities for change. In the fall of 1989 no one understood this. No one could have told you that those surprising IWC Tigers were on to something that would have an impact beyond the rolling prairie of southeastern Iowa.

13

No Good Deed Unpunished

In the spring of 1989, before his first season at IWC, Hal and athletics director David Johnsen had attended the first meeting of the Illini-Badger-Hawkeye Football Conference in Chicago. It had been a happy occasion. Iowa Wesleyan had just joined the conference, which meant that it had found a home among its small-college brethren. And the brethren were delighted—thrilled, actually—to welcome into their ranks a perennial loser, with a four-year record of 9-31, which could be counted on to make all their homecomings a success for years to come. The member schools were, for the most part, much richer than Iowa Wesleyan, with endowments, dormitories, student centers, and athletics facilities IWC could not match. It was perhaps with such inequality in mind that the athletics directors and coaches at the assembly gave their compatriots from Mount Pleasant a warm welcome. If Hal seemed a bit out of place and not quite sure yet how things worked here in the northern heartland, so much the better.

One year later, in March 1990, Hal and Johnsen walked into the same annual meeting, only this time there were no hearty handshakes or well wishes. This time there were sullen, downcast gazes and barely concealed hostility. The meeting's first order of business, in fact, was a proposal to evict Iowa Wesleyan from the conference. The members' thought process went something like this: They had all heard rumors on the recruiting trail that Hal was throwing buckets of scholarship money at Texans and other exotics to come to southeastern Iowa to play. To the members he was thus violating the ethos of the Illini-Badger-Hawkeye Conference, where big money and national recruiting were not welcome. The fact that Hal had hung an average of 38 points per game on them that season only seemed to underscore the grievance: He was giving out too many scholarships, he had too many good players, he was tampering with the spiritual balance of small-college football in the Midwest.

Hal and Johnsen sat in numb shock while the rest of the coaches and ADs discussed their fate as though they were not in the room. Representatives of some of the competing schools, like Concordia University (Illinois), were furious and could not be placated. They were wrong, of course. Hal had, in reality, a total of $12,000 in scholarship money to give out. IWC's scholarship program was exactly what it had been in 1988, when the team had gone 0-10, and its method of helping players pay for college was in general much like what the other schools in the conference (half D-III, half NAIA) were doing. He had only gone out of state because nobody in-state would play for him.

No one appeared to have thought for a moment that what was beating the competition so badly was not twenty phantom players on full rides but the most innovative passing offense in America.

And then the Illini-Badger-Hawkeye Conference voted to kick Iowa Wesleyan out.

Because of the I-B-H's rules, IWC had to be granted one year of grace before the full banishment kicked in. But the individual schools could still cancel their upcoming games with the Tigers. And cancel they did, with a vengeance. For the 1990 and 1991 seasons Dubuque, Culver-Stockton, Grinnell, the University of Chicago, Central Methodist, and Trinity all called off their games, leaving gaping holes in IWC's schedule. A few teams did not go along: The ever-feisty Max Bowman and his Greenville team kept Iowa Wesleyan on its schedule, as did Eureka and Concordia.

Hal's immediate problem was how to fill three canceled games for the imminent 1990 season. It was this need that led him into another confrontation over the future of the IWC football program, this time with his own people. President Prins's vision for the school had been to use an improved football team to boost enrollment. His plan was working. From 1989 to 1990 full-time enrollment would rise 21 percent. But Hal had a grander vision. His idea was to turn Iowa Wesleyan, a traditionally cellar-dwelling NAIA school, into an NCAA Division II power. Since there was only one Division II team in the state, he figured, Iowa Wesleyan could offer good local athletes a way to stay close to home. They would, of course, have a well-coached team. On its face, Hal's proposal was breathtakingly ambitious: D-II schools in general were much bigger and better funded, and gave out many more athletic scholarships. It was, he thought, a great idea.

Though IWC was a small school that played at a tiny stadium, Hal pushed to play major Division II powers.

But it was just this sort of great idea that drove members of IWC's administration and faculty to distraction. Most of them hated it. As they saw it—and here they were in agreement with the members of the I-B-H Conference—Hal was tampering with the very nature of the college. They did not want big athletic budgets. They did not want lots of athletic scholarships. They liked their antique gymnasium. Division II sports would happen at IWC around the time that goats and monkeys rained from the sky. Though Hal had become friends with a number of university people, he had always had the impression that many of them saw him as an arrogant cowboy. There was no longer any reason to doubt that.

If his plan sounded to cloistered academics like pure insanity, one might imagine their reaction when Hal scheduled two of his first three games with top NCAA Division II teams. It was as though he was carrying out his idea anyway. The first game was against traditional football power Morningside College, from Sioux City, Iowa. The second was against Portland State University, one of the elite teams of Division II football. It had been runner-up for the national championship in both 1987 and 1988. Because PSU was 2,000 miles and two time zones away, the Tigers would fly to the West Coast on a chartered aircraft and would be paid $10,000 for their trouble. The third game would be against Midwestern State, in Wichita Falls, Texas, a school ten times IWC's size and a thousand miles from anywhere IWC had ever played before. The Tigers would need to charter a large airplane to fly there, too.

All of this was, or looked very much like, big-time football, something IWC had rarely, in nearly a century of playing the game, been within sniffing distance of. Here was the insanity itself, only not in some theoretical form. If the Iowa Wesleyan faculty could have stopped Hal from scheduling these games, they almost surely would have. But Prins was letting him run, seeing what would happen. Hal was merely being Hal: pushing hard, taking on things much bigger than himself. Playing great teams was always part of his ambition, even though the idea sounded, indeed, completely crazy, like a Division II college playing the Dallas Cowboys.

With such competition looming, Hal spent the off-season thinking about opposing defenses. He had deliberately built his offense around the idea of attack—aggressive, continuous assault of all parts of the field that would force the defense to adjust to his team, not the other way round. Still, he could not ignore defenses altogether, especially ones that were now being carefully adapted for the express purpose of bringing Iowa Wesleyan's aerial circus down. When the Tigers' offense had taken flight after the first two games of 1989, only one team had come close to stopping it—Trinity, which IWC had beaten, 28–18. Led by their brilliant coach, Leslie Frazier, Trinity's defenders had intercepted Dustin Dewald four times. Frazier had employed a defense known as 46, which had been invented by Chicago Bears defensive coach Buddy Ryan and had become famous when he used it to annihilate the New England Patriots in the 1985 Super Bowl, 46–10.

There were two essential parts to Ryan's defense. First, there were the eight men he put in the "box" (the area near the line of scrimmage, 3 to 5 yards deep and the length of the interior offensive line), who were designed not only to crush the run but also to bring more bodies against the quarterback than the offense could block. Second, there was the way Ryan's defensive backs covered the receivers. Because 46 brought so much manpower to the box, the defensive backs had to play man-to-man coverage, bumping the receivers hard at the line of scrimmage and disrupting the short passing routes that were critical to beating the relentless rush. When the system worked, it was brutally effective. Coach Bill Walsh of the 49ers said in an interview that he "had to use every bit of knowledge and experience and wisdom I had" to attack it. The Bears had been rocking the NFL with it, and it was catching on in colleges. Trinity had knocked Dewald's receivers off their patterns and had hit him repeatedly. Frazier had found a weak point, and he knew it. In Iowa Wesleyan's last game of the year, Lambuth University had also used 46 against the Tigers some of the time. The word was obviously out. Other teams would do the same.

One of the biggest problems when facing the 46 was the difficulty receivers had shucking their defenders, extricating themselves from the street fight at the line of scrimmage. In college football (unlike in the pros) defensive backs were allowed to bump receivers anywhere on the field as long as the contact was in front of the defender and a pass was not in the air. By holding up a receiver at or near the line of scrimmage, the defenders could destroy the timing of pass plays and throw the quarterback's reads off. Hal needed to learn how to coach the receivers to use their hands and bodies to avoid getting jammed. He needed a teaching technique.

Of all the teams in the NFL, the Green Bay Packers were the best at beating Ryan's 46. The two teams were in the same division, played each other twice a year, and knew each other well. Packers head coach Lindy Infante, one of the unsung passing gurus of the era, had taken his team from a record of 4-12 in 1988 to 10-6 in 1989. He had been named the AP Coach of the Year. His quarterback, Don "Majic Man" Majkowski, had led the NFL in passing. Infante had beaten the Bears twice. His receivers had evidently figured out how to release against bump-and-run coverage.

Because no one had told Hal that he could not just drive over to Green Bay and ask Lindy Infante personally for his advice, that is what he decided to do. He had only the thinnest of connections to the Packers, via a receivers coach from his UTEP days. But he called anyway and asked if he could visit, and the Packers told him he was welcome. In early February 1990, he packed Mike Leach, (volunteer) assistant coach Kirk Soukup, and Mount Pleasant High School coach Bob Jensen into a car for the eight-hour trip north across the frozen prairie to Green Bay. It was a sort of buddy trip from the Lord of the Rings trilogy: young men in search of secret knowledge.

To their mild amazement, the Packers let them all the way in. Hal and his cohorts found themselves in the locker room watching number-two draft pick and offensive line phenomenon Tony Mandarich jerk weights around as though they were made of sawdust. They were taken to the film room to watch Green Bay beat Chicago's press coverage and then were schooled by receivers coaches on how to teach it. They took detailed notes. Best of all, Infante, a quiet, gracious man with a Florida drawl, talked to them. They got what they came for: a rapid-step drill the Packers called footfire and other drills showing receivers how to use their hands to grab the defenders' hands or slap them away.

There were collateral benefits to the trip, too. While watching film of quarterback Majkowski, Hal had noticed how effective one of those passing plays was. It was called smash. It was Infante's own invention, a vicious little diagonal stretch meant to defeat the Cover 2. Hal saw immediately that it embodied everything he was trying to do to defenders: make them cover the entire field, while simultaneously pulling them crossfield and downfield, and forcing them to make choices they did not want to make. Hal asked for and got, from Infante and others, a detailed explanation of how the Packers ran the play.

In its basic form, smash consisted of routes run by two receivers on the same side of the field. The outside receiver ran a short hitch while the inside receiver ran a corner route—straight downfield, then 45 degrees to the sideline.* In a mirrored smash, wide and slot receivers on both sides of the field ran identical routes. The concept is easy to teach: Put vertical stress on the cornerback, forcing him to choose between coming up to play the hitch route in front of him or dropping back to the corner route behind him. Smash in fact shared common mechanical traits with one of IWC's most effective short plays, Y-stick.† Both were triangle stretches that isolated defenders on the sides of the field by pulling them simultaneously in opposing vertical and horizontal directions. Though both included receivers who ran downfield, the main purpose of those routes was to put strains on the defense; the goal was really a short completion. The

---

* The "smash" component of the original play entered when the outside receiver hit the defensive back as though to block him before making his cut.

† The original inspiration for Y-stick was Bill Walsh's 49er team. Hal shortened it and eventually changed it significantly, making it a signature play of his offense.

key was extremely precise routes, which threw an automatic warp into the receiver-safety-cornerback triangle and bought a few tenths of a second of open space. Enough to complete a pass. Smash simply gave Hal another way to use one of his favorite techniques.

Hal and his companions stayed for three nights. They worked hard during the days, interviewing coaches and watching film, then went out to bars and restaurants at night. One afternoon they went to a bar owned by legendary Packer offensive tackle Fred "Fuzzy" Thurston, where Thurston himself told them stories of Green Bay's glory days. On the long drive home, Hal sat in the backseat with Jensen, drawing up routes and talking about them, sifting through all of the things they had seen and heard.

Hal and Leach made another foray in search of NFL tutelage that winter, this time to Chicago for a coaching clinic run by the Bears. The idea: Find out how the Bears taught their cornerbacks to jam receivers at the line of scrimmage. This would help their own defense, of course. But mainly it would show them what was coming at them. The trip had none of the mythic qualities of Green Bay, but they came back loaded with information. The winter trips marked a shift in Hal's relationship with Leach. As offensive line coach, Leach was an integral—Hal often thought *the* integral—part of the passing attack. If Dewald didn't get three or more seconds, there was no offense. Leach was the ideal student. For all his other interests—he had many and they just seemed to proliferate—he was also capable of focusing intensely on the game of football. He was, if anything, even more aggressive by nature than Hal. And now he was learning the other aspects of the offense. It was the next step in what was fast becoming a formidable partnership.

14

Bumps in the Road

Everything was different at the start of the 1990 season. And better. Hal had transformed the Iowa Wesleyan football program in his first year as head coach. He had established one of the nation's most prolific passing offenses. His recruiting had gone so well, fueled by his team's success, that he now had enough players to field a junior varsity. Some of the new players, like 230-pound Hawaiian linebacker Soakai Soakai, offensive tackle York Kurinsky from suburban Chicago, and receiver Bruce Carter from Dallas, were exceptional talents. Dustin Dewald was a preseason pick for the NAIA Division II All-America team.

Better still, Hal had made an improvement more fundamental than just release techniques and the smash route: The Tigers would now operate mostly from the shotgun formation, with the quarterback 5 or 6 yards behind the center. There were two reasons for the change. First, he worried that his quarterback was wearing himself out making 45 to 60 drops in each game. In the shotgun he would take far fewer steps. Second, he expected that his team would face the full fury of 46-style defenses, with their incessant blitzing and press coverages. He needed to buy Dewald time, and distance from the center equaled time.

Like so many innovations involving the forward pass, the shotgun had traced an erratic and discontinuous path through the 20th century. An early version had been used by Dutch Meyer and

Sammy Baugh at TCU in the 1930s. Baugh took every snap from the traditional tailback position, well behind the line of scrimmage. The double wing "Meyer spread" was devastating and produced unprecedented passing yardage. And while Baugh took deep snaps as late as 1944 for the Washington Redskins, he eventually went back under center, and, with few exceptions, the formation was abandoned. The contemporary shotgun was "invented" by San Francisco 49ers coach Howard Wayne "Red" Hickey in 1960 and used for two seasons with John Brodie at quarterback, until Hickey concluded that it could not work against NFL defenses. In the 1970s, quarterback Roger Staubach and the Dallas Cowboys ran it some of the time, as did the Kansas City Chiefs and the Joe Namath–era Jets, the latter to save the quarterback's knees. In the 1980s it made modest gains in popularity, though most of the truly proficient college passing offenses, such as BYU, the University of Houston, and the University of Miami, did not use it. Nor, in the NFL, did the San Francisco 49ers under Bill Walsh or the San Diego Chargers under Don Coryell.

By the time Hal adopted the shotgun, it had become almost exclusively a passing formation, used mainly on third down. Hal intended to use it *most of the time*, which meant that it would be the main platform for his running game, too. This was a very advanced idea in 1990. Most coaches felt that it was foolish to give up the inherent advantages of operating from under center, which included the deception of handoffs and play fakes and the automatic, built-in timing of the quarterback's three-, five-, and seven-step drops. But Hal was going to do it anyway, and, typically, he was going to do it in a way that had not been done before. His team had worked hard in the off-season to install the new formation, and Mike Leach had somehow figured out how to teach the long shotgun snaps. The effect, along with the ever-wider offensive line splits that Leach was deploying, was to create even more open space in IWC's already capacious offensive formation. By traditional football standards, the whole thing looked astoundingly porous and structurally weak, the antithesis of anything that could ever keep a defense out. It was remarkable that something so spindly and tenuous-looking could be so deadly. There was nothing in American football that year, in fact, that looked quite like it.

It was thus with great hopes and high expectations that on September 1, 1990, the IWC Tiger football team traveled by bus to Cedar Rapids and then by plane to Sioux City to play Morningside College. Flying was not only a radical departure from IWC's normal traveling habits, but many of the players had never flown before. But in Hal's world everything had to be bigger, and that included charter planes instead of buses, longer trips to games, and bigger dreams of victory and glory. That he was still running all of this out of the basement of a dilapidated 1922 gym on a shoestring budget might have struck some observers as funny.

Morningside demolished them, 55–3. Hal and his coaches hadn't seen it coming. In the films, they had seen a team of modest talent. What arrived was anything but. As they later learned, Morningside had a new coach, who had brought a group of large, fast players with him. They ran a wicked trap play out of a wing-T formation that IWC could not stop. Morningside's defense, meanwhile, harassed Dewald all afternoon. He completed only 11 of 33 passes for 139 yards with 3 interceptions.

The highlight of the game was a first-quarter brawl, the worst many of the players and coaches had ever seen. Both benches emptied, and the fighting spread past the sidelines and into the stadium. It was in certain ways emblematic of the Hal Mumme era at IWC. First-year Tiger linebacker Marc Hill saw it as the result of two colliding principles: the Iowa Wesleyan players' strong conviction, instilled in them by Hal, that they should never back down, and the sudden realization that they were facing something much bigger, faster, and stronger than they were—the very thing they were not supposed to back down from. IWC's players, like their coach, were brash and self-assured. They talked trash. They thought they could beat anybody. It didn't always work out that way.*

The disaster that befell the Iowa Wesleyan Tigers the following week was at least predictable. This was Portland State, ranked first in one national poll and sixth in another, a team built around 35 full scholarships. Dewald was shut down again, completing only 18 of 45 passes for 91 yards. Portland State rolled over the Tigers with 575 yards of total offense and won, 40–3.

Only two weeks into the season, Iowa Wesleyan had lost to two D-II opponents by a combined score of 95–6. Hal's opponents in the administration, as well as his own defensive coach, Charlie Moot, had strongly opposed playing these schools. (Moot had replaced Mike Major, who had left to take another job.) They believed that it bordered on irrationality, and they had instantly been proved right. Hal could have easily picked teams he could have beaten. But that was not in his nature. He was not afraid of anybody, even when he should have been, and he invariably sought to play teams that were better than his teams.

In this case that instinct served him poorly. The disastrous defeats would later seem an appropriate prelude for the rest of the 1990 season, which, if it was not quite a step backward, did not show great progress. The season had an odd, bumpy quality to it. There was the outright whipping of IWC by Greenville, 30–14, the team the Tigers had come so close to beating the year before. A loss to Lindenwood College was determined by holding and clipping calls that stopped six IWC drives. Dustin Dewald showed his old magnificence in a 65–13 victory over Concordia (Illinois), throwing for 4 touchdowns in the first half, and in the 51 unanswered points he engineered to beat Blackburn. There was the heartbreaking 31–27 loss to Concordia (Wisconsin), which cost IWC the conference

---

* In 1994 Morningside College was placed on a three-year probation by the NCAA for "major football violations" that included playing ineligible athletes during the years 1989–92. Morningside was required to forfeit all victories in which ineligible players played.

title, and a sweet win over Olivet Nazarene, a team with the leading offense in NAIA D-II.

No one could say exactly what was wrong. There was an inconsistency to the team's play that Dewald attributed to the new arrivals, of which there were many, including receivers like Bruce Carter and Dana Holgorsen, who had to learn Hal's system. (Holgorsen had played a year at another college, then transferred to Iowa Wesleyan.) The shotgun was new; there were new plays like smash to learn. The defense, under its new coach, had not quite found itself. Opposing defenses had gotten a bit smarter.

The Tigers finished with a 7-5 record. Considering their abysmal start, they had done well enough. They had lost to two Division II teams and two ranked NAIA D-II teams. They were still better than anything Iowa Wesleyan had ever seen, and they had still put up big passing numbers. Dewald led the NAIA with 33 touchdown passes (he was third among college quarterbacks at all levels in touchdowns) and led the NAIA D-II in passing yardage. He had broken so many Iowa Wesleyan records that it was becoming hard to keep track of them all. Carter, his 6-foot-2-inch, 205-pound slotback, finished second in the league with 90 catches. At the end of his second season, Hal's win-loss record was a cumulative 14-9. He and his team had done extraordinary things. But it was impossible not to notice that Iowa Wesleyan's football team had not fulfilled the scintillating promise of that first season.

There was absolutely no doubt, however, that the team had completely reordered the largely white, largely rural culture of Iowa Wesleyan. The center of the upheaval was McKibbin Hall, the men's dorm, a low-slung, three-story, beige-brick-and-concrete affair with painted cinder-block walls and old linoleum floors. Of the 200 students who lived there, some 90 were football players. In addition to the Texans, blacks, Hispanics, and various out-of-staters there was a new, highly visible group: Polynesians.

If the urban black kids seemed mildly exotic in white-bread Iowa, the Polynesians were something else entirely. A dozen or so had arrived in Mount Pleasant in August 1990. Their presence was the handiwork of Mike Fanoga, Hal's new defensive line coach, and a special sort of recruiter. He was an American of Samoan descent who had played linebacker at UTEP when Hal was coaching there. He also had an immense number of contacts in the Polynesian community, both in the United States and overseas. Polynesians were good at many things—music, dance, and art—and, often, they proved to be especially good at football. This was at least in part because they tended to be bigger, stronger, and faster than ordinary human beings. There were many Polynesians in the NFL.

When Fanoga arrived he brought with him more than a dozen recruits from Hawaii, American Samoa, and California. They were large, friendly people with double names like Epinosa Epinosa, Soakai Soakai, and Pati Pati, and they came with their elaborate culture fully intact. They roamed the campus wearing sandals and lavalavas, the traditional knotted skirts of Polynesia. They would gather in various places on campus to play their ukuleles and sing. They put on dances and luaus, building underground ovens and roasting pigs on campus. Fanoga and his wife looked after them. It was not uncommon to see him traipsing across the main quad toward the library, trailed by a group of enormous Polynesians.

They were not always docile. The dean of students, Carol Nemitz, considered them to be "the nicest young men you would ever want to meet"—until they started to drink. They had their own ideas about morality and law enforcement, too. On one occasion, one of them caught some young men stealing gasoline from a city building. He settled the problem with his fists. When the police charged him with assault, he protested. "That's what we do at home!" he cried. "If we catch someone stealing, we take care of it!" Hal engaged his personal attorney Gary Wiegel, who managed to get the charges dismissed.

The Polynesians were crammed, along with everybody else—including a group of Japanese students from Prins's early recruiting forays—into McKibbin Hall, which had become a testosterone-infused cultural melting pot. York Kurinsky, a 6-foot-4, 265-pound recruit from the Chicago area, was astounded by the sheer insularity of the place. There was nowhere in town to go, no mall, no stores anyone wanted to shop in, no pizza. There were no fraternity buildings to host parties in. Everything happened here. And the place jumped. There were the usual beer parties, of course, and in winter the "naked bell runs" to the college's prize bell, as well as constant sorties up Route 218 to Iowa City and the University of Iowa in search of parties. Plenty of mischief was afoot, too: Fire alarms were pulled, curfews violated, girls' dorms invaded. Occasionally fights broke out. But most of the trouble was minor. Hal had managed to run off the worst offenders. He had a code of conduct that, like his offense, was elegantly simple: (1) Players should never do anything to hurt the team, and (2) Hal would be the sole judge of what constituted hurting the team. Doing drugs hurt the team. Missing class or practice hurt the team. Getting arrested hurt the team. Taking cheap shots at opponents hurt the team.

Perhaps the most remarkable thing about this variegated collection of young men was that, by and large, everyone got along: whites, blacks, Hispanics, and Polynesians; Texans, Iowans, and everyone else. Marc Hill, the linebacker from Mount Pleasant High who had arrived with Kurinsky and the Polynesians, found it remarkable that the players adjusted to one another "so fast and so quick." He thought, too, that the harmony came directly from the coaches. There was something tolerant and easygoing about them, he thought, some sort of chilled-out Jimmy Buffett vibe that somehow trickled down to everyone else. Still, the players had come a long way to play football for Hal Mumme, and they wanted to win.

15

Pilgrimage to Margaritaville

If the opening losses of the 1990 season had been a disappointment, the looming 1991 season held the potential for a full-scale disaster. Hal, who had insisted on changing IWC's status to NAIA Division I—a major move upward—and scheduling yet more tough, ranked teams, was more aware of this than anyone. To some observers his impatience in building his program was beginning to look like a fatal flaw. He wanted too much too soon. And now, in the off-season, he was coming to terms with the alarmingly real possibility that his team could start the season 0-4. IWC would open again with two big NCAA Division II schools, then play two tough, ranked NAIA teams. The schedule, in fact, was stacked top to bottom with dangerous opponents—full of killers the likes of which no Iowa Wesleyan football team had ever faced. Greenville College, which had beaten the Tigers twice in a row, was just one worry among many. With a record of 0-4, Hal could very quickly seem less like the young genius of the forward pass and more like a talented coach who had lost his way in the quirky world of small-time college football. His many doubters would be wonderfully vindicated.

So Hal did what he usually did when he was worried: He went on the road, looking for ideas. In the winter of 1991, the pretext was recruiting in the South—one of their targets happened to be a kicker who lived in Key West, Florida—but the goal was something a good deal more elusive. As Hal saw it, he needed some advantage he did not already possess. He had only vague ideas about what that might be. He had worked hard to come up with his plays and formations, which in his hands had become brilliant pieces of moving, three-dimensional geometry. He did not believe he needed any more plays. He thought, in fact, that he perhaps needed fewer of them. But something was still missing. Some magic he had not yet learned.

He took Mike Leach with him. The two men, nine years apart in age, had become close friends. They had made trips to Provo and Green Bay and Chicago, and various sallies out into the Midwest looking for pieces of offense, plays, refinements of plays, ways of thinking about passing. (In the days before the Internet, football coaching clinics were the main way football knowledge was passed along; dissemination of new information was dead slow.) They went to high schools and junior colleges and made phone calls to coaches far away. They picked up a screen pass from a coach at the University of Montana. They scavenged where they could, picked up shards of wisdom as they found them, then got together and drew everything up.

Leach had by now caught up to Hal in his understanding of the offense. He knew what the receivers and backs were supposed to do. He understood option routes and coverages. Though his main job continued to be coaching the offensive line—where he was making his own innovations, including larger splits and all the highly specialized mechanics that went with them—he also excelled at the many jobs Hal had given him, which he pursued with an almost reckless single-mindedness. As the team's sports information director, he pestered papers from the *Burlington Hawk Eye* and the *Des Moines Register* to *USA Today* for coverage of Iowa Wesleyan football, and in fact succeeded in getting the college a few mentions. This attracted the attention of Iowa Wesleyan's actual public information officer, whose job it was to deal with the press. She was furious and asked President Prins to intervene. When challenged, Leach told her he believed that her office "couldn't get

Iowa Wesleyan College into *USA Today* unless there was a mass murder." As punishment for the sins of overreaching and for his impolitic language, Leach was banished from campus for three days by President Prins.

Leach was a superb recruiter, too, badgering prospects relentlessly at all hours. All the while he was paying strict attention to the close, complex relationships Hal had with quarterback Dustin Dewald and his receivers.

For men with such different personalities, the two had many similar interests. They both read a great deal and took books seriously—especially histories—and liked the exchange of non-sports-related ideas, which made them extremely unusual in coaching circles. Much would be made later about Leach's eclecticism, but Hal's interests bore the same catholicity and range: He was widely read in American history, especially the Civil War. (Stonewall Jackson was his hero.) Leach was fascinated by Winston Churchill, George Washington, Daniel Boone, and the painter Jackson Pollack, among others. The two men liked to drink, too. While they endured the brutal, endless Iowa winter, they played Jimmy Buffett music and dreamed of beaches in tropical Margaritavilles. There was more than a bit of the beach rat in both of them, or at least the idea of the beach rat.

Above all they were bound by their passion for football. Leach had believed in Hal and his radical ideas about football when no one else did, and his faith had been rewarded. Hal really *was* that brilliant. Hal thought Leach was one of the smartest people he had ever met, and Leach had turned out to be the perfect sorcerer's apprentice. He had begun to function as Hal's football conscience, pushing his mentor to take even more risks, throw the ball more, eschew punting, and in general avoid all forms of conservative play. Hal had instilled these beliefs in Leach in the first place, and now Leach was more or less permanently perched on his shoulder, whispering "keep attacking, keep attacking." Hal was still very much head coach, and Leach, as junior officer, was not immune from the occasional reprimand. But Hal was, by nature, quick to forgive, and they reconciled their differences easily. Though they cared deeply about each other's views on football, they cared very little about what the rank and file of American coaching thought. It was a point of honor not to care. They held deep contempt for traditionalists of all stripes and for what they saw as the ossified coaching systems of the contemporary game. They were subversives, loners together.

Their search for knowledge had taken them to obscure corners of the football world, but none quite so obscure as the organization they visited in Florida in March 1991. This was the Orlando Thunder, another team in the brand-new and soon-to-be-extinct World League of American Football. The reason for the visit was to call on a living legend—at least to people living north of the borders of the United States—known to many of his fans simply as "the Don." This was Don Matthews, the second-winningest coach in Canadian Football League history, winner of five Grey Cups, in exile now after a losing season in Toronto. It was like journeying to sit at the feet of the CFL's version of the Dalai Lama.

Hal had one question for him, which was as open-ended as Hal's own thoughts about how he was going to avoid going 0-4.

"What's your best drill?" he asked. He thought that Matthews would give him some sort of exercise for an individual position.

Instead, the Don replied: "Watch the end of practice. That's where we practice the two-minute offense. We call it Bandit."

The two-minute offense—playing at a breakneck pace and without huddles as time is running out—had been part of football for a long time. Johnny Unitas, of the Baltimore Colts, made it famous in the 1958 NFL Championship Game against the New York Giants, when he engineered a spectacular 86-yard, 13-play drive without huddles leading to Steve Myhra's 20-yard field goal, which tied the game with seven seconds left. (The Colts won it in overtime.)

Bandit was the practice version of that offense, and it turned out to be a brilliant exercise in high-speed football. The ball would be placed on the offensive team's 30-yard line, and then the offense would run a play against the defense. No matter what happened on the play, the otherwise idle punters and kickers would immediately spot the ball 10 yards farther down the field. The offense would run up to the line without huddling and call and run another play. The ball would be instantly spotted again. And so on down the field. The motion on the field was frenetic and nonstop. Offensive players sprinted on and off the field, while defensive players tried desperately to match up with the offensive alignments.

For Hal the drill was like watching those first BYU films: a pure, instantaneous revelation. He had always thought that the most exciting part of NFL football was the two-minute offense. He had watched Bill Walsh's 49ers win Super Bowls with it. Matthews's drill was so good not only because it mimicked the frenzied moments of a desperate drive at the end of a game, but because it was so straightforward and easy to coach. The little exercise was, actually, just what Hal needed, though not in the way the Don might have anticipated.

The rest of the Florida road trip was a splendid success. Hal and Leach signed five new recruits, including the kicker from Key West. They visited the University of Miami, in Coral Gables, where they learned some of the secrets of the Miami receivers' seemingly amazing ability to make catches on deep balls. Head coach Dennis Erickson himself, the guru of the one-back spread, padded out in his boxer shorts and met with Hal and Leach in the locker room. He stood at a chalkboard for an hour diagramming a simple, ingenious technique. Though what he described was a minor change, a slight turn to the middle of field instead of to the sidelines, it would have a profound effect on IWC's long passing game.* In Key West, Hal and Leach hit the beach and set up happily at the bar at Captain Tony's Saloon, whose owner, Tony Tarracino, was the subject of Jimmy Buffett's song "Last Mango in Paris." At some point Hal

---

* See Chapter 18 for a full description of what Hal and Leach learned from Erickson.

turned to Leach and told him how impressed he had been with the Bandit drill. Leach enthusiastically agreed.

"But what if," Hal asked, "we just did that all the time?"

The no-huddle offense had long been a staple of American football. There had been no huddles at all in the game until quarterback Paul Hubbard of Gallaudet University (for the deaf) organized one in 1893. He had to have a way to conceal his hand signs from the other team. It wasn't until the 1930s that huddles became the norm. As the game became more complicated, they allowed plays to be discussed and set, and let the quarterback give instructions for specific positions. They provided a space for private communication in an often noisy stadium, and allowed time for substitutions. In the modern era few teams had ever shown interest in running without a huddle outside of the final two minutes.

But attitudes were changing. When Hal had played at Tarleton State University in 1974, his opponent Angelo State had run without a huddle continuously for a quarter. The tactic had surprised and confused Tarleton State's defense, which had trouble setting up and substituting so quickly. Angelo State had scored on three straight drives. Hal had been so impressed that eight years later, in 1982, as offensive coordinator at UTEP, he had run a continuous no-huddle for the same amount of time against Arizona State. It had resulted in a couple of long drives. From 1982 to 1985, head coach Archie Cooley at Mississippi Valley State used a no-huddle offense most of the time with great success (abetted by his star receiver, Jerry Rice, and star quarterback, Willie Totten).

In 1988 the Cincinnati Bengals, under head coach Sam Wyche, became the first NFL team to run a wire-to-wire no-huddle offense, though it was not a pure no-huddle as it would be conceived today. The strategy involved several subroutines, including walk-bys and frequent sugar huddles, where the team gathered in a loose group a few yards from the line. The main idea was to limit defensive substitutions (based on the rules at the time), make it hard for defenders to call plays or match personnel, and tire them out. As soon as a play ended, Wyche would send new players onto the field and give his quarterback, Boomer Esiason, a hand signal for the play. If the defense tried to substitute, Esiason would go right to scrimmage and take a snap. Two years later, the University of Houston, under head coach John Jenkins, was doing something similar. In January 1990, the Buffalo Bills, under coach Marv Levy and quarterback Jim Kelly, became the second NFL team to run a full-time no-huddle offense, which they did in a divisional playoff loss to the Cleveland Browns.

These were the pioneers of the modern no-huddle offense.

While they were changing the pace and character of the game, however, what these innovators were not doing was *playing with the blazing speed of an actual two-minute drill,* where a new play was launched 15 to 20 seconds after the whistle ending the previous one. "No huddle" and "hurry up," as it turned out, were two different things. There were good reasons for this. Running superfast meant that the quarterback's play calls at the line of scrimmage had to be brutally short, which meant that the coaches' voluminous playbooks became quickly useless. It was impossible to run a complex offense in a full-game, high-speed, no-huddle format. Two-minute offenses, moreover, often ran just a few pre-scripted plays—6 to 10—that would be far too limited for an entire game. Finally, running that fast for four quarters could throw your own offense off balance, making it hard to pick up blitzes or adjust to major changes in defensive formations. Operating their no-huddle, for example, the pioneering 1988 Bengals ran an average of only *61.5 plays per game*, just below the NFL average. Wyche boasted that he could run his entire offense through the no-huddle, which, considering how fast his team played, was probably right. The no-huddle was effective and changed a fundamental piece of the game. What it was not was very fast.

As the Iowa Wesleyan Tigers met for their spring practice, Hal and Leach and the rest of the coaching staff began to teach this new high-speed offense. Hal called it, simply, "playing fast." The absence of a huddle was merely a subset of the pure speed of play. They based it off the Bandit drill, which was as brilliantly instructive as Hal had believed it would be. He had added several twists to it. To start the exercise, the ball would be placed on the goal line, making it a 100-yard drill, and the line of scrimmage would zigzag down the field by setting up on the left hash mark, then the right. The drill would last 20 minutes, during which time the team would run off 50 furiously fast plays. Since his days at Copperas Cove, Hal had been doing drills in which the players were instructed to run down the field and score a touchdown every time they touched the ball. He had learned this from Bill Walsh and had come to believe that it was one of the best parts of his practice. He now adapted it to Bandit: The man with the ball scored on every single play.

Considering that no one had ever played consistently at this speed for an entire game before and that it was the single most significant change Hal had ever introduced, the new system carried a great deal of risk.

Just how much risk became clear in the first few days of spring practice. It became quickly apparent that Hal's All-American quarterback, Dustin Dewald, didn't like the new system. He was overwhelmed by it. He was even more disturbed by another unprecedented change Hal had made. Dewald was about to become the only college or pro quarterback to have full authority to call plays from goal line to goal line. The idea was that he could see and react to the field better than Hal could—he could spot a sagging cornerback, for example—and Hal refused to cede those critical seconds that it would take to signal in every play. There would be times when Dewald operated with Hal on a "check with me" basis—looking at his coach on the sidelines as he approached the line of scrimmage for a signal—but he was essentially trusted to make the call. Quarterbacks, of course, had once called all the plays themselves, but by 1991 quarterback play callers did not exist.

Dewald's problem was that, in spite of IWC's lack of a playbook and minimal numbers of plays by anyone else's standards—15 passes and 6 runs, through multiple formations—this was too much information for him to process in a few seconds at the line of scrimmage. And a few seconds was all that he would have. Unlike the other no-huddles in operation, this one was going to run at breakneck, two-minute-drill velocity. Hal joked that Dewald was suffering from a condition he called "paralysis by analysis" and moved quickly to fix it. He reduced the number of formations from which plays would be run (two backs, one back, mirrored slots and wideouts, three receivers on a side, and so on). And he reduced the pass plays from 15 to 12 and the runs from 6 to 3. The offense was now even more starkly simple than it had been before. His play calls would be four words or fewer.

To make things even easier for Dewald, IWC would be using a script for the first 10 plays of the game. This was another trick Hal had learned from Walsh and had been doing since his days at Copperas Cove. The idea was to open the game with a coherent, tactically unified set of plays that had been both decided on away from the hurly-burly of the game field and practiced in order by the team. Dewald carried it on his wrist.

The result: By the time fall camp rolled around in August, Dewald, who had mastered the shotgun the year before, had come to like the fast no-huddle. It played to his greatest talents, his ability to see the field, read the geometric patterns unfolding in front of him, and find open grass. He grew to love the pure speed, too. It was yet another way in which Hal's teams were not playing the same game everyone else was.

16

Rise of a Great American Offense

On paper there was little difference between Portland State, the NCAA Division II team that had annihilated Iowa Wesleyan in 1990, and Northeast Missouri State, the team that it would play in its first game of 1991. Northeast Missouri, a state-funded football dynamo with 9,000 students 90 miles from Mount Pleasant, was probably the better team. The previous year the Bulldogs had gone 9-1, finishing the season ranked ninth in NCAA Division II. Their quarterback from the previous year, who had been a finalist for the D-II equivalent of the Heisman (the Harlon Hill Trophy), had been replaced for the 1991 season by a 6-foot-5-inch, 235-pound transfer from the University of Missouri. The Bulldogs were opening the 1991 season ranked 10th.

The Tigers, who had not played Northeast Missouri since the Truman administration, were 25-point underdogs. The two teams were playing now only because, as the Bulldogs coach Eric Holm had put it to Hal when they scheduled the game, "nobody wants to play either of us." And, of course, because Hal liked nothing better than to pick a fight with someone much bigger than he was.

In spite of the odds, fans turned out in numbers that few Iowa Wesleyan teams in history had ever seen. They came from Mount Pleasant and Burlington and other nearby cities, but also from Iowa City, Illinois, and Missouri. By game time, more than 3,000 of them had packed Maple Leaf Field, the small high school stadium three blocks from campus where the Tigers played. Tickets, which were free when Hal first arrived in Mount Pleasant, were going for $8 to $10. Cheerleaders bounced across the field, trailing purple-and-white Iowa Wesleyan banners.

One of the onlookers was Rob Ash, the head coach at Drake University, in Des Moines. He had driven down to Mount Pleasant to scout Northeast Missouri as a favor for another coach. Iowa Wesleyan meant nothing in particular to him. Still, he was astounded at the differences between the two teams when they took the field. Northeast Missouri looked to him like full-on Division I-A: big, physical, and fast, with immaculate uniforms and state-of-the-art equipment. The team was attended to by a cohort of clipboard-toting coaches, all wearing identical color-and-logo-coordinated clothes. Across the field, the Iowa Wesleyan Tigers reminded him of a "rag-tag, junior high team." Hal was never fastidious about his players' appearance, in or out of uniform, and today was no exception. This was apparent as his group shambled onto the field with shirts untucked, hairstyles that ranged from the white players' shaggy mullets to the black players' high-top fades. Some wore bandannas. To Ash, they made Northeast Missouri State look like Notre Dame.

Then the game began. Hal, who was nervous about the debut of his radical offense, had instructed his players to huddle for the first five plays from scrimmage. The idea was to run at normal speed for a few minutes, settle the boys down, then step on the gas.

They followed his instructions. They settled down. And then, on the sixth play, they went into full Bandit-drill mode, and they never slowed down. Northeast Missouri had never seen any such thing. No one had.

The first known attempt in modern football history to play at wide-open throttle full-time, however, was just part of what the Bulldogs were looking at. Some of it would have been apparent to the crowd in the stands. There were the splits in the offensive line, for example. Since Hal had instructed Mike Leach in the summer of 1989 to put space between linemen, Leach had been experimenting, making the gaps even wider. Putting so much air in the O-line, of course, made each man more of an island than part of a solid wall, so blocking techniques had to change, too. Twisting or stunting defensive players had to be accounted for; blitzes had to be picked up; protections had to be adjusted; ground had to be stood. Leach had done all this quite brilliantly, but he had gone even further than Hal had expected. By the Northeast Missouri game he was very likely employing wider splits—five feet or more between guards and tackles—than any contemporary coach had done. Certainly Ash thought so; he had only ever seen anything like it on trick plays. And only once or twice. The ultra-wide splits were hard to see from the sidelines, where there was no lateral perspective. Viewed from the end zones they were flat-out astonishing. They looked big enough to drive a pickup truck through. And these were IWC's *standard* positions; they were not reserved for passing downs or other special downs. The O-line guys were in those oddball two-point stances, too, which was shocking enough when pass-blocking but almost unheard of when you were trying to fire in unison into a zone-blocking scheme ahead of a running play.

The Bulldogs were also getting a look at Hal's fully adaptive offense. Dewald was cleared to change the play at the line of scrimmage, and he often did so in a way that was virtually unprecedented in American football. He would see defenders shifting then scream out a new play. If the defense shifted or feinted again, he would scream out another play. A cheating safety or a blitzing linebacker was immediately called to account.*

Other changes would have been apparent, too, that were so uncommon that few coaches had seen them, such as using the shotgun formation as a platform for your running game—or even

---

* Football audiences would not become familiar with such at-scrimmage play changing until Peyton Manning played for the Indianapolis Colts in the late 1990s and early 2000s.

the idea of running the shotgun full-time.* Or having the quarterback call most of the plays at the line of scrimmage in the 15 seconds that elapsed between plays. Or spreading passes all over the field, deep and short, sideline to sideline, stretching the field of play by using every inch of the 35-yard-by-53.33-yard rectangle in front of him.† Or that Dustin Dewald was throwing 70 or more percent of the time.

Then there were innovations that no one on the outside could see, like the absence of a playbook. Like the radical simplicity of an offense that had been made to look vastly complex and indecipherable. Like Hal's unique formula for decoding the field—the read progression—and the receivers' ability to read and react on their own to defenses.

Taken together, these elements constituted an offense that, it is safe to say, no other football team had ever faced.

Still, this was big, bad Northeast Missouri, not the Little Sisters of Mercy. There was an obvious physical mismatch between the two teams, and the enemy was not going to get down on his hands and knees and surrender to Hal's brilliant ideas. He had to be beaten. That did not happen right away. The first half went to the Bulldogs. The Tigers moved the ball well but had trouble putting it in the

---

* In the middle of the 1991 season, about a month after the IWC–Northeast Missouri game, head coach Rich Rodriguez put in a full-time shotgun formation at Glenville State College, in West Virginia. The two events were unrelated. He ran a version of the run-and-shoot out of it. There were experiments like this here and there, but most coaches across the country still saw the shotgun as a third-down or passing-down formation.

† It is important to note that Hal never called his offense a "spread," a term that generally refers to the practice of expanding the offensive formation to fill most of the width of the field and to spreading four or five receivers wide at all times. Hal had one and sometimes two backs in the backfield, and neither the slots nor the wideouts were excessively wide. To Hal, and to Leach, too, "spread" meant mainly two things: the O-line splits and the fact that once the receivers crossed the line of scrimmage, they indeed forced the defense to cover the entire field. At Texas Tech Leach would change this and indeed spread the field with a single back. Hal is often considered, incorrectly, to be one of the fathers of the spread offense.

end zone. They had some bad luck: a fumble, a blocked punt that was run in for a touchdown.

At the half Northeast Missouri led, 24–7.

And then something interesting happened. Hal, with memories of Morningside and Portland State and the prospects of an 0-4 start still dancing in his head, was trying to think of something he could say to motivate the team at halftime, something to give them a fighting chance. As he walked through the locker room, he encountered Shawn Martin, a talented offensive tackle whom Hal had always found a bit shy. When their eyes met, Martin's gaze fixed itself on Hal. "Don't worry, coach, we're going to win the game."

In spite of his small size, quarterback Dustin Dewald
put up astounding passing and scoring numbers.

Perplexed, Hal moved deeper into the locker room, where he met an equally upbeat Dewald.

"You don't need to say anything at halftime, coach," Dewald said. "We're gonna kick their ass."

Around him, Hal now realized that he saw no bowed heads or downcast eyes. Everybody was pumped up and ready to go.

What the players had experienced were the devastating effects on the defense of both their unrelenting speed of play and the constant screens and short passes into the flats and short crossing patterns like mesh that, by design, had forced the linebackers and linemen to sprint back and forth across the field. It was only halftime and the Bulldogs were already gassed. Everyone on the IWC offense could feel it.

What followed was an astonishing display of offensive prowess by a physically overmatched team that, in the words of booster club president John Lance, "made the hair on the back of my neck stand up." Hal had long worked on redefining space on the field—its contours, curves, and folds. Now he had redefined *time*, too. The Tigers would run 82 plays that game—the equivalent of five quarters of traditionally paced football. (Later in the season they would run 100, which was like adding another full half of play.) The crazy tempo, which should have been a burden, was actually the instrument of liberation, the thing that made everything else cohere. It was now as much a part of Hal's system as the quarterback's read progressions.

Iowa Wesleyan dominated the second half of play, scoring 27 unanswered points. As the game went on, and Northeast Missouri's defense ran out of breath and patience, the Tigers gained momentum. Dewald hit Marcus Washington for 30 yards to set up a 9-yard touchdown to wide receiver Chann Chavis. In the fourth quarter the Tigers drove down the field three times, moving the ball at will and alternating downfield passes with their usual maddening flurry of screens, short curls, and crossing routes. They attacked the flat with a vengeance. The ground game was popping, too, as the fear of short and deep passes spread defenders across the field and the gaps between linemen opened natural running lanes.

One of the game's most spectacular plays happened with 3 minutes and 24 seconds left on the clock and the Tigers holding a fragile lead of 28–24. Dewald set his team up at the line of scrimmage in the shotgun formation and called Y-cross.* As he did, he saw Northeast

---

* See Chapter 18 for a diagram and full explanation of Y-cross.

Missouri's two big inside linebackers lining up in the gaps on either side of the center. Dewald did not change the call. Instead he ran up to the center, took the snap underneath, took one step back, and looped the ball over the heads of the onrushing linebackers into the empty space they had abandoned and into the waiting arms of Washington. As the Y, or tight end, Washington was supposed to run under the strongside linebacker and over the middle linebacker toward a spot 22 yards deep on the far sideline. But because this was Hal's offense, Washington was also given enormous freedom. If the linebackers were blitzing, then Washington could snap off his route and run just behind the line of scrimmage and parallel to it. Because he and Dewald saw the same defensive shift, this is what he did, cutting directly to the space where the linebackers had been. He caught the ball, deked the safety, and scored a 51-yard touchdown to ice the game. That afternoon he led all IWC receivers with 6 catches for 128 yards. (He had also turned into an outstanding student who was elected homecoming king that year. His old friend Dereck Hall had been runner-up for king the year before. Washington would later be named to the All-America team.) The play would never have worked if IWC receivers had not been trained to read the field and find open grass on their own, or if the quarterback had not been given the authority to change plays at the line of scrimmage. The play could not have worked if Hal had not completely redefined the tight end position. Traditionally it required a large body who could block like a tackle and run the odd route. At IWC the Y position became a playmaker—as evidenced by the number of key plays whose names featured him: Y-cross, Y-sail, Y-stick, Y-corner.

Iowa Wesleyan won, in front of its delirious small-town crowd, 34–31. There was no doubt in the stadium, campus, or town that it was the greatest victory in the school's history. The game had not been as close as the score suggested. The Tigers had piled up 537 yards of total offense compared with NMS's 322. Dewald had completed 41 of 54 passes for 454 yards and 5 touchdowns.

IWC had rushed for 92 yards on 22 carries. Dewald broke his own single-game yardage record, which he had set in 1989 against Greenville.

After five years of trial and error and thousands of napkins and credit card receipts crammed with Xs and Os and countless practices trying out this or that drill, the Northeast Missouri State game marked the moment of full synthesis, the moment when all of Hal's innovations and semi-innovations and borrowings from other coaches and minute adjustments of time, speed, and distance finally came together in a single place. All the banners were flying, trumpets blowing. American football changed that day. But it would take many years before anyone would begin to understand that.

Over the next nine games of the regular season the Tigers ran high speed all the way. Facing an unforgiving schedule that included eight teams with winning records and seven that were ranked at one time in their divisions, they put up astounding numbers. Against Concordia (Wisconsin), the team that had beaten them the previous year to kill their chances of a conference championship, IWC completed 45 of 79 passes for 454 yards in a runaway 59–29 victory. They destroyed a tough, ninth-ranked (NAIA D-I) Baker College team, 42–14, completing 41 of 57 passes for 349 yards and 5 touchdowns. They stopped a ranked MacMurray College team, 31–0, and Division II powers Missouri University of Science and Technology and Wayne State and finally disposed of nemesis Greenville, 30–14. They were 10-1 in the regular season and made the national playoffs, where they lost to fourth-ranked Moorhead State University, 47–14. The game took place in a snowstorm with a high wind and a wind chill of 20 degrees below zero that made passing the ball extremely difficult. Moorhead State was located in the icebound upper reaches of Minnesota, near Fargo, North Dakota. The Moorhead players didn't seem to have any problem with the weather.

The Tigers finished the season 10-2.

Perhaps the best measure of what Iowa Wesleyan had done in

1991 lay in Dewald's statistics, especially when measured against what was going on simultaneously in the worlds of college and professional football. In a year when he averaged 60 passes per game, completing 66. 2 percent of them for 344 yards, NFL quarterbacks attempted 31 passes per game and completed 57 percent of them for 199 yards. Though aggregate numbers are not available for the many divisions of college football, in 1991 it lagged the NFL by a considerable margin in all passing categories.

The achievements of the leading NCAA D-I quarterbacks, the nation's greatest collegiate passers, on the other hand, are easier to quantify. Dewald outperformed them all in the categories of attempts, completions, attempts per game, completion percentage, touchdowns, and total yardage, as the table below illustrates:

1991 PASSING STATISTICS		
Type	NCAA D-I Leaders	Dewald
Attempts	David Klingler (Houston) – 497	665
Completions	David Klingler – 278	400
Atts. per game	David Klingler – 45	60
Percent complete	Matt Rodgers (Iowa) – 65.4%	66.2%
Touchdowns	Troy Kopp (Pacific U.) – 37	45
Yards passing	Ty Detmer (BYU) – 4,031	4,102

At the end of the 1991 season, Dewald became just the sixth quarterback in collegiate history, at any level, to pass for more than 10,000 career yards and 100 touchdowns. He ranked second all-time in career passing touchdowns, with 128, behind only Willie Totten's 139. He was fifth all-time in passing yardage with 12,045. Ahead of him in the latter category were Ty Detmer (BYU), 15,031; Kirk Baumgartner (Wisconsin–Stevens Point), 14,847; Neil Lomax (Portland State), 13,220; and Totten (Mississippi Valley State), 12,711.

But each of those quarterbacks had taken four years to amass their statistics. Dewald's were all earned *in only three years* at Iowa Wesleyan.*

The most amazing thing of all about Dustin Dewald that year was not statistical. In the fourth game the Tigers had played one of their toughest opponents: Harding College, the fifth-ranked NAIA D-I team in the country with the top-ranked pass defense. IWC played most of the game without its best receiver, the All-American Bruce Carter, who was out with a sprained ankle. The game was sensational. The lead changed hands four times in the second half. Late in the fourth quarter IWC was holding on to a 31–28 advantage when Harding blocked a punt and scored three plays later to win the game, 35–31.

Several things had happened in the game that were not immediately apparent to the crowd that day. The first was that Dewald had set the all-time American college football records for both pass attempts and completions. He had gone a mind-boggling 61 for 86. Nothing like it had ever been done before. Nor could the crowd appreciate that fully 52 of those pass plays were something called 92, or mesh. Most important of all, they were unaware of a serious injury to Dewald himself. With 10 seconds remaining in the first half, Hal signaled to Dewald to call a version of a Hail Mary. Dewald, who hated the play, looked back at his coach and said, "No." Hal, yelling now, told Dewald to run the play. He did, and his pass was intercepted. Dewald himself tackled the ballcarrier. When he did, he felt a sharp pain in his shoulder. "Good goddamn call," he yelled to Hal as he walked off the field, his shoulder throbbing. He woke up the following morning in severe pain. He was diagnosed with a partially torn rotator cuff and given the choice of having immediate, season-ending surgery or finishing with a damaged shoulder that

---

* To see how far ahead of his time Dewald was, merely prorate his three-year touchdown numbers—128—and add the average to the total. In a hypothetical four-year career, Dewald might have passed for 171 touchdowns. Even with a subpar fourth season, he would have exceeded the current mark of 155, set in 2011 by the University of Houston's Case Keenum.

would limit his ability to throw. He chose to play. That meant both that his passes in games would lack velocity and that he would not be able to throw in practice. He thus put up those numbers for the last eight games of the season without a single practice rep. He did it all with a busted shoulder.

Iowa Wesleyan College was a respectable institution and a pleasant enough place, but it had never had anything like a culture of winning. Life there unfolded in shades of gray and brown. Now there were nationally ranked football players swaggering through McKibbin Hall and the student center and high-fiving ordinary students in the library. Polynesians were roasting pigs in underground ovens and singing and playing ukuleles. There was a joy in the dorms and on campus that had not been there before. It was impossible to miss. Everyone there felt it. Enrollment was up, too, meaning that Dr. Prins's plan was working.

It was against this background of change and optimism and celebration that Prins summoned Hal to his office two days after the Harding game. When Hal arrived it was about six o'clock. The administration building was empty, most of the lights turned out. Prins was waiting for him in the reception area.

"What's up, Dr. Prins?" Hal asked.

Prins paused for a long moment, then said somberly: "After this season is over, you've got to go away."

Stunned and confused, Hal replied: "When I first came here, I told you that if you ever want me to leave, just call me and tell me. But I don't understand why you want me to leave at this point."

"You're overbudget."

"No, sir, we're not overbudget. That's not true."

"Yeah, you're overbudget," Prins snapped. He was apparently not in a mood to be argued with.*

* Dr. Robert Prins died in 2010.

Hal said: "But I still don't understand what you mean by 'go away.'"

"I mean that, after the season is over, you and all of your coaches have to go find other jobs. We're not going to pay you anymore after your December check."

"What about the three-year contract I signed?" Hal replied, more testily now.

"Your lawyer can talk to my lawyer," Prins said.

Furious, Hal rose to leave.

"There's one more thing," Prins said.

"What thing is that?"

"Make sure your staff knows that they're not getting paid after December. And if any of them want the job of head coach, tell them to come see me."

Hal went home and told his wife, June, who was as angry and confused as he was. She thought there must be some other reason, something he had done wrong that she did not know about. Hal assured her that there was not. He had not even exceeded his budget. As Johnsen would point out to Prins himself that day, Hal was actually a bit underbudget. The next morning Hal told his staff, passing on Prins's strange choice of words and his stated reason for letting Hal go. They were all furious, all in disbelief. Then they talked about what to do next. Hal believed that there were two very big pieces of news that needed to stay secret. One was the medical status of Dewald's shoulder, which Hal had just learned. The second and deeper secret was that he had been fired.

"We're not going to tell anybody," Hal told his staff, "because if we tell anybody we're going to blow this season. We've got a really good team. We might be able to win out and get to the playoffs. If we do, I could probably get another job and everybody can go with me. But we're not going to win if our players find out about this. Y'all can't tell anybody this."

And they didn't. The season played out. Rumors did swirl, to the point that the booster club circulated a petition to keep Hal in

Mount Pleasant. But no one, the press included, learned that Hal was leaving until two months after the football season had ended. Hal and Prins thus became, oddly, coconspirators. Hal wanted to preserve the illusion in order to find a new job, on the theory that as most prospective employers would see it, a coach with a 10-2 record and a national ranking who gets fired is either sleeping with the college president's wife or cheating or drinking too much or abusing his players, or some combination of all of those. Prins wanted to preserve his legal fiction that Hal wasn't being fired so he would not have to pay out on a three-year contract. That was the belief of Hal's lawyer, Gary Wiegel, anyway, who thought that the evasive language was all legalistic.

In any case, the entire grand experiment would be over in a matter of weeks. Hal Mumme would be part of Iowa Wesleyan's past. Neither Hal nor Prins would ever comment publicly on what happened between them. Which left everyone to speculate. There was no question that some members of the faculty and board believed that IWC was focusing too much on football and that football was detracting from the mission of the college, which did not involve an emphasis on sports. Hal wanted to build a nationally ranked Division II program, and it is likely that almost no one else in the university community shared that desire. Dean of students Carol Nemitz believed that Hal had "brought some glory years to Iowa Wesleyan" and had involved the community in a way she had never seen before, but that "he had just gotten too big for the college." She believed that his ambitions and need for larger budgets would severely strain the college's resources. Johnsen thought it came down to ego: Hal was getting more headlines than Prins.

Just before Christmas, Hal received his last paycheck from Iowa Wesleyan, which came with a handwritten note from Prins making sure that Hal understood it would be the last. That same day Hal, along with other full-time employees of the college, received a free Christmas turkey, with best wishes from Prins. Hal of course wanted nothing to do with such a gift. He left the office, while behind him he heard a voice call out, "Hey, coach! Don't forget your Christmas turkey!" An hour later Charlie Moot—Hal's defensive coordinator, who was about to take over as head coach, with Hal's help—arrived at the Mumme house carrying the turkey. He thought he was being helpful. Hal, who now had the impression that he was being pursued by Prins's turkey through the streets of Mount Pleasant, took the bird from Moot, carried it two blocks through the snow to Prins's stately home, and flung it over the fence.

17

The Street Value of
an Aerial Circus

While Hal's astounding little football team was putting up record numbers and beating schools ten times its size and leading the nation in most passing categories in the last half of the season, he was busy trying to find a new job. He believed he had the credentials to move up. He had hope. There was an opening for a head coach at South Dakota University (D-II) that looked promising. The team had been losing consistently and was looking for the sort of turnaround Hal had engineered at IWC. There was another at Missouri Western State University, a school that played in the same Division II league with Missouri University of Science and Technology and Northeast Missouri State. Hal had beaten both of those teams; his name would surely carry some weight in that conference. He had connections at Stephen F. Austin State University, in Texas, where another head coaching job had opened. He sent résumés to these and other schools. He solicited references. He followed up.

The result: He did not get a single interview for a college job. Nobody wanted to talk to him.

He was considered for the job of head coach at Bryan High School, in Bryan, Texas—a step backward for Hal, who had proved his ability as a college coach—but he was ultimately rejected for that job, too.

It was as though the same veil of silence that cloaked his employment status had now descended on his achievements at Iowa Wesleyan. The beauty of IWC and its relative obscurity was that Hal had been left alone to pursue his vision with little interference. He could try apparently crazy things, like throwing the ball 70 or 80 times a game or splitting his offensive linemen five feet apart in two-point stances or running at two-minute-drill speed for 60 minutes, without the alumni and board of directors experiencing aneurysms and trying to remove him. The problem was that very obscurity: Few people paid any attention to the NAIA or to Division III, a tightly circumscribed world of small schools in small towns with small stadiums that played in the deep shadow of the larger NCAA divisions. There were no such things as the Internet or social media or smartphones or the wild proliferation of cable channels that would come later, no way for news of a great game or an individual achievement to move through a nonexistent digital landscape, no way for most information to bypass the mainstream channels of the big-city newspapers, national magazines, and network television stations.

There were occasional sniffs of interest from the outside, when some big-city media outlet would dispatch a reporter to the wilds of southeastern Iowa. In October 1991, an Associated Press staffer based in Des Moines wrote a story about Dustin Dewald with the headline "Nation's Most Prolific Passer Found at IWC," pointing out that "big-time throwers" like BYU's Ty Detmer, the University of Houston's David Klingler, and Florida State's Casey Weldon were "not even close" to Dewald's passing yardage (Detmer was the only one within 1,000 yards at that point).

But such stories were rare. Local news tended to stay local. It was a fact, too, that Dewald had made his numbers against competition that wasn't going to be confused with Michigan State. Seen in the larger context of college sports, what he and Hal had done at Iowa Wesleyan was a major achievement in a minor league. Nobody who wasn't paying close attention could possibly understand the meaning of the astounding victory over Northeast Missouri State. In the media's eyes, the nation's hottest passing offense was the University of Houston, which was operating the run-and-shoot and racking up fun-house numbers. Quarterback Andre Ware had won the Heisman Trophy there in 1989. There were lots of national stories about Houston's wide-open, gunslinging offense, nothing about the small revolution taking place in the Illini-Badger-Hawkeye Conference.

More significant still was the breathtaking ignorance, on the part of most of the people who saw Iowa Wesleyan play, of what lay behind those dizzying statistics. The local papers understood *records* just fine. When Hal's team or players broke IWC school or division marks, the papers covered it happily and in detail. They understood rankings and, to some extent, raw yardage. But they had no sense of context, no appreciation of exactly how a coach and his team could pile up such wild statistics, how utterly different their style of football was from almost everything else being done, how far beyond NFL and collegiate statistical averages IWC was, or why a play like mesh was different from any old pass play. They just saw what most people saw: receivers running and quarterbacks throwing and somehow, mystically, passes getting completed. Who knew how? And who knew the difference between a good pass and a bad pass? To read the various newspaper accounts in Mount Pleasant and other towns, you would not have had the remotest clue that, beyond throwing the ball a lot, Tiger audiences were seeing what amounted to a reinvention of the game of football. Opposing teams certainly knew that Hal's offense was radically different. They, too, did not know how it worked, and the proof was that they could not come close to stopping it. In the end most outsiders did not really care to understand it. There was the traditional bias, almost as old as the sport itself, that held that pass-first offenses amounted to a sophisticated form of cheating that would soon be suppressed.

There was, of course, the possibility that Hal's moment had already passed, that what he and his players had done—fully in keeping with football's habit of shelving its best inventions—was destined to live on only in the minds of his players, the archives of Iowa Wesleyan, and the morgue of the *Mt. Pleasant News.*

Hal's wife, June, was even more upset than Hal by what had happened. She had allowed herself to believe that they had finally left behind the grinding, desperate, knife-edge life of the small-time football coach, that the days of dragging around from town to town after jobs and having to do everything herself—house, kids, banks—because Hal was always working and new jobs always started yesterday, were over. Their three children—now 16, 14, and 8—were settled in a decent school system. They lived in a comfortable old house on a prosperous street. They could afford vacations. They could also afford to live on Hal's paycheck alone, which meant that June could finish the college degree she had started so many years before at LSU. She had graduated from Iowa Wesleyan in 1990 with a business degree and had gone to work for the booster club, marketing Hal's football program. She raised funds, produced posters, sold ads for Hal's weekly radio show and for the game-day programs. She pitched sponsorship packages. She got a cut of the fund-raising. She was good at it.

All that was gone in an instant. Christmas in 1991 now looked a lot like that hopeless Christmas in 1985 after Hal had been fired at UTEP. It meant the end of the family's income. It meant the end of Mount Pleasant and the start of God only knew what.

Around that time there arrived what was, from June's point of view, a fresh horror to add to the horrors of joblessness and penury and selling the house and moving and pulling the kids out of school. This was the news that Hal had accepted a job with very likely the flakiest organization in all of football, one that would not even pay for his plane ticket to the team's training camp. June would be left behind again to sort things out, and this time she was really furious.

The job was offensive coordinator for the Washington Marauders of the brand-new, nine-team Professional Spring Football League, or PSFL, as it was known to the few people it was actually known to. The idea was, the teams would be assembled from NFL rejects and near-misses, they would practice in the winter in Florida and other warm places, then start their spring season in cities around the country. Hal's team would play in RFK Stadium, in Washington, D.C. He was hired by his friend Guy Morriss, who was the head coach. Morriss had played offensive line in the NFL for 15 years for the Patriots and Eagles and had coached for the Patriots for two years. Hal would be the offensive coordinator, and an energetic 30-year-old rising star named Rob Ryan, who had been coaching at Tennessee State, would coach the defense.* The job paid $50,000 a year.

Or would have, had Hal ever received a single paycheck. As it was, he spent three weeks in January at the Marauders' camp at a high school field in Orlando, Florida, sharing a room with Ryan at a Best Western Hotel. They would practice during the day, and at night the two men would sit up drinking beer and diagramming plays, trading the chalk back and forth. Ryan would draw up versions of his father Buddy Ryan's 46 defense and tell Hal how he was going to kick his ass. Hal would draw up mesh and explain that, in fact, it was Ryan's ass that was going to get kicked. On into the night, and ultimately to no end: The league would never make it to its first game. Ryan would never see a paycheck either.

While Hal was laboring to teach his offense to professional football players, a process was under way in a small southern town 200 miles from his football camp—unbeknownst to Hal—that would soon change everything.

During one of Mike Leach's winter recruiting trips he had passed through the town of Valdosta, Georgia, in the southern part of the state, near the Florida border. He had been impressed by how pretty the town was. He later learned that it housed the even prettier Valdosta State College. VSU was, in fact, one of the loveliest campuses in the South, which was saying something. There were fountains

---

* Ryan would later become defensive coordinator for the Oakland Raiders, Cleveland Browns, Dallas Cowboys, and New Orleans Saints.

and gardens and palm trees everywhere, immaculate green lawns and grand old mission-style buildings with red-tile roofs. It soon became clear to Leach that, compared to Iowa Wesleyan, Valdosta State was a five-star recruiter's paradise. If he and Hal could draw decent players to the bleak, existential emptiness of the frozen plains, imagine what they could do with this lush, sun-warmed utopia. Who wouldn't want to play football at Valdosta State? At the time, there were no job openings there for football coaches.

By the late fall of 1991 that had changed. Valdosta was looking for a head coach. When Leach heard the news, he hustled into Hal's office.

"You really ought to go after this Valdosta State job," he said. He explained about the palm-tree-lined campus.

Hal, who found this mildly amusing, replied: "It would be a waste of a stamp, Mike. They're too provincial. They're not gonna hire anybody from Iowa, especially when they find out I'm from Texas."

Because Leach was an extremely persistent person, he returned to Hal's office later to plead his case. "You need to apply to Valdosta State," he said, more forcefully this time, explaining in greater detail his recruiting concept.

"If it means that much to you," Hal replied, "go and tell Sharon [Leach's wife, a team secretary] to put a résumé in the mail." And that was that. Leach was placated. Hal was off in pursuit of all those jobs he did not get.

But that was not the end of it. As Hal would later learn, Leach had not only sent his résumé to Valdosta State. He had also included a videotape of the team's 48 touchdown passes from the 1991 season, edited by him personally and set to the music of John Mellencamp's "Small Town." Leach had originally made the tape to raise money for IWC's playoff trip to Moorhead State. But this seemed to him like a good way to put it to use. Hal, meanwhile, forgot that he had even applied for the job.

Leach's tape, meanwhile, had come into the possession of Valdosta State's brand-new athletics director, a compact, strong-willed former star placekicker named Herb Reinhard, who became one of the first people outside of Mount Pleasant to begin to understand what Hal had done. Valdosta State had fielded a football team for only 10 years, most of which were undistinguished. Reinhard was looking for something to make it stand out, something different. As he searched for a coach, he found himself watching Leach's tape over and over. He even made his wife watch it. Whatever else you could say about IWC's oddball offense, it looked nothing like the kind of football that was being played in his part of the country. "I can sell tickets to this," he told her. He and his search committee interviewed Hal in January. On February 4, 1992, Reinhard called Hal and hired him, over the objections of some members of the committee. Hal was barely two months shy of his 40th birthday. At the press conference introducing him to the curious and somewhat perplexed football world of Valdosta, Georgia, he got the name of Valdosta State's conference wrong.

18

Air Raid

When word got out that Valdosta State had hired a Texan from Iowa who passed the ball all the time, the consensus of opinion in south Georgia was immediate and unambiguous: There is no way that sort of football will ever work here. He will never get away with it. There was a good deal of disdain in this reaction, too, as though what was being proposed were illegal or unsanitary or both, but in any case not something that local people wanted their children doing.

If prejudice against throwing a football continued to run deep in America 86 years after the first official pass, it ran twice as deep in south Georgia and in the pretty, prosperous antebellum town of Valdosta in particular. This was one of the great football regions of America, one of the most prolific producers of high school talent, and one of the great cradles of coaches. Valdosta High School was the winningest high school football program in American history. Since 1913 its record was an astounding 712-141-33. The school had won 22 state championships and 6 national championships. It won by playing rugged, deeply traditional, run-oriented football and doing it better than anybody else. The town's other high school, Lowndes, was a power in its own right, winning a state championship in 1980. It was no accident that Hal was about to become the third-highest-paid football coach in town.

Though Valdosta State's football team had experienced only modest success in the 10 years of its existence, with a record of

57-45-3, the league in which it played, the Gulf South Conference, was the toughest in NCAA Division II. Its best teams—the University of North Alabama, Jacksonville State University, Mississippi College—could have beaten many NCAA Division I-A and I-AA teams. Among them, those three teams alone would win five of seven national Division II championships from 1989 to 1995. The Gulf South was, moreover, a close cousin of the Southeastern Conference. The coach of the best team in the Gulf South Conference, Bobby Wallace, of North Alabama, had come from Auburn, where he had coached defensive backs. The man Hal was succeeding at Valdosta, Mike Cavan, had once been the backfield coach at Georgia. The coaching staffs of Gulf South teams were full of such SEC pedigrees, and the GSC had long been considered a proving ground for future SEC head coaches. For that reason their teams often ran mirror-image SEC playbooks. The Gulf South was known for its ground-based offenses and its crushing defenses. Just like the SEC. In both conferences the basic idea of offensive football was to line up in an I formation, toss the ball to the tailback, and grind the opposition to death.

Into this land of hard-nosed, ultra-traditional football came Hal Mumme, Mike Leach, and the rest of the irregulars from Mount Pleasant, bringing their subversive ideas with them. It was no secret that Hal was going to throw the ball 50 times a game and that he did strange, unnatural things, like putting his linemen in two-point stances. Nor was he shy about explaining his coaching theories to the curious denizens of south Georgia, including his belief that practices should include very little hitting and no wind sprints at all.

In Valdosta this was blasphemy. In the 19th century, Yale's Walter Camp had protested that the forward pass would "sissify" the game. One hundred years later, the local reaction to Hal's ideas could be summarized the same way. Football here was all about raw power and the ability to cram your will down your opponent's throat. Valdosta High coach Nick Hyder was proud that his players never hit dummies: they always hit live meat. Football was about meat hitting meat and who felt the most pain. Down here there were no light practices. Down here everybody sprinted till they puked.

From his earliest days in Georgia Hal had heard from local fans that, while his radical methods might have worked at some flyspeck of a college in a middle-of-nowhere conference, he could never win with them in the Gulf South. He would see, they said. Just watch what happens to your precious quarterback. But it was not until two months after his arrival that he fully understood just how deeply unpopular he was with the Georgia football community.

Hal had decided that to help introduce himself to Georgia high school coaches—who would be critically important to his recruiting—he would put on a clinic for them in April. Many college head coaches did this, including Hal's predecessor at Valdosta State. Hal worked hard on it, securing a lineup of guest speakers that included NFL assistant coaches from the Chicago Bears and Washington Redskins, a BYU assistant coach, and two high school coaches who had won state championships. There would be a full day of football theory with experts speaking on their areas of specialty. Hal would meet the coaches, who he hoped would send him their best players.

Nobody came. No Georgia high school coaches wanted any part of Hal's heresies, let alone a clinic where they could learn how to coach them. While there was plenty of natural aversion to the idea of the forward pass, there was also the feeling among football people that throwing the ball *down here*—as in, Gulf South and SEC country—would not work. Their jobs depended on winning, and what Hal was proposing, on a purely practical level, was a formula for losing. Once it became clear that no one was going to show up, the speakers went ahead with their lectures anyway and listened to one another. It was Hal's first big event as head coach.

In all other ways Valdosta looked to Hal like a dream job. The place was just as Leach had described it: one of the most beautiful campuses in the South. Walking across the immaculately manicured front lawn, he would gaze up at the palm trees or watch the Frisbee games and think how much better this was than the relentless, ice-bound midwestern winter. The world was a sweet, hopeful place that spring. Hal was making a good salary—$58,000, plus income from his own radio and TV shows and summer camps—and June had found a nice home in a good neighborhood. His son, Matt, a talented quarterback, would be playing football for the greatest high school team in American history.

Hal had the coaches he wanted, too. Leach was the most important of these. With his intimate knowledge of the offense and his ability to find players to execute it, he was now critical to Hal's success. He would carry the title of offensive coordinator (as he had in 1991 at IWC) and would officially coach the receivers instead of the offensive line. This was in part to give him wider experience of the offense and in part because Hal had hired Guy Morriss to coach the O-line. Morris had lost his job as the head coach of the Washington Marauders soon after Hal had left, and he had accepted Hal's offer of employment. (Hal offered Rob Ryan a job, too, but Ryan chose to return to Tennessee State.) Mike Major, who had been the defensive coordinator at Copperas Cove and for Hal's first year at Iowa Wesleyan, returned to coach the defense. He and Hal were friends, and Hal trusted him, which was important, since Hal spent almost no time worrying about defense. Defense was just something the rulebook said he had to have. With Major was another IWC veteran, John Wiley, who would coach the secondary. (The other key defensive coach, Mike Fanoga, remained at Iowa Wesleyan, in part to help shepherd his Polynesian flock. He would join Hal the following year, as would former receiver Dana Holgorsen, as a graduate assistant.)

Most important, Hal had inherited a good football team instead of a wreckage of one, as he had in his previous three posts, at UTEP, Copperas Cove, and Iowa Wesleyan. Though the Valdosta State Blazers had started the previous season 1-3, they had finished strong, ending with a 6-3-1 record. The defense had looked solid, especially Antonio Edwards, the 1991 NCAA D-II Defensive Player of the Year. Hal would have some fast, talented receivers to work with and an experienced offensive line. (He would also benefit from his own import, the redoubtable blindside tackle York Kurinsky, who had migrated south with Hal from Iowa Wesleyan.)

But to Hal the most interesting part of the team he inherited was a scrawny, 5-foot-11, 170-pound sophomore who looked like Tom Sawyer's younger brother and was easily mistaken for the equipment manager. His name was Chris Hatcher. He had played quarterback at a small private school in Macon, Georgia, then had walked on as a freshman at Valdosta State the year before Hal arrived. He was a typical coach's son: a diligent, hardworking gym rat who loved the game but lacked great physical talent. Because of his diminutive size, average arm strength, and subaverage speed, he was relegated to the nether regions of fourth- and fifth-string players who were never going to see playing time.

But something happened in his freshman season to change that. The Blazers started losing. They scored a total of 10 points in their first three games, in significant part because their quarterbacks could not complete routine passes. They especially could not throw curl routes, common and relatively low-risk patterns in which the receiver sprints hard straight downfield for 8 to 12 yards, then turns sharply and comes back to the ball. Valdosta State head coach Mike Cavan thus began a descent through the ranks of quarterbacks until he found someone who could throw a curl route. That was Hatcher. He was a little guy with a baby face who had a conspicuously non-bazooka-like arm, but he was reasonably accurate. He was one of the reasons the team started winning. Over the last seven games as a starter he averaged 12 completions in 21 attempts (57 percent) for an average of 155 yards per game. He threw 8 touchdown passes. By Gulf South Conference standards, that made him a prolific passer. He was rewarded with a full scholarship.

Now, under Hal, Hatcher would be the key to everything. Though a quarterback in Hal's offense did not have to be big, strong, or fast, he did have to understand how the read-progression system worked, how option routes worked, how to call plays at the line of scrimmage, and how to get rid of the ball quickly. The one obvious weakness in Hal's system was its dependence—some might have said overdependence—on the quarterback. It was impossible not to notice that for four of the six years that his offense had been in operation—three at Copperas Cove and three at Iowa Wesleyan—Dustin Dewald had been its quarterback. (Dewald graduated the year Hal left.) Which meant that it was possible that Hal had simply gotten lucky. Hatcher would be the test case, the opportunity to prove that the system was transportable, that it could be taught to quarterbacks who were not named Dewald.

Thus in spring and late-summer camps Hal set about teaching Hatcher—and 100 other players who had never seen anything like his system—a new way of playing football. While there was no overt resistance to these changes, Hatcher and many others wondered why, since the team had been playing at a high level at the end of the preceding season, the coaches wanted to fix something that was not broken. Their old system was working just fine, thank you. They had finished with five wins and a tie. If there was no audible grumbling, there was an abiding skepticism among the returning players. Which meant that the coaching staff had to work especially hard. Everything had to be taught from scratch, explained patiently and in great detail. By the start of the season, in September, the players would be ready to go.

Or so the coaches wanted to believe. What happened over the next six games was a small-scale disaster that unfolded in slow motion. In the Blazers' first three losses, to Georgia Southern, Jacksonville State, and Troy State, which took the team to a 1-3 record, Hal's high-scoring air attack scored a total of 29 points. By the time Valdosta State was blown out by West Georgia 42-28 on October 17, their record was 2-4 and they were in free fall. Hatcher was playing poorly, looking more confused all the time, and the more hesitant and confused he was the angrier Hal became.

Their differences came to a head in the West Georgia game. Valdosta State had blown a 28–7 halftime lead in part because Hatcher was refusing to throw the ball downfield to open receivers and was instead doing what Hal called "dinking" the ball. He had suddenly become conservative in his approach to passing; he had become like every other quarterback in south Georgia. Hal told him he was going to bench him. A talented freshman backup named Lance Funderburk would start, Hal said. The two exchanged heated words. Hal wasn't budging. "You are not taking my team away from me!" Hatcher yelled, and proceeded to hustle at the next week's practices as he had never hustled before. He was evidently deeply upset about his poor performance and his failure to please his coach.

But as Hal would soon come to understand, the problem was not Chris Hatcher. The problem was Hal. He had committed a fundamental football sin. He had been so busy being successful and breaking records and reading his press clippings that he hadn't seen it. His apostasy could be summarized in a single word: *complexity*. It was a very big sin in Hal's private universe and had been one of the first things he had rebelled against when he started coaching. The most common temptation for any football coach is to add plays and variations of plays and formations to his playbook. This begins as an exercise in self-improvement: more is better, especially if it confuses defenses. If a halfback sweep left is good, a halfback sweep with a cutback option and a pulling guard is better. There was no virtue in simplicity. More also *looked* better: A bulging playbook that players complained about having to learn was a badge of merit, a sign of how hard the coach had worked to amass so much football knowledge and how hard his offense would be to predict. The process was additive; nothing was ever lost.

At Iowa Wesleyan Hal and Leach understood this. They had

battled constantly to pare down their playlist, fighting their natural desire as coaches to add plays without subtracting any. Each year Leach would conduct an analysis of all the plays they had run. The two men would discuss them and agree to drop anything that did not average more than 5 yards. And then, of course, there had been the reduction in 1991 when they had begun to play fast. Simplicity and all it brought—great ability to focus, higher repetitions of plays in practice, the ability to play fast because players were not hesitant or confused—was the cardinal virtue of the system, the grease that made everything work. And Hal had stuck to it while he watched rival systems that had once been simple—the run-and-shoot and the West Coast offense in particular—grow dense and intricate.

But in the transition from Mount Pleasant to Valdosta Hal's playbook had grown. He had convinced himself that the players in the football-crazed South had a larger capacity to learn than players elsewhere. He had added formations. He had added plays and had violated his own rule that required subtracting a play for every one added. His system was still far simpler than anything else in the game, but his players now had to absorb every piece of it—and this was the thing he really did not see—*in a matter of months.* Dewald had had four years to learn an offense that had been tailored in part to fit him. Hatcher had to learn everything between April and September.

Hal realized that he was crushing his quarterback with information. And the overload had caused Hatcher and everybody else on the offense to lose sight of the oddest and most unusual feature of the system: that it was less about Xs and Os and more about *attitude, optimism, and a way of thinking.* To make this offense work, you had to believe you were going to score from any part of the field anytime. You had to be fearless. You had to stop worrying about what the defense was going to do to you. You had to be prepared to flex as the systems built to stop you flexed; you had to move freely in space and you had to feel the space around you as though it were a tangible thing and adjust to its movements. The game was to find open grass and possess it for a tenth of a second, and that was supposed to be, yes, fun, as Tiger Ellison had preached. What had happened in the first six games of 1992 wasn't anything like fun. University of Texas football coach Darrell Royal once observed that a confused player cannot play fast. And, he added, "You can take that to the bank." Hal now found himself with a team full of confused players.

So Hal performed radical emergency surgery in the middle of the 1992 season. He chopped his offense down to a level of simplicity that had never existed before. He got rid of all but two formations: the one-back set with four wides ("ace") and the two-back set with three wides ("blue"). (Hatcher believed that there had been as many as 20 different formations at the beginning of the season, if you counted every variation of every back and receiver.) He also got rid of most of the plays. Though the number would rise a bit later on, Hal gave Hatcher a handful of basic plays and he let Hatcher call them.

Hal had not really intended to bench Hatcher, but he let Funderburk play a quarter anyway in the next game against American International just to scare him. It worked. On his first play from scrimmage Hatcher checked from a scripted screen pass to 6 (Four Verticals) and threw an arcing 80-yard touchdown pass to receiver Calvin Walker. From that point forward everything changed. The component parts of the system kicked in. Hatcher got it. The next week, VSU beat a formidable Mississippi College team they had never beaten, 28–14, as Hatcher completed 36 of 47 passes for 350 yards and 3 touchdowns. The following week, he went 30 of 45 for 358 yards and 4 touchdowns in a 45–7 blowout of traditional power Delta State. In its last game, VSU tied North Alabama, one of the top D-II teams in the country, 24–24. For the season Hatcher passed for 2,548 yards and 21 touchdowns. His completion rate was a remarkable 66 percent. His top receiver, Walker, who had caught only 8 passes for 84 yards the previous year, caught 71 passes for 867 yards. The team ended with a 5-4-1 record, which sounded to many people, including the ubiquitous skeptics, like business as usual for Valdosta State. It was really anything but.

Hatcher's struggles early in the season had forced Hal to return to one of the most elemental principles of his offense: *the idea that technique and execution were more important than scheme.* That statement was subscribed to by few coaches in the game of football. Most believed that the complexity of their playbooks, more than the way plays were executed, was what defeated defenses. Hal, meanwhile, was not necessarily trying to deceive anyone. He would be happy to draw up mesh for you, show you how it was going to disembowel your middle linebacker, then proceed to actually dis-embowel your middle linebacker. Because of the innate simplicity of his system, the mind-numbing repetition of the same plays at his practices, and his opponents' inability to practice enough to counter it, his players could execute their plays better than their defenders could execute theirs. Knowing where his receivers were going or what options they had would not help the defense very much. This was always the greatest mystery behind the offense, the part that defensive coordinators could never figure out, no matter how many hours of film they watched. They always assumed it was all about scheme, about necromancy and voodoo and giant playbooks and indecipherable play sets.

In the spring of 1993 Hal made yet another radical move to simplify the offense. In a conversation years before, Bill Walsh had told Hal that he did not believe that a team had to have left and right versions of all its plays. If you ran a sweep to the right because you had a great pulling guard on that side who made it work, that did not mean you had to run the identical sweep left. The practice of running asymmetrically was not unknown. Fred Biletnikoff, the Hall of Fame receiver for the old Oakland Raiders, always lined up on the right. But the notion went dead against conventional wisdom in football. Though most coaches had a natural right-handed bias, they practiced and ran mirror images of most of their plays. The belief was that if you did not flip your plays, you would become too predictable, easier to stop. The idea of running exclusively right-handed or left-handed made little sense. Why not just flip every play, make the defense adjust?

Hal had been pondering Walsh's idea for years. Running the offense from one side—meaning that the X receiver was always far left, the Y and Z on the right, in the backfield the H usually left and the F right—would offer huge advantages. It cut the number of total plays roughly in half, and therefore allowed him to double the number of repetitions each play got in practice. Hal had already begun to run certain plays almost entirely right-handed. That spring two events intervened to resolve the matter.

The first was the decision, by both college football and the NFL, to move the hash marks on the field closer together, more toward the middle of the field, which meant that teams would no longer have to run plays jammed up against one sideline or the other. The second was a trip Hal and Morriss took—one of those off-season journeys into the football heartland Hal loved—to visit Raymond Berry in Denver. Berry had played for the Baltimore Colts and had been famous as one of Johnny Unitas's main receivers. He had been the head coach of the New England Patriots from 1984 to 1989. He had just been fired as quarterbacks coach of the Denver Broncos and had some time on his hands. While his wife, Sally, cooked, he and Hal and Morriss talked offensive football. Hal diagrammed mesh for Berry, who loved it and thought it would work in the NFL.

Hal then told Berry that, because of the hash mark changes, he was thinking about running his offense from the right side only and asked him what he thought of this idea. Berry responded by enthusiastically grabbing the marker and diagramming the "brown" set from the old Baltimore Colts days: Berry was the X receiver, Jimmy Orr was the Z, John Mackey was the Y. Berry explained that he had *always* lined up on the left. Always. Every down-and-out pass route the great Raymond Berry had ever run for the Colts was run from the same side. Contrary to all perceived wisdom, this did not make Berry any easier for the defense to cover. "We did it in the NFL," Berry told Hal. "You can do it at the college level."

So Hal changed everything again at practice that spring. Valdosta State would now run entirely right-handed. He thereby effected yet another quiet revolution that no one noticed. The combined effect of the radical paring of plays in 1992 and the decision to run right-handed only in 1993 was to create a stripped-down football machine that did not exist anywhere else. It was the culmination of all of his work on the idea of simplicity. The team went 8-3 that year, finishing in second place in the Gulf South behind the eventual NCAA Division II national champion, North Alabama. In midseason, VSU was ranked seventh in the D-II nation. One of its losses was to North Alabama. Another was an aerial shootout that ended in the near-upset of NCAA I-AA power Central Florida, 35–30.

The team's statistics at the end of that second season showed the remarkable progress that had been made. In 1993 VSU ranked fourth in the nation in passing offense and fifth in scoring offense and led the Gulf South in both categories. Hatcher, who was named a first-team All-American, set 20 school, 13 conference, and 5 national passing records. His 37 touchdowns were a new conference record. Most impressive of all was his stratospheric 71 *percent completion rate*, fully five points up from the previous year, a difference accounted for entirely, Leach and Hal believed, by the decision to run right-handed. Berry was right. To put Hatcher's 71 percent into proper perspective, consider the completion rates of other passing giants of his era:

Player	Team/Org	Year	Completion %
Robbie Bosco	BYU	1984	61.8
Dan Marino	Miami Dolphins	1984	64.2
Willie Totten	Miss. Valley St.	1985	60.4
Andre Ware	Univ. of Houston	1989	63.1
Ty Detmer	BYU	1990	64.2

There was, moreover, proof that the five-read system successfully spread the ball around into the hands of a number of playmakers, which was one of the fundamental goals of Hal's offense. This was apparent in the statistics for VSU's receivers in 1993:

Receiver	Catches
Calvin Walker	82
Steven Greer	70
Robert Williams	47
Sean Pender	32
Stanley Flanders	31
Dominique Ross	24

Finally, it was clear that the passing game really did work to set up the run. Even though VSU passed the ball 65 percent of the time and used just a few running plays, halfback Dominique Ross gained 1,030 yards on the ground, which placed him fifth in the run-heavy Gulf South. Hal's pass-first system worked just exactly the way everyone in Georgia said it could not.

Hatcher had emerged, too, as something more than just a deadly accurate thrower. Where Dustin Dewald had been a quiet, serious leader, Chris Hatcher was loud and voluble. He loved walking into the room and saying, "Hey, boys, it's a great day to be a Blazer!" Then he would proceed to tell his teammates exactly why. He was a ringleader, an organizer. He was full of ideas, and he was persuasive. Sometimes he would convince the backs and receivers that they needed to go "throw some routes" in their spare time, extra practice just for the fun of it. Sometimes he organized parties. By now he and Hal had resolved whatever tensions there had been in the first year. Like Dewald, Hatcher also concerned himself with the shortcomings of his teammates. At one point Hal had threatened to cut the team's star running back, Dominique Ross, from the team for his failure to show up for weightlifting and other team activities. When Hatcher heard about it, he came to Hal and said: "I will be responsible for him." Hal said: "Okay, you go and tell him you are responsible for him. If he misses a single workout it is on your head and I am cutting him." Hatcher—and Ross—pulled it off. (Ross went on to play for the Dallas Cowboys.)

It is impossible, within the scope of this book, to address all of the tweakings, adaptations, and wholesale changes that had determined how each of Hal's plays worked on the field in the autumn of 1993. His process was like that of most other coaches: constant tinkering. There was also a constant matching of talents of particular players with particular features of his passing game. The classic play Y-cross illustrates a few of the many ways Hal adjusted his system to accommodate players and also to make individual plays more efficient. To understand how the play was modified you first have to understand the play itself.

The diagram was LaVell Edwards's, but it might have come straight from the Tiger Ellison playbook: Four of the five receivers had the ability to adjust their routes on the fly. One of those four could also have his route changed by the quarterback at the line of scrimmage. The idea—you could argue it was the idea underlying much of the passing revolution that Hal was part of—was to give the entire whirling clockwork the ability to react to what the defense was doing. Only one receiver, F, ran a strictly prescribed route. Y-cross was structured to put great strains on the defense: Three receivers crashed the zones on the weakside of the field, stretching defenders vertically and horizontally. The play worked because it was elegantly designed, but also because Hal's ultra-minimal playbook allowed the quarterback and receivers to repeat it hundreds of times in practice in routes on air. The players knew it so well that—here was the key—reading the options off the base plays became second nature for both quarterbacks and receivers.

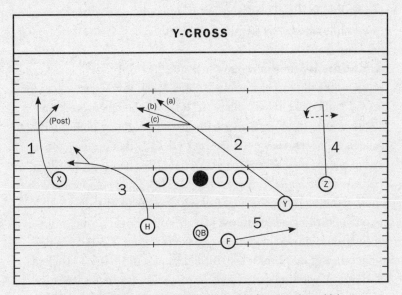

Former BYU head coach LaVell Edwards's favorite play, which
also could have come from Tiger Ellison's playbook, in which four of five
receivers are given the freedom to adjust their routes as they go.

Y-cross, like mesh, is best explained as a sequence of quarterback reads:

1. With the snap of the ball, the quarterback, who was 6 yards back in shotgun formation, took three steps back, then looked for his first read, X. X took off as if he was shot out of a cannon, got the best release he could off the cornerback, then headed straight downfield. If the quarterback saw single coverage—if the free safety was not moving off his hash mark to help the cornerback—he took an immediate vertical shot, aiming for the receiver's outside shoulder. If the quarterback thought the safety was cheating too far forward, he had the option of using a hand signal to tell X to run a post pattern, angling toward the grass in the center of the field the safety had vacated. But if the safety came off the hash

to cover X—the more likely event—then the quarterback's eyes moved immediately to his second read, Y.

2. Y's basic assignment was to run inside the strongside linebacker, then over the top of the middle linebacker. But Hal gave him a wide range of choices after that. If he was being covered man-to-man, he climbed in an arc toward an imaginary point on the far sideline 22 yards downfield (a). He had other options, too. If the middle linebacker blitzed, Y could divert and run a shallow route just behind the line of scrimmage (c). This was how Marcus Washington drove the final nail into Northeast Missouri State's coffin, turning a blitz into a 51-yard touchdown. If the middle linebacker moved toward one side or the other, Y could just find open space in the middle of the field and settle in it. He also had the option of simply flattening his route (b) against man coverage. If Y was tangled up in the middle of the field, the quarterback moved on to his third read, H.

3. H was the first safety valve if the quarterback felt pressure. His job was to check the weakside linebacker, then release on a 3-yard route in the flat. If the defense was sitting back in a zone, he would break the route off and settle outside the end.

4. Z, the fourth read, ran a 10-yard curl. When he made his break, he had the option of moving either inside or outside.

5. F ran a short route on the right side behind the line and was the ultimate fail-safe. In the face of an all-out rush, the quarterback always knew that F was waiting out in the flat.

Like most of Hal's plays, Y-cross could also be tailored to take advantage of the talents of a single player. Hal's H-back at Valdosta State that year was sophomore Sean Pender, a 5-foot-8, 165-pound speed merchant out of Jacksonville, Florida. Pender's singular talent was to find open grass within 10 yards of the line of scrimmage. Thus Hal adjusted both the route and the quarterback's sequence to accommodate Pender. He called it 95 H option. He made H the quarterback's first read, instead of his third, and then let the receiver do pretty much whatever he wanted to find open grass. He could run a hitch to the inside at a depth of 3 yards; he could simply turn inside and settle. He could break out on the flat. What was required here was both quickness and the ability to read the defender's body language. Pender had both skills. He was also deadly in the open field with the ball in his hands. By his senior year he would become, with 247 career catches for 2,072 yards, the most prolific receiver in the history of the Gulf South Conference. He did a lot of that on 95 H option.

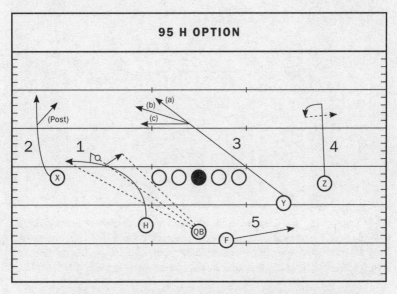

95 H OPTION

In this variation on Y-Cross, H becomes the quarterback's first read. H is also given great freedom to find open grass within a few yards of the line of scrimmage based on the behavior of the defensive backs.

Y-cross also offers an illustration of how Hal made adjustments to the actual mechanics of route-running. In this case it involved the

X receiver, who was the quarterback's first read. One of the most valuable pieces of information he had gathered from his trips to visit other coaches had come from Dennis Erickson at the University of Miami in the spring of 1991. Miami had an amazing ability to complete long passes at percentage rates other teams could only dream about. Hal had asked Erickson why. Erickson's response was to show Hal a small but actually critical adjustment that helped lift Hatcher's percent-completion numbers into previously unexplored realms.

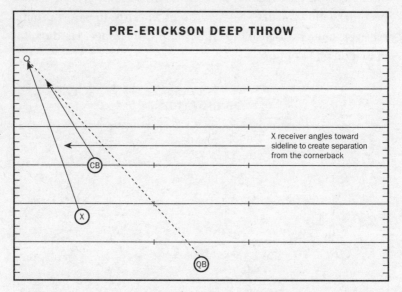

PRE-ERICKSON DEEP THROW

X receiver angles toward sideline to create separation from the cornerback

This shows the way Hal's receivers ran deep routes before his meeting with University of Miami head coach Dennis Erickson in the spring of 1991. Note that, as the receiver, X, tries to get separation from the cornerback, CB, he actually allows CB to achieve an angle on him and place himself in the line of the throw.

The diagram above shows the path that Hal's receivers took on deep balls before he and Leach met with Erickson. The premise is that the X receiver has beaten the cornerback and is a step or two ahead of him. Having gotten a step on his man, the receiver drifts toward the sideline in an effort to create even more separation. This was what most coaches in America believed he should do. It was the classic way to run an "up" route, and it did, in fact, put additional distance between the receiver and the cornerback. But it also left the defensive back directly in the line of the throw, making it easier for him to recover on a ball that was thrown short.

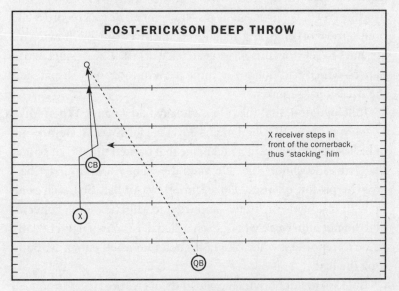

POST-ERICKSON DEEP THROW

X receiver steps in front of the cornerback, thus "stacking" him

CB

X

QB

How "stacking" the receiver works. By stepping in front of the cornerback, CB, X opens a clear passing lane with his own clear angle to the quarterback.

What Erickson taught Hal was to "stack" the defensive back, a move that was deeply counterintuitive. In Erickson's version, the receiver did not angle toward the sideline. Instead, as soon as he got behind the cornerback, he stepped in front of him. Now the cornerback was behind him, no longer in the path of the throw and no longer with a critical angle on the receiver. This greatly reduced the defender's ability to make a play or recover on an underthrown ball. Hal immediately understood the revolutionary implications of what Erickson was saying. He was astounded by how apparently simple the adjustment was. It would change the way this team threw deep passes.

Nineteen ninety-three was the year large numbers of people finally started to pay attention to what Hal was doing. Attendance was up. The North Alabama game on November 6 drew a record VSU home crowd of 9,148. High school coaches were finally showing up at games to see how this passing attack worked. The Atlanta newspapers, which had not covered the team in 1992, now dispatched the occasional reporter.

It helped, too, that the offense finally had a name. When Mike Leach was trying to solicit media coverage for Iowa Wesleyan, one of his ideas was to invent a nickname that packed the sort of punch that "run-and-shoot" did. He liked the name Steve Spurrier had given his passing offense at Duke University: Air Ball. So Leach came up with his own—Air Raid—and tried to sell Hal on the concept. Hal did not much care what Leach called it. Leach then pitched the name to reporters, who were not much interested either. Nobody took the bait.

But Leach, stubborn till the end, did not give up. He reintroduced the idea at Valdosta State, this time with an accomplice. Receiver Sean Pender's father happened to own an authentic air raid siren from an old aircraft carrier. It made a horrifically loud, earsplitting noise. He would hook it up to a big electric battery and wheel it into the stadium on a dolly, then crank it up every time Valdosta scored or made a big play. As it turned out, that was all the time, which meant that everyone on the Valdosta State campus and many of the residents of Valdosta itself knew about every touchdown the team scored. The siren was hugely popular and had the added feature of driving opposing teams to distraction. Complaints were filed. Soon the Gulf South had a new rule prohibiting "noisemakers" in conference stadiums, aimed directly at Valdosta. The team's response was to mount the siren on top of the Kappa Alpha fraternity, right next to the stadium, where it continued to wail away.

By the off-season of 1993–1994, there was no longer any doubt that Hal's oddball, sissified version of football would work in the Gulf South Conference. He was, in fact, on the verge of dominating it.

19

High, Wide, and Handsome

In 1994, 18 years after he began coaching football, Hal Mumme finally broke out, once and for all, of all the boxes and categories his peers had tried to put him in and the dustbins they had consigned him to. It was the year the national media finally discovered him and began to understand what he had done. And it was the year that scrawny little Chris Hatcher, running Hal's stripped-down, open-throttle passing machine, lit up the football world. Though VSU's schedule had started officially with a routine destruction of Knoxville College, 36–0, on September 3, the real season, the legendary season, the one everyone would always remember, began with the University of Central Florida game on September 10 at the Citrus Bowl, in Orlando.

It was one of those games where the bigger, better team pays the inferior team good money—in this case $25,000—for the privilege of beating them up in front of a large, joyous, hostile home crowd. This was how football teams padded their early schedules with lopsided victories, why you saw games that inexplicably pitted the Alabama Crimson Tide against the Charleston Southern Buccaneers, or the Arkansas Razorbacks against the dreaded Nicholls State Colonels. The bigger, better team in this case was UCF.

Just how much better, at least on paper, was readily apparent before the teams even took the field. The 24,000-student University of Central Florida was one of the principal powers of NCAA Division I-AA, a full notch above Division II, where Valdosta State played. It was in the process of moving up to Division I-A. One measure of the difference between the two divisions was the number of scholarships: VSU had 36 full rides to give out, UCF had 85. Central Florida had gone to the national playoffs twice in four years and was ranked sixth in the nation. Valdosta State, ranked 17th in its division, was a two-touchdown underdog.

When the game began, the crowd at the Citrus Bowl noticed that UCF's star running back, Marquette Smith, a future All-American and NFL player, was on the sidelines wearing headphones. He had some soreness in his ankle, and, well, the Central Florida Knights did not really think they would need him. Their feelings on this subject would change abruptly in the second quarter. Though the Knights scored first, Hatcher led the Blazers on two pitch-perfect touchdown drives, mixing runs with short and long passes. Classic Air Raid stuff, spreading the field and throwing to multiple receivers. Smith was soon hustling back to the locker room to put his uniform on.

Central Florida managed to score early in the third quarter, but that was the last time the Knights would find the end zone. The second half belonged to the Blazers, who scored 17 unanswered points to win, 31–14. They were under full sail, operating from the shotgun, warping the field with wicked vertical and horizontal stretches, using huge line splits, playing fast. Hatcher had what was by his standards a modest afternoon, completing 26 of 34 passes for 278 yards and 2 touchdowns. But he had been nearly flawless. He had thrown no interceptions and had completed an astounding 76.5 percent of his passes. Nobody else in the country was close to this sort of accuracy. Nobody in the modern history of the game had ever been able to hit 70-plus consistently, which Hatcher was now doing.* Most of the great passers of his age were in the upper 50s. A few of the more extreme cases, like Andre Ware running the

---

* Sammy Baugh completed 70 percent of his passes for the Redskins in 1945. His career percentage in college was 46 percent; his NFL career average was 56.5 percent.

run-and-shoot at the University of Houston or Dan Marino in his epic 1984 season with the Miami Dolphins, got into the lower 60s.

This was in some ways the biggest revolution embedded in Hal's offense. It realigned the conventional risk-reward equation of the game. At 65 or 70 percent, going for it on fourth down—one of the riskiest decisions a coach could make—started to look like a reasonable statistical move. Such efficiency was no accident of talent or circumstance. It was the direct product of Hal's drastically simplified, right-handed scheme, of Hatcher's freedom to adjust plays at the line of scrimmage, his skill at checking through Hal's five reads, and his receivers' aptitude for finding open grass.

Part of it, too, was that Hal had effectively reinvented and expanded the short passing game, where the percentages and efficiencies were automatically higher. One of its critical components was what was known as a "receiver" screen, an area of offense that Hal had pioneered. Traditional screen passes were thrown to backs who set up behind a "screen" of blockers. The Air Raid's screens were still thrown for few or no yards past scrimmage, but now the ball was moving horizontally to new targets. Hal's first innovation had been the quick screen, the lightning-fast horizontal pass to a wide receiver that had become a major part of his strategy. But just as devastating was a play that came to be known as a "tunnel" screen, in which the slot receiver takes two hard steps forward, turns, and comes back toward the quarterback before moving along the line of scrimmage toward the center of the play. The play's history was typical of the Air Raid. Hal and Leach had learned it from a short-lived pro team called the Sacramento Surge, which played in the World League of American Football in 1991 and 1992. (They had originally named it "surge.") They tweaked it, put it into heavy rotation, and made it famous. In both plays the blocking was key, particularly of the cornerbacks. The effect was quintessential Air Raid, too: The ball was delivered quickly into the hands of the team's best playmakers, who often ran for many yards after they made the catch. What was maddening for defenders was Hal's willingness to call the tunnel screen on any down, no matter what the distance or defensive formation.

All of this was on display in the Central Florida game, and of course all of it was made possible by VSU's terrific offensive line and its ultra-simple protections, which allowed Hatcher time to throw. And his passes set up the fleet Dominique Ross, who rushed for 102 yards. The VSU defense, meanwhile, was better than anything Hal ever dreamed he would have; it held Smith to 46 mostly meaningless yards in the second half.

For the next seven games VSU's offense would run free and wild, unstoppable, while the defense would allow more than one touchdown only once. By now opposing defensive coaches had been watching film of VSU games for three years. They had been looking at the same handful of plays over and over, dutifully recording every move, every cut. And they still could not stop the Blazer offense. Most could never grasp the brilliantly cloaked central mystery of the Air Raid, the stunningly simple fact that their defenses were being out-executed: The Valdosta players had learned a few plays really well, and they could beat you at those few plays. Period. The scores tell most of the story:

VSU	50	6 .	Fort Valley State
VSU	63	6	Clark Atlanta
VSU	63	0	Livingston*
VSU	38	7	New Haven
VSU	49	33	West Georgia
VSU	24	7	Mississippi College
VSU	57	10	Delta State

The Blazers were winning in deeply unconventional ways, too. In the victory over West Georgia, which had beaten them twice in a row, Valdosta State was trailing, 27–7, in the second quarter

* In 1995 Livingston University changed its name to the University of West Alabama.

when Hal made the decision that the Blazers would not punt again, an extreme version of his own natural preference. For the rest of the game, they went for it on *every* fourth down. They scored 42 points to West Georgia's 6 and won the game, 49–33. They crushed Livingston University, 63–0, while possessing the ball for only 20 minutes, underscoring Hal's belief that time of possession, to the overwhelming majority of coaches the critical factor in winning a game other than the score, was one of the most worthless metrics of all. At home against the University of New Haven, VSU faced a nationally ranked team that had lost only once in 25 games and featured running back Roger Graham, who had won the Division II's top award, the Harlon Hill Trophy, the previous year. Hatcher—who had finished fourth for that award—picked New Haven's defenses clean. He went 39 of 44 for 318 yards and 5 touchdowns, completing 88.6 percent of his passes against one of the country's better D-II teams. *Sports Illustrated* named him Player of the Week. The much-touted Graham, who would go on to play in the NFL for the Jacksonville Jaguars, rushed 11 times for 35 yards.

In *Run and Shoot Football,* Tiger Ellison had written about his offense as a state of mind as much as a series of plays and formations. To him it was about putting balls in the air and not being afraid of what happened when you did. Working from Ellison's blueprint, Hal had spent years tampering with the fundamentals of the game, with the *premises* of the game, shifting and altering time and space, breaking sacrosanct rules, and dragging football into the looking-glass world of the Air Raid. And that was *fun*. Yes, it was. As Ellison had prophesied, the fans came to love it. They turned out in unprecedented numbers. They loved seeing balls in the air and receivers running pass patterns that expanded kaleidoscopically across the field. They adored the *siren*. On autumn afternoons people in the streets of the sleepy Georgia town would look up when they heard it and smile. It meant victory. It meant glory. The town finally went wild for its college team, too.

As the Valdosta State Blazers steamrolled into the month of

November, they were undefeated through nine games. With 41 touchdowns, only 5 interceptions, and a 75.6 percent completion rate, Hatcher led the entire collegiate nation in passing and was rewriting division and conference record books. His receivers held the top four spots in the conference rankings in yards gained. The team was averaging 508 yards of offense per game and was ranked second in the country.

With an apparently perfect sense of dramatic timing, on November 5 the white-hot Blazers arrived in the town of Florence, Alabama, to play the number-one-ranked University of North Alabama. This was the first of two games between the two teams that year that would put Hal Mumme on the American football map for good.

That was because the North Alabama Lions were more than just a number-one team. They were arguably the greatest NCAA Division II team ever to play the game. They were midstride in a run of three straight national championships (1993, 1994, 1995), with a collective record of 41-1. The only team that had beaten them during this run was Youngstown State, the monster of Division I-AA, coached by Jim Tressel, which had won national championships in 1991 and 1993 (and would win again in 1994).* UNA had lost a squeaker to them earlier in the season, 17–14.

The Lions were loaded with enough talent to destroy most of Division I-AA and a large swath of Division I-A. Much of it was concentrated in the defense. On the line, tackles Israel Raybon and Marcus Keyes were All-Americans and future NFL draft picks; defensive end Reggie Ruffin was also an All-American. They had twin All-American linebackers in Keith Humphrey and Ronald McKinnon; the latter would play 10 years in the NFL.

North Alabama was, moreover, the opposite of VSU in every conceivable way. The Lions operated a potent triple-option offense that,

---

* Tressel was later head football coach at Ohio State University from 2001 to 2010, where he compiled a record of 94 wins and 22 losses and won a national championship.

in its fluidity and ability to stretch defenses, was oddly similar to the Air Raid. UNA ran the ball almost every play. Thus the contestants were perfectly, oppositely matched: the best ground game and toughest defense against the nation's best passing attack, one that no other team in the Gulf South Conference was within 2,000 yards of. The press, including the national media, loved it and showed up in large numbers for the game, which was televised on SportSouth. It was only the second time that VSU football had ever been on television.

Sports Illustrated was there, too. In his article about the game, *SI* writer Douglas S. Looney asked Hal how his program differed from North Alabama's. "We don't stretch, we don't run sprints, we don't practice on Mondays or Fridays," Hal told him. "And when we do practice we never go longer than an hour and forty-five minutes. All this is so we don't waste the players' time, and we never scrimmage in the fall, to avoid injuries. So when I recruit offensive linemen I say, 'Look, all you have to do are three things—lift, jump rope, and eat. There's probably one of these three that you like already.'" You could almost hear the sound of snickering rising from the red dirt of Alabama.

Looney wrote that UNA head coach Bobby Wallace, by contrast, "believes ardently in stretching, sprints, fall scrimmages, and Monday and Friday practices, and his practices last a lot longer than one hour and forty-five minutes." UNA was a possession team, one that preferred grinding out successive 12- to 13-play drives and leaving the opposing offense almost no time to deal with the Lions' vaunted defense. While Hal did not disdain long drives, his offense in practice was all about quick strikes. Many of his team's "drives" lasted less than two minutes; many lasted less than one.

The Blazers, pumped up and full of confidence, came onto the field for pregame warm-ups jawing at their opponents, telling them what they were going to do to their quarterback, how badly they were going to beat them. The UNA players, so accustomed to deference, were shocked. They had never heard talk like this. And it made them mad. When Lions receivers coach Rob Likens walked into the locker room before the start of the game, he was stunned by what he saw. His usually unemotional North Alabama players were fighting one another, throwing each other around, looking for anything human to hit. Likens had never seen anything like it.

And then they went out onto the field and in a driving rainstorm destroyed Valdosta State, dominating every aspect of the game. The Lions won, 38–21. The reason was clear and uncomplicated. VSU had no answer for North Alabama's defensive linemen and linebackers. The physical mismatches were too extreme. The Blazers could not block Raybon and Keyes and could not keep them out of the backfield. They could not match the speed and power of Ronald McKinnon, one of the best college defensive players in the country at any level. McKinnon's very existence suggested that there were limits to what a team could do to neutralize a middle linebacker.

Since Valdosta's line could not protect Hatcher, he spent the afternoon running for his life. In the previous year's game, a 31–21 loss, he had been held to 238 yards passing. He had been harassed so badly that he had thrown 5 interceptions. This time, against virtually the same UNA defense, roughly the same thing happened: Hatcher passed for 222 yards and was intercepted 4 times. Though North Alabama's offense played well—221 rushing yards and 152 passing yards—it was defense that won the game. VSU, the unstoppable force, had finally met the immovable object.

But that wasn't quite the end of the story.

Three weeks later a chastened 10-1 Valdosta State team played the undefeated University of North Alabama again, this time in the quarterfinals of the 16-team national playoff for the NCAA Division II championship. The Blazers' prospects were, if not quite hopeless, very grim indeed. The Lions had beaten them twice in a row, convincingly; they had clobbered everybody except Youngstown State. Hal's mind was occupied by images of Hatcher fleeing from lightning-fast defensive linemen who outweighed him by 120 pounds, of the most accurate quarterback in America throwing interceptions again and again. To quantify his agony, Hal had his young assistant coach Dana Holgorsen compile game-by-game statistics comparing how many times Hatcher had been hit or sacked with his completion percentage. It was no surprise to learn that they were inversely proportional.

Hal liked to think while he jogged and did some of his best thinking while pounding down the street, and his staff had come to fear the moment he returned, bursting with new ideas that of course meant more work for them. One such moment happened in the week before the second North Alabama game. When he had toweled off and assembled his staff, he said, "You know, guys, we are doing it all wrong. We are trying to stay ahead of these guys. But we actually need to be down by, like, eleven points at halftime. We need to be *losing the game*." Assistant coach Scott Preston could see the other coaches' eyeballs rolling back into their heads. Was Hal serious? Yes, he was. "We need to make them play football," Hal went on. "We need to run the ball, tire them out. Then, maybe in the third quarter, when we have them where we want them, we go back to doing what we do." To Preston and the rest of Hal's assistants, this seemed desperate if not absurdly impractical. But there was no talking the head coach out of it.

This time in the pregame warm-ups the Valdosta State players said nothing at all. Hal had told them explicitly not to. UNA coach Likens was amazed at how silent the field was. The Blazer players did not even look at the North Alabama players, who had been so built up for this moment, so ready for the verbal confrontation, that they now seemed uncertain how to act.

For those in the stands who expected to see the nation's most prolific passing offense in action, what happened next came as a profound shock. The Blazers came out in a conservative, tightly packed offensive formation that looked like something from 1945. There were two tight ends, narrow line splits, two backs in a conventional backfield, and a single slot receiver. It was as though Hal had undone all his innovations. VSU ran the ball up the middle, over and over. Hal double-teamed the two big tackles and ran the ball right at them. Instead of pursuing Hatcher across the open savanna of the VSU backfield, Israel Raybon was being hit head-on almost every play. VSU punted like a normal team, too. Wallace was stunned by the approach. He kept waiting for it to change, for VSU's offense to resolve itself into its usual mode of play. He was amazed above all at Hal's patience. Like Muhammad Ali in his 1974 "rope-a-dope" fight against George Foreman in Zaire, Hal would not come out of his closed stance; he would not fight in the open. The television commentators and everyone else watching the game could not quite believe what they were seeing. Herb Reinhard, VSU's athletics director and Hal's boss, was positively mystified.

So the contest plodded forward on a sodden field in the rain and fog, ground game against ground game. It was a Grantland Rice sort of game. At halftime the score was North Alabama 14, Valdosta 3. To the astonishment of his assistant coaches, VSU's deficit was exactly what Hal had said he wanted it to be: 11 points. Half of the third quarter passed, and still Hal waited. At that point the score was 17–3. It was then that Hal gave Hatcher the signal to unleash the offense, and VSU finally snapped back into its open passing formations.

Hatcher and his offensive line saw the change immediately: UNA's usually hyperaggressive defensive line and linebackers were visibly tired. They had nothing left to rush the passer. Hatcher proceeded to rip through the UNA defense, moving 77 yards and completing 7 passes—the last one a 21-yard touchdown strike to Flanders. After a fumble on the kickoff, Hatcher drove down the field for another score, this time on a 4-yard pass to Robert "Beanpole" Williams. The score, at the end of the regulation period, was 17–17. North Alabama scored first in overtime, characteristically driving 25 yards in six running plays to score a touchdown. Hatcher countered, in Air Raid fashion, with a 25-yard touchdown strike to Williams on VSU's first play. In the second overtime, VSU missed a field goal attempt. UNA did not. Final double-overtime score: UNA 27, Valdosta State 24.

The next day the Florence newspaper proclaimed that what the fans had seen in those miserable weather conditions was the greatest NCAA Division II game ever played. Likens thought it was also one of the greatest pieces of coaching he had ever seen. Hal's tactic had not won the game, but it had come shockingly close, and everybody on both teams and coaching staffs knew it. For Hal it was a sort of backward triumph. The game marked the end of his season, an 11-2 affair marred only by the twin defeats to the University of North Alabama, which would go on to win the national championship.

When the dust had finally settled after the 1994 season, what remained was a pile of offensive statistics that would have been beyond imagining for a team in the Gulf South Conference two years earlier. Topping it all was Hatcher himself, who completed 367 of 508 passes (72.2 percent) for 4,076 yards and 55 touchdowns, with only 10 interceptions. To understand how radical this achievement was, the quarterback closest to him in the Gulf South Conference that year, West Georgia's Mark Eldred, completed 82 of 162 passes for 1,532 yards and 15 touchdowns. In his four-year career at VSU, Hatcher had passed for a collective 11,363 yards. He had thrown 121 career touchdowns, breaking the Division II record of 100 held by Grambling State's Doug Williams. Hatcher held 21 national records. In 1994 he was awarded the Harlon Hill Trophy as the best D-II player in the nation.

There were other accolades as well. On a pass-first team that had only a handful of highly predictable running plays in a nonexistent playbook, Dominique Ross finished the season as *the rushing leader* in the Gulf South, with 1,473 yards.* Hatcher's receivers held down the first four conference rankings in yardage and receptions:

Name	Catches	Yards	Touchdowns
1. Robert Williams	86	1,167	21
2. Steven Greer	81	829	7
3. Stanley Flanders	70	1,083	20
4. Dominique Ross	64	492	3

In all conceivable ways, 1994 was Valdosta State's best season ever. For Hal it was payoff for two decades of begging and borrowing

---

* Ross would go on to play for the Dallas Cowboys in the NFL.

ideas and of diligently subverting the great traditions of the game. He had been told repeatedly that his offense could not possibly work in the real world, and he had proved over and over that it did. Considering the numbers of high school and college coaches now coming to sit at his feet and receive wisdom—a group that included assistant coaches from Auburn, Florida State, and Georgia—he had perhaps proved his point once and for all. In November 1994 Hal's career choice was finally, all things considered, starting to look like a pretty good idea.

That year the Valdosta State Blazers were on the leading edge of one of the biggest changes ever to sweep through the American game of football. This was not apparent to the average fan. And most people inside the conservative, tradition-driven world of football saw Hal just as they had always seen him: as a wild-eyed dreamer playing a gimmick-driven game that veered perilously from the bedrock principles of the game and stood no chance of survival in the long run. The doubters certainly had the percentages on their side: There were still only a handful of college and NFL coaches who really believed in using the forward pass as their principal offensive weapon.

Whether the traditionalists liked it or not, however, the game was changing in important and fundamental ways. The NFL was a good barometer of the shift. In 1975 teams had passed the ball 43 percent of the time. By 1995 that figure would increase to 56 percent—in historical terms a paradigm-altering rise. Over that same two-decade period, roughly coincident with Hal's career, passes per game would increase 30 percent, from 27 to 35 per game, and passing yards per game would go up 36 percent, from 163 to 221—hardly a revolution but still an unmistakable upward drift. To the old way of thinking, such an increase in volume should have meant a comparable rise in incompletions and interceptions—the two bad things that were going to occur when you put a football in the air. But—and this was the more telling change—the reverse happened. Passing efficiency was, in fact, on the rise. In 1975 NFL quarterbacks had completed 52 percent of their passes; in 1995 they'd complete 57 percent. Concealed within that number was an even more telling statistical swing: Interceptions had dropped from 6 percent of passes to a mere 3 percent. A century and a quarter after the game's inception, it was finally official that passing was no more dangerous than running. The latter changes spoke to fundamental attitudes about the air game and confirmed what Hal had long theorized: that the more you passed, the better you got at it.

Leading this change was that same tiny group of vastly outnumbered pioneers of the forward pass. During that time, six distinct and highly influential passing systems emerged, all of which had their roots in the 1960s or 1970s: Don Coryell's timing-based deep and mid-range passing game, known as Air Coryell; LaVell Edwards's BYU system; Bill Walsh's West Coast offense; Dennis Erickson's one-back spread (from Granada Hills High School coach Jack Neumeier via Jack Elway); the run-and-shoot; and the Air Raid. Those offenses were different in many ways, but they shared certain characteristics: They all forced defenders to cover the entire field, all used option routes to one degree or another, and all employed short passes to shift the play-action away from the core of the defense. Only the Air Raid was a hybrid of three others (run-and-shoot, West Coast, and BYU). The West Coast and one-back spread were balanced or slightly run-heavy; the other four were pass-first.

Their methods and tactics seeped steadily into the larger football world of the pre-Internet age—through television broadcasts, the game films that coaches were always watching, coaching clinics and camps, and the constant migrations of head and assistant coaches. It is impossible to quantify the influence of any single system; football in America is just too vast, too diffuse. Most of the change was undocumented: a high school coach in a small town adopting the run-and-shoot here, a state college coach installing the one-back spread or the West Coast offense there. Maybe the local papers recorded those events; most likely they did not. Most of the media did not have a clue that this shift was going on, or that the entire game was changing right in front of them. It was common, moreover, for coaches to adopt pieces of the various high-profile passing offenses, as Hal had done, rather than adopting the systems as a whole. Like Walsh's idea of using short passes as part of a ball-control offense, or Ellison's concept of letting receivers read the defense themselves. Those changes were even harder to quantify. Still, people in football could see and feel the difference. Passing was on the rise, stealing ever-larger chunks of the clock from the running game.

The most visible way the changes moved through the sport was by means of what might be called a disciple system. Assistant coaches who worked for the various masters became offensive coordinators or head coaches and took the wisdom with them, in turn spawning new disciples. A typical example would be Mike Holmgren, a former quarterbacks coach under Bill Walsh at the San Francisco 49ers, who later used Walsh's West Coast offense to win a Super Bowl as head coach of the Green Bay Packers in 1996. Below, the principal pioneers of the four offenses are grouped with selected members of their coaching trees who were head coaches:

Pioneer	Disciples Who Became Head Coaches
Don Coryell	Joe Gibbs (Redskins), Norv Turner (Redskins, Raiders, and Chargers), Mike Martz (Rams), and John Madden (Raiders)
Bill Walsh	George Seifert (49ers, Panthers), Mike Holmgren (Packers, Seahawks), Sam Wyche (Bengals, Buccaneers), Jim Fassel (Giants), and Dennis Green (Vikings, Cardinals, Stanford University)
LaVell Edwards	Mike Holmgren (Packers, Seahawks), Ted Tollner (USC), and Norm Chow (University of Hawaii, offensive coordinator at USC, Titans, and UCLA*)
Dennis Erickson	Mike Price (Washington State, Alabama, UTEP), Scott Linehan (Rams), and Joe Tiller (Wyoming, Purdue)

* Though Chow was an offensive coordinator and not a head coach, I have included him here because of his influence on the passing game. He also spawned his own coaching tree.

In the mid-1990s, when Hal was at Valdosta State, the most influential passing system in the country was probably the West Coast offense. While Hal owed much to Bill Walsh, their offenses were in many ways very different. The West Coast offense was a balanced attack in which runs roughly equaled passes. The Air Raid was pass-first, pass-most-of-the-time. Nor did most of Hal's routes require the ultra-precise timing Walsh's did. On many of the 49ers' pass plays, the ball would hit the receiver's hands as he came out of his cut, without his looking for or following it. In Hal's system the quarterback mostly threw to visibly open receivers, which accounted in part for his freakishly high completion rates. He preferred the idea of aggressively attacking open spaces to relying on perfect synchronization. Hal's quarterbacks usually read the field deep to shallow; Walsh's did not. Hal's quarterbacks read the field sideline to sideline; Walsh's read only half the field. Finally, much of the effort Hal put into his offense was meant to simplify it, to make it so easy that no one would ever need a playbook and the players could play fast and instinctively. As Walsh's West Coast offense developed, it became known for its complexity.

Despite the popularity of Walsh's ideas, by far the most extreme and productive passing offenses to emerge in the late 20th century were the run-and-shoot and the Air Raid. Measured by passes attempted and completed, yardage gained, touchdowns thrown, and emphasis on the passing game, nothing else was really close to them. They represented the most radical challenges to football's status quo. They also happened to come into full flower at roughly the same time, making comparisons inevitable. The Air Raid grew up in the deep shadow of the run-and-shoot. Hal's small-college offense received little attention compared with a passing system that had succeeded at professional and major-college levels and received barrels full of media ink.

Mouse Davis had done miraculous things at Oregon high schools and then at Portland State with the run-and-shoot. But it was the system's second rise, when head coach Jack Pardee and his offensive coordinator John Jenkins showed up at the University of Houston in 1989, that got most of the national attention. That year Houston quarterback Andre Ware threw for an NCAA record 4,699 yards and 46 touchdowns. He threw an average of 53 passes a game and completed 33 of them for 474 yards and a completion percentage of 62 percent. Major college football had not seen numbers like these. Ware won the Heisman Trophy. In 1990 Jenkins took over from Pardee as head coach and his quarterback, David Klingler, actually outpaced Ware's numbers, throwing for 5,140 yards and 54 touchdowns.

Pardee, meanwhile, took the run-and-shoot to the Houston Oilers of the NFL, where, in 1990 and 1991, quarterback Warren Moon averaged nearly 300 yards a game with it and threw 37 touchdown passes in a season. By 1991 the run-and-shoot had been adopted by the Detroit Lions, where Mouse had migrated, and the Atlanta Falcons, where Mouse's former quarterback June Jones was now offensive coordinator. Tiger Ellison's old offense, now updated by Mouse and Jenkins, was so successful, and such a mystery to defenses trying to stop it, that it seemed as though it might be poised to take over a large chunk of American football.

In fact the reverse was true. Implosion was imminent. Even as U of H's Klingler was throwing 11 touchdown passes to beat hapless Eastern Washington, 84–21, and throwing for 716 yards against Arizona State, the seeds of the run-and-shoot's decline were being sown. The engine of destruction was a defensive strategy known as the zone blitz. The idea behind it was to switch out apparent rushers at the last minute, causing them to drop back into pass coverage, while the defenders who had appeared to be in pass coverage rushed the passer. The key was to make the switches at the last second, which did not allow the offense to adjust. Since the run-and-shoot was all about adjusting to defenses on the fly, the zone blitz caused great confusion for both quarterbacks and receivers. The run-and-shoot protections broke down; their blitz-defeating hot reads and break-offs no longer worked as well either.* There were other problems with the pure versions of the run-and-shoot. Since there were no fullbacks or tight ends, the quarterback was unusually vulnerable, especially in the NFL, and it was difficult to use runs to control the ball. The half roll that the quarterback did on most plays was at the same time chaotic and predictable.

Though the moment the tide turned against the run-and-shoot is debated, there is general agreement that there were two landmark games in the offense's latter-day decline. The first was the nationally televised game between the University of Houston and the University of Miami on September 9, 1991. Miami, under coach Dennis Erickson, used a relentless zone blitz and won the game, 40–10. Though that didn't shut down the Houston scoring machine, it showed how to beat it. Jenkins would win only seven more games. He went 4-7 in 1991 and 4-7 in 1992 and was fired in the spring of 1993 amid allegations of NCAA violations of which he was later found innocent.

The second game was the 1992 American Football Conference wild card game between the Houston Oilers and the Buffalo Bills. The Oilers, with Moon at quarterback, were up 35–3 at the half. They passed the ball 22 times and ran it 4 times in the second half and lost, 38–35. The analysis was roughly the same: They could be stopped with the right sort of blitz.

Then, just as quickly as the run-and-shoot had gained in popularity, teams moved away from it. Mouse's version of it had always been something of a temperamental child, difficult to coach and requiring athletic quarterbacks to run. It had also gotten vastly more complex than the simple offense Ellison had run at Middletown High School or that Mouse himself had run in his early years. One outward sign of this was that at the University of Houston Jenkins

---

* For an excellent analysis of the troubles encountered by the run-and-shoot—and why it had been able to beat blitzes for so long in the first place—see Chris Brown's July 2, 2007, post "What Killed the Run and Shoot" in his SmartFootball.com blog. I have followed his general line of thought here. For his take on the run-and-shoot at the University of Hawaii, see the December 15, 2007, post, "Switch It."

issued an updated 350-page playbook to his players every week. While the Air Raid required receivers to read only man or zone, the run-and-shoot required them to see and identify five different defensive formations and to adjust accordingly.* The run-and-shoot was sometimes seen, unfairly, as an unsportsmanlike gimmick. Much of the mainstream media as well as the coaching world viewed it this way, echoing age-old prejudices against the forward pass, and they were collectively thrilled when it finally showed weakness. Jenkins's habit of leaving his starters in to run the score up on opponents abetted this view. (From 1990, scores included: 60–0, 84–21, 66–15, 69–0, 65–7, 66–10, 64–0.) Critics noted that no run-and-shoot team had ever won an NFL or college championship. There were problems at college levels of the sport, too. Many coaches whose jobs were in jeopardy had looked to run-and-shoot to save themselves; they installed it without understanding it and ditched it the moment they realized they couldn't duplicate the offbeat brilliance of a coach like Jenkins. When blood went into the water in the early 1990s, the media sharks circled, the system crashed.

But the run-and-shoot did not vanish from the scene. A small number of schools continued to run it. Jenkins won a Grey Cup with it in the Canadian Football League with the Toronto Argonauts in 1997. Doug Flutie was his quarterback. June Jones continued to use the run-and-shoot as the head coach of the Atlanta Falcons until he was fired in 1996 after a 3–13 season. He resurrected a version of it at the University of Hawaii in 1999 and used it with great success. Jones's quarterbacks Timmy Chang and Colt Brennan set national passing records. By this point, however, Jones's offense was considerably modified from the classic run-and-shoot. One huge change was that the new version operated from a shotgun formation. Another was that the run-and-shoot's signature move, the quarterback's half roll right or left, had been dropped.

---

* The defenses were (1) three-deep zone, (2) two-deep zone, (3) two-deep man under, (4) man free, and (5) four across man (blitz).

It is more accurate to say that, while the run-and-shoot in its original form disappeared from American football, its ideas, concepts, and many of its option-driven plays have taken deep root. To read Ellison's book today is to understand how many contemporary passing offenses work. Spreading the field and teaching receivers to read defenses and adjust on the fly have become integral parts of the game. The Air Raid, of course, was profoundly influenced by the run-and-shoot. Seen in retrospect, Mouse Davis was a prophet of the new age.

But if it was true that by the mid-1990s the run-and-shoot was in a steep decline, it was also true that the Air Raid, the surviving radical pass offense with no apparent design flaws, was starting to take off. Hal's coaching clinics were attracting more interest and within a few years would become wildly popular. Where once he could not draw a single coach to them, they were now sold out in advance. Everybody wanted to know how you could run a passing offense that could not be stopped. They wanted the secret of the perfect pass.

20

Stars in Their Courses

Hal's coaching career at Valdosta State lasted five years. That was long enough to rewrite the record books both in the Gulf South Conference and in NCAA Division II football and to finally break the curse of the small-college football coach. He had followed his nose through seven different jobs, in places and with teams that he might not have otherwise chosen; he had worked those impossible hours for pitiful wages and lost a lot of football games and been run out of town. But what was sometimes a grotesque imbalance between work and life and happiness and misery had finally righted itself in this balmy, palm-tree-lined southern campus. The *Atlanta Journal-Constitution,* which in earlier days had declined to send a reporter to cover his games, was now calling Valdosta State the best college football program in Georgia, a state that took its football seriously and was home to the likes of the University of Georgia, Georgia Tech, and Division I-AA power Georgia Southern.

Hal's last two years there—1995 and 1996—extended his phenomenal run. Though 1995 was a retooling year due to the loss of 10 starters on offense and 10 on defense, the Blazer offense again put up record-breaking numbers. That was in part because Hal and Leach and the other coaches had gotten better at teaching the system and partly because Hal's new quarterback, the 6-foot-5-inch, 220-pound Lance Funderburk, was as successful at torching opposing defenses as Chris Hatcher had been. Hal had by now figured out how to teach his offense to anybody, starting with the quarterback. The Air Raid was built to be fully portable and democratic, which made it different from most other passing systems. In 1995 Funderburk set conference records for the most completions and highest average yards per game, while his main receiver, Sean Pender, set records for the most catches in a single game (20) and most catches in a season (111). Playing the toughest schedule in program history with a group of younger players who had never started, VSU went 6-5. This sort of performance was now the Air Raid's baseline.

The following season, Hal's last in Valdosta, his Blazers won the trifecta: They beat North Alabama, won the Gulf South Conference championship, and made it again to the national playoffs (quarterfinals). Funderburk passed for a conference record 4,226 yards and threw 38 touchdowns. He was the Gulf South's MVP and the runner-up for the Harlon Hill Trophy. VSU ended the season ranked second in the nation in total offense.

With all this success came, finally, some of the perks that people at the top of Hal's profession routinely got. In his last three years at VSU, between his salary, his weekly radio and television shows, and his summer camps and clinics, he made comfortably more than $100,000 a year. But the money was just part of it. He received a complimentary new Pontiac Bonneville every 4,000 miles, with insurance paid by the athletics department. His dress clothes, including suits, blazers, shirts, ties, shoes, and slacks, were provided by a local men's store in exchange for game tickets and credit on the television show. All athletic apparel for him and his family was provided free of charge by the local sporting goods store. Hal's 2,800-square-foot home was built for him by a local builder at cost on a half-acre lot in a country-club neighborhood and was financed by a bank with no closing costs. And his $5,000 annual membership to the Valdosta Country Club was paid for through his radio show. Though what Hal received was just a fraction of what Division I-A coaches from the power conferences got in perks and salary, he had a good deal and he knew it. It was nice to be wanted.

That is not to say that the job was easy. Hal battled daily with athletics director Herb Reinhard, usually over money. Reinhard thought Hal was a great coach but a terrible administrator, one who believed that he could spend a dollar 10 different ways. Hal did not dislike Reinhard but felt that the stubborn AD was impeding his quite reasonable ambition to build a nationally ranked football program. Hal, as usual, wanted things. He wanted a new stadium instead of the current one he had to share with Valdosta High. He insisted on air travel even though many times that meant grueling, same-day, round-trip "commando raids" on discount charter planes to save hotel bills. On one occasion, when Reinhard had told him he could not have extra scholarship money, he signed several junior college players anyway and raised the money later with a golf tournament. He was, in other words, the same old Hal, pushing hard and relentlessly for what he wanted. Sometimes he pushed too hard. At one booster luncheon he complained publicly about the lack of a decent stadium and how embarrassing it was to have to share one with the high school, an expression of sentiment that didn't go down well with his bosses.

But those were minor bumps in the road, certainly compared with what happened to June Mumme in the fall of 1996. She was diagnosed with breast cancer, news that was shattering to the family and provided a horrific counterpoint to the victories on the field. She underwent a radical mastectomy on October 18. While she was recovering from that surgery—three days later, in fact—the Mummes' world was turned upside down yet again. Hal received a phone call from the University of Kentucky to see if he was interested in coaching football there. Hal and June were astonished. SEC schools—even ones in the cellar, as Kentucky was—simply did not recruit their head coaches from Division II. It just didn't happen. *Of course* Hal was interested, though he did not give himself much of a chance. At the very least it was a thumping validation of the program he had built at Valdosta State. June, in spite of her fragile condition and facing a long period of recovery, encouraged Hal to go after the job. She decided to defer her chemotherapy until early

December and see what happened. (She would eventually, after multiple surgeries, make a full recovery.)

Ten days later the university's legendary athletics director, C. M. Newton, was sitting in the Mummes' living room questioning Hal about how his offense worked. Newton had decided that he could sell the idea of a "fast break on grass" to a university that had long been enamored of its dominant basketball program but deeply ambivalent about games that did not involve round balls and hoops. The coach he had just fired, Bill Curry, was a straitlaced fellow who reminded some people of General George Patton. His record in seven seasons was 26-52. He had tried and failed to play smashmouth football in the ultimate smashmouth conference. Newton thought that Hal—whose loosey-goosey irreverence reminded people more of *M*A*S*H* character Hawkeye Pierce—might be a refreshing change. Three weeks after that the president of the University of Kentucky and four officials from the athletics department came to Valdosta to meet with Hal. They wanted to know if there was anything in Hal's past that the university needed to know about. Hal told them that he had been dismissed at Iowa Wesleyan. And he described June's cancer. They expressed concern for her illness but seemed unfazed by it. One of them did call Bob Prins, who said that even though Hal had won a lot of games, certain people at IWC believed strongly that the team's success was diverting attention from the mission of the school. So they had asked Hal to leave. That was as close as Prins would ever come to making a public statement on what happened to Hal at Iowa Wesleyan.

On November 23, VSU beat Albany State, 38-28, in the first round of the national playoffs. Three days later Newton, armed with a strong recommendation of Hal from LaVell Edwards, called to offer Hal the job as head football coach at the University of Kentucky. Hal accepted. Though the official announcement would not come until December 2, rumors were already running wild. By the time the Blazers played Carson-Newman in the second round of the playoffs, a small media circus was circling Hal. VSU lost that game, 24-19, which ended its season. Instead of returning to Valdosta with the team, however, Hal and June were whisked away to Lexington in Kentucky's private plane. Before they landed, and before the hiring was even announced, the chorus of pessimists and doomsayers was getting warmed up. Hal's hiring was a spectacularly bad idea, they said. Worst mistake Newton had ever made. Throwing passes all the time might work in Division II, they theorized, but it would never, ever work in the SEC.

Ten months later, on October 4, 1997, the University of Kentucky football team played the Alabama Crimson Tide at Commonwealth Stadium, in Lexington, Kentucky. The rivalry, if you could call it that, was one of the most lopsided in the SEC and in college sports in general, a showcase for Alabama's exceptional talents and Kentucky's woeful shortcomings. Kentucky had not beaten Alabama in 75 years. This year Alabama, ranked 20th in the nation, was expected to slaughter the Wildcats again. It was business as usual in the SEC.

But the strangest thing had happened in the first four weeks of the season that led up to the game. Against all expectations, Lexington, and indeed all of the Kentucky football world, had fallen in love with Hal Mumme and his eccentric offense. This was not a subtle sort of love. This was crazy, over-the-top, skywritten love. There was already a cult of Hal Mumme. The street running next to Commonwealth Stadium had been renamed Hal Mumme Pass. Songwriters wrote ballads about him. The game was dubbed Mummeball. Cardboard Mumme masks mounted on wooden sticks were ubiquitous. Fans did interviews in the masks; Leach and the other coaches conducted conversations in front of Hal wearing the masks, which Hal tolerated gracefully. The Kentucky company that made Maker's Mark bourbon put up ads on highway billboards featuring a huge bottle of their liquor wrapped in gauze—like a mummy—and bearing the words "The Mark of a Great Coach." Jimmy Buffett music blared from the stadium PA and inspired decals that said "Come Mumme, It'll Be

All Right," a reference to Buffett's hit song "Come Monday." All of which seemed to fit the style of the coaches themselves, Hal cool and relaxed and slightly scruffy, wearing Oakley shades and a Panama hat, Leach in his trademark Hawaiian shirts. Fans loved all of it; they cranked air raid sirens and showed up at games in record numbers.

Hal's Wildcats had begun the season with a victory over longtime rival Louisville. No one had given Kentucky a chance to win. At least not until they saw Hal's 6-foot-5-inch, 220-pound quarterback, Tim Couch, running the Air Raid offense. Couch had been the most famous schoolboy quarterback in Kentucky history. His freshman year had been uneventful, and he had only stayed in Lexington because he wanted to play for Hal. Couch, in combination with his new coach, was actually as good as SEC favorite Peyton Manning, of Tennessee, a fact that the rest of the world was about to learn. Couch went 36 for 50 for 398 yards and 4 touchdowns in a 38–24 victory in which the Wildcats gained 519 yards to Louisville's 291 yards. Kentucky lost a close game to Mississippi State, 35–27, then clobbered Indiana, 49–7. Couch piled up huge passing numbers along the way, averaging 35 completions in 50 attempts per game (70 percent) for 381 yards and 5 touchdowns.

In the season's fourth week Hal was again granted his inveterate wish to play a team much better than his. In this case it was the University of Florida, ranked number one in the country, packed with future NFL players, and coached by Steve Spurrier. Kentucky was playing at home. The first part of the game unfolded as everyone expected. At the end of the first quarter, Florida led, 28–0. This was fully in keeping with recent tradition. In the previous two years the Gators had outscored the Wildcats 107–7.

Then something happened that did not quite follow the script. Early in the second quarter Kentucky faced fourth-and-long on its own 14-yard line. The team's punter waited 15 yards deep while 10 Florida players with their knuckles on the ground prepared to end the game right there. Except that Kentucky did not punt. Hal had called a fake. *From Kentucky's own end zone. Against Florida.*

The snap went to walk-on running back A. J. Simon, who threw a pass to a walk-on tight end named James Whalen, who made it to the 50-yard line before he was tackled. Fans screamed for joy. The Wildcats scored a few plays later. Then they executed a perfect onside kick. The home crowd roared. Later they onside-kicked again and scored. Kentucky, in a deep hole against the nation's best team, had somehow awakened from its dream of certain defeat.

Mike Leach was a critically important part of Hal Mumme's football operation. By the time he and Hal got to Kentucky, they were one of college football's most successful coaching teams.

The Wildcats also ran the play Hal's teams had practiced once a week since Iowa Wesleyan: the one where they were backed up to their own end zone and scored a touchdown. They got their opportunity in the second quarter when Florida nailed a perfect punt that was downed on the Kentucky 1-yard line. Instead of being despondent, as they ought to have been, the Kentucky players were actually thrilled. They realized that they were finally in the desperate situation they had practiced for so long. Here, against an NFL-level defense, was their great chance. The Florida coaches must have been mystified by their opponents' apparent happiness. What the hell was going on? The ball was snapped; the line moved in zone-blocking, elephants-on-parade mode to signal the run that everyone in the world thought was coming; the defense charged; and Couch lofted a perfect spiral while the fans stood and screamed bloody murder. The pass hit his receiver on the hands just short of midfield. The receiver dropped it.*

But the *spirit* of that play took hold.

The result was that for the game's final three quarters Kentucky played the redoubtable Florida dead even, scoring 28 points to the Gators' 27. Florida could not stop Couch, who ended up 34 for 60 for 369 yards and 2 touchdowns. The final score of 55–28 sounded to the world like a blowout, but the hometown fans knew better. At the end of the game the second-largest crowd in the history of Commonwealth Stadium—59,224—rose and gave the team a standing ovation. Losing by four touchdowns made the fans love Hal and his Air Raid more than ever.

Many of those fans also had a strange notion, based on no rational evidence whatsoever, that they could win against Alabama the following week. The press picked this up. One AP writer actually predicted that Kentucky would upset Alabama. In Birmingham, a sportswriter even conceded that Kentucky had "become an opponent to lose sleep over." Hal had the same weird thought, too, which he shared with his quarterback. Hal had been reading Shelby Foote's three-volume history of the Civil War and had been interested in Foote's title for his chapter about Gettysburg, a paraphrase of the Bible that suggested that what happened on that battlefield had been destined to happen. Standing in the parking lot of a Lexington

---

* The next season, Hal called the same play against Florida in roughly the same situation. It resulted in a 98-yard touchdown pass.

hotel with Couch on the cool, clear Friday night before the game, Hal said, "You know, Tim, I think we're going to win this game tomorrow night. I can just feel it. I think it is just the *stars in their courses*." Couch thought so, too.

The game was a dogfight, pitting a traditional run-dominant SEC team against Hal's aerial combat unit.* The numbers reflected that: Alabama, with its All-American running back Shaun Alexander, gained twice as many yards on the ground as Kentucky did.† Kentucky, relying on mesh, Four Verticals, Y-cross, and its assortment of receiver screens and short passes, passed for twice as many yards as Alabama did. Alabama won the time of possession battle, 35 minutes to 25 minutes. Alabama huddled and ran behind its talented and tightly spaced offensive line. Kentucky never huddled, played blazingly fast, and spread the field.

The lead changed hands five times. Trailing 34–31 with four seconds left on the clock, Alabama kicked a 37-yard field goal to tie the game. In overtime Alabama, which had the first possession, lost the ball on a fumble, and Kentucky took over. On third-and-11 from the 26-yard line, Couch hit receiver Craig Yeast on a curl route. Using his best settle-and-noose technique, Yeast spun away from the defender, headed straight downfield, broke a tackle inside the 10-yard line, and sprinted into the end zone. The final score was 40–34—more points than Kentucky had ever scored against Alabama. Couch had completed 32 of 49 passes for 355 yards and 4 touchdowns. He had completed passes to nine different receivers.

---

* Alabama that year, under head coach Mike Dubose, contained a virtual who's who of coaching talent, including offensive coordinator Bruce Arians, now the head coach of the Arizona Cardinals; wide receivers/tight ends coach Dabo Swinney, now the head coach of Clemson; defensive backs coach Curley Hallman, formerly the head coach at LSU; and Ellis Johnson, the former defensive coordinator at Auburn and current linebackers coach at South Carolina.

† Alexander would later star in the NFL for the Seattle Seahawks and Washington Redskins.

When Yeast broke into the end zone, there was an odd instant of silence in the stadium, like the gap between heartbeats. People who were there remember it. It was as though the nearly 60,000 fans could not quite believe that the overtime was really over, that Kentucky had won the game. And then they erupted into pure, screaming, blue-and-white pandemonium that spilled in a torrent onto the field. While thousands of fans took a knee with the team for a post-game prayer at midfield, thousands more ripped the goalposts apart, an event that had never occurred in the stadium's 24-year history. Athletics director Newton told the police to leave them alone. "If I wasn't so old, I would have jumped up on the damn thing myself," he would later say. While the mayhem exploded on the field, the Kentucky band struck up Bruce Channel's 1961 song "Hey! Baby." Tens of thousands of people danced and sang joyously along: "*Heyyyy, hey, hey baby / I want to know-oh-oh / If you'll be my girl.*"

One of Hal's favorite sayings was, *Play the next play.* The words were a combination pep talk and theory of life, perfectly aligned with his coaching philosophy. The gist was, life, like football, is a headlong dive into the future. There is no past, as least not one you should worry too much about. If you lose, let it go. Don't panic. If you win, don't be too satisfied. *Play the next play.* The future awaits. There are so many possibilities. And the moment was always better if the next play was an onside kick or a fake punt in one's own end zone or a certifiably crazy attempt to throw a touchdown pass from one's own 1-yard line. Because the Air Raid was such a malleable concept, there were any number of futures out there. *Anything* could happen, and if anything could happen, then there was no point in dwelling on the past. *Play the next play.*

For football coaches there is always a next play, too. Life goes on, in victory and defeat. For Hal there would be many more games, on different fields with different teams. But if there ever was a moment— just one thunderous moment—when a coach might be tempted to rest in the blinding glory of the present, this was it. Beating Alabama was probably as good as it was ever going to get.

Epilogue: The Game Changes

"Talk all you want about the gridiron genius of Nick Saban, Gus Malzahn, or Chip Kelly," wrote Kevin Van Valkenburg in a feature story in the September 19, 2014, issue of *ESPN The Magazine*, referring to the then head coaches of Alabama, Auburn, and the Philadelphia Eagles. "But it's Hal Mumme who brought you the game you're watching today. . . . He wasn't the only one to drag football out of its ground-and-pound dark ages. But as Kentucky's coach in the late 1990s, he is the one who brought video game offenses to the SEC, the game's motherland. And it was there that football changed forever."

Van Valkenburg's thesis was that Hal was the most influential American football coach of the previous 20 years. That sentiment is shared by a growing number of media analysts, football fans, coaches, and former players. Chris B. Brown, whose books and columns (SmartFootball.com) are among the most influential in the sport, wrote of the Air Raid's "incredible rise . . . and its almost shocking omnipresence, in one form or another, at every level of football."

The consensus has been a long time building.

It has been driven by the extraordinary growth of the passing game since Hal coached at Iowa Wesleyan, Valdosta State, and Kentucky and by the simultaneous viruslike spread of his Air Raid offense through thousands of high schools, hundreds of colleges, and into much of the NFL. While the other dominant passing systems were fading from view in the new century's first decade, the Air Raid was rapidly gaining in popularity and visibility. Unlike the run-and-shoot, it had no apparent flaws or weaknesses; there was no single defense that could solve it. By the second decade its influence was unmistakable at all levels of football. When New England Patriots quarterback Tom Brady threw touchdowns and won Super Bowls using Air Raid plays like mesh and Y-cross or their close equivalents, or when the top college offenses played at two-minute-drill speed for entire games and threw for 400-plus yards, those were *Air Raid* legacies. When Washington State quarterback Connor Halliday passed for a mind-numbing 734 yards against the University of California in 2014, that was the *Air Raid* in action.

Hal's influence on football—both on the methodology and frequency of the forward pass and on the speed with which the game is played—is most visible at the college level. The change that has taken place there in a relatively few years—since Hal's full-blown transformation of the game in 1991 against Northeast Missouri—is astounding. Before 1991—Dustin Dewald's senior year at Iowa Wesleyan and 85 years after the forward pass was first made legal—only 5 NCAA Division I quarterbacks had thrown for more than 10,000 yards in their college careers. Since then, *90 more have done it.* Of the 92 times in NCAA history that quarterbacks have thrown for more than 4,000 yards in a single season, *78 have occurred since 2000.* Before 2000 only 3 Division I quarterbacks had passed for more than 10,000 yards and 100 touchdowns. All of them played in the 1980s and 1990s. Since 2000, *18 quarterbacks have hit that mark.* Maybe you have heard of Rakeem Cato (Marshall), Timmy Chang (Hawaii), and Dan LeFevour (Central Michigan), maybe you haven't. You almost certainly haven't heard of Division III superstar Alex Tanney, of Monmouth College (14,249 career yards passing, 157 touchdowns), or Division II luminary Jimmy Terwilliger, of East Stroudsburg (14,350 career yards, 148 touchdowns). They have all recently joined the likes of Ty Detmer, Colt McCoy, and Case Keenum as members of the ultra-elite 10,000 yards/100 TDs club.

Inside those raw production statistics is an even more reveal-ing sign of the passing revolution. One of Hal's major advances was in completion percentage. What Chris Hatcher did—staying consistently above 70 percent for two full seasons—had not been done before.* Tim Couch's three-year average of 67.1 percent set an NCAA career record. But by 2015 fully 51 college quarterbacks had averaged 65-plus percent over their careers. All but 2 played after Hatcher. Perhaps the most telling statistic is that 7 of the top 10 college leaders in career passing percentage—all above 68.6 percent—were Air Raid quarterbacks.

Though passing in the NFL lags the stratospheric production levels of the college game, a revolution has been under way there, too. You can see this in the increased frequency of NFL quarterbacks passing for the sort of yardage that would have been unthinkable twenty years ago: Peyton Manning threw for 5,477 in 2013; Drew Brees, 5,476 yards in 2011; Tom Brady, 5,235 yards in 2011; Matthew Stafford, 5,038 yards in 2011; Ben Roethlisberger, 4,953 in 2014; and so on. Between 2005 and 2015 alone, NFL passing yardage rose 20 percent and passing touchdowns increased 30 percent. Pass completion rates have soared along with everything else. In 2015 Kirk Cousins, of the Washington Redskins, led the NFL with a 69.3 percent completion rate, followed by the New Orleans Saints' Drew Brees with 68.3 percent. That year 25 NFL teams had completion rates above 60 percent. The game-altering statistical shift Hal pre-dicted has finally arrived. What was once radical is fast becoming normal. Walter Camp is spinning in his grave.

The game's speed these days is an even more visible Air Raid legacy. In the 2015 season, 52 major college teams averaged more than 75 plays per game; 18 of them ran more than 80. That sort of

---

* The only major football division quarterback to hit 70 in a single season before Hatcher was Doug Gaynor at Long Beach State in 1985 with 71.2 percent. Sammy Baugh completed an astounding 70.3 percent of his passes for the Washington Redskins in 1945. But he could not sustain it; he completed 46 percent of his college passes and 56.5 percent of his passes in his NFL career.

sustained speed—in effect adding the equivalent of a quarter to the traditional game—was unknown before Iowa Wesleyan did it against Northeast Missouri State in 1991. The Air Raid's velocity finally penetrated the NFL as well. Between 2007 and 2012, use of the no-huddle offense increased by 100 percent. In 2012 the New England Patriots averaged 74.4 plays per game, an astounding pace for the NFL. In order to play fast, of course, professional teams had to radically reduce their gigantic playbooks, which was itself an enormous change in game strategy. The term "up tempo"—as distinct from "no huddle"—has now become part of football's vernacular.

The key to the timing of the big shift, as Van Valkenburg suggested, was Hal's startling demonstration, beginning in 1997, that he could post huge passing numbers against the SEC's lockdown defenses. Almost no one had believed this to be possible. After Kentucky beat Alabama, interest in the Air Raid exploded. A steady stream of coaches and players showed up in Lexington, wanting to learn the magic. The coaches included rising stars like Urban Meyer, then the wide receivers coach at Notre Dame, and Sean Payton, then the quarterbacks coach for the Philadelphia Eagles. The following summer 6,000 high school players and many of their coaches attended three continuous weeks of Air Raid day camps at the University of Kentucky. Requests poured in from all over the NFL for Kentucky game films.

The other focal point for the spread of the Air Raid was Mike Leach. In 1999 he left his job at the University of Kentucky with Hal's blessing to become offensive coordinator at the University of Oklahoma. The school's football program was in decline, and a new head coach named Bob Stoops figured he would take a chance on Hal's young protégé.* As defensive coordinator at the University

---

* When Stoops called Hal to ask whether he should hire Leach, his first question was, "Does he call the plays?" Hal said no but assured him that Leach knew everything about the offense and how to coach it.

of Florida (1996–1998), Stoops had seen at close range the dazzling work of Kentucky's offense and felt his own helplessness in trying to stop it. He gave Leach complete freedom, which Leach used to install the exact system he had been coaching under Hal for a decade, down to the precise details of practice. To find a quarterback he traveled to Snow College, a two-year school in Ephraim, Utah, where he recruited a relative unknown named Josh Heupel. Heupel, who couldn't run and had what was considered to be a weak arm, had been a bust because of an injury at another Utah school, Weber State, and had been playing only half the time at Snow. Leach liked his accuracy and his intelligence. Everybody in Oklahoma thought Leach was crazy. At least until the intra-squad game in the spring of 1999, when Heupel hung 700 yards on the Oklahoma defense, causing what defensive coordinator Brent Venables later described as a "deep, deep state of depression in the locker room afterwards."

That fall Leach more than doubled Oklahoma's points scored per game, from 17 in 1998 to 37 in 1999, while the offense went from 101st in the nation to 11th and from last to first in the Big 12. Leach's amazing performance won him the job as head coach at Texas Tech the next year. Oklahoma, meanwhile, with offensive coordinator Mark Mangino now running the system Leach had taught him—and with Leach's triggerman Heupel at quarterback—won the national championship in 2000. (To date it is Stoops's only national championship.)

In the years that followed, with Leach's Texas Tech offense as a model, the Big 12 steadily turned itself into a pass-first conference. It is now an Air Raid–dominated conference. The head coach at Texas Tech is Kliff Kingsbury, Leach's first great quarterback at Tech; Texas Christian University's offensive coordinator is Sonny Cumbie, Leach's third great quarterback at Texas Tech; Baylor head coach Art Briles was an assistant coach under Leach at Texas Tech; West Virginia head coach Dana Holgorsen was a receiver at Iowa Wesleyan under Hal, an assistant at Valdosta State, offensive coordinator under Leach at Tech, and then offensive coordinator at Oklahoma State. Sonny Cumbie's offensive co-coordinator at TCU is Doug Meacham, who was Dana Holgorsen's assistant at Oklahoma State. Kansas offensive coordinator Rob Likens, who had been an assistant to North Alabama head coach Bobby Wallace, later moved with Wallace to Temple University where it adopted the Air Raid.

By the time Graham Harrell hit Michael Crabtree for the game-winning touchdown against the University of Texas in 2008, Mike Leach was already a legend, and thousands of high school kids wanted to be like his quarterbacks and receivers and score horrific numbers of points on opponents. Though Texas was not the only place where people were experimenting with wide-open passing offenses, it became the nation's principal breeding ground for phenomenally productive high school passers like Chase Daniel, Todd Reesing, Andy Dalton, Matthew Stafford, Colt McCoy, and Harrell. In 2008 one-fifth of all NCAA bowl participants had starting quarterbacks from Texas high schools. This was partly because Texas was also ground zero for the rise of seven-on-seven summer leagues, which drew inspiration from the Texas Tech offense. The seven-on-sevens—competitive, no-contact, pass-only games on a 40-yard field—trained receivers and quarterbacks in the techniques of reading defenses and running options off their basic routes. The game might have been invented by Tiger Ellison. It grew hand in hand with the spread of the Air Raid into American high schools.

Individual players have also been notable beneficiaries of Air Raid systems. Trevone Boykin, a lightly recruited high school player from Mesquite, Texas, had mixed success in his first two years at TCU. When TCU installed the Air Raid system in 2014, Boykin's college career exploded. He threw for 3,901 yards—best in the Big 12—and 33 touchdowns, leading TCU to a 12-1 record and a number-three national ranking.

Baker Mayfield, a walk-on at both Texas Tech and Oklahoma, is another example. Though Oklahoma's Stoops had introduced the Air Raid to the Big 12, he later abandoned it. But in 2015 he decided he no longer wanted to be the coach who was *not* running the Air Raid. He hired Lincoln Riley, who had been an offensive coach under Mike

Leach at Texas Tech for seven years and had averaged 533 yards of offense per game as offensive coordinator at East Carolina University under head coach and former Leach defensive coordinator Ruffin McNeil. Under Riley's tutelage, Mayfield became one of the country's leading quarterbacks, throwing for 3,700 yards and 36 touchdowns and finishing fourth for the Heisman Trophy. He led Oklahoma to the national playoffs, where the Sooners lost to Clemson in the semifinals.

Two of the most celebrated college quarterbacks of the past decade in other conferences ran the Air Raid, too. Case Keenum played for the University of Houston under head coach Kevin Sumlin and then–offensive coordinator Dana Holgorsen. With Holgorsen calling plays in 2008–2009 and his successor Kingsbury calling them in 2010, Keenum set all-time NCAA records for both passing yards (19,217) and touchdowns (155). Sumlin and Kingsbury then moved together to Texas A&M, where their quarterback, Johnny Manziel—who added his phenomenal athleticism to the basic Air Raid concepts—lit up the SEC and won the Heisman Trophy.

Sometimes Hal's influence circled back on itself. In 2005 a coach named Robert Anae, who had played and coached at BYU and was later an assistant coach for Leach for four years at Texas Tech, was hired by, of all places, *BYU* to install the Air Raid there. Amazingly, Hal's LaVell Edwards–inspired offense was returning to the place of its birth.

Since Hal's ideas about football are now the coin of the realm, what of the man himself? Why isn't he coaching a team in the NFL—much of which now employs some form of the Air Raid—or a major college team?

The answer is in some ways as complex as Hal. But a large part of it lies in Kentucky, where things went very well in the beginning and very badly at the end. Kentucky was both his moment of glory and the instrument of his undoing.

In his first year there, 1997, the team finished 5-6. But in Kentucky terms it was a spectacular, mesmerizing, and unprecedented 5-6.

Wildcat nation was riding high. The Alabama dragon had been slain. The following spring 30,000 fans showed up for the team's spring intra-squad game. Hal and his team did even better the next year. They beat LSU in Death Valley on a field goal as time expired. They whipped Jackie Sherrill's Mississippi State, lost a heartbreaker by two points to Georgia, and made it to the Outback Bowl, where 40,000 Kentucky fans showed up in Tampa, Florida, to watch their team lose to Penn State and finish with a 7-5 record. Tim Couch had a brilliant season, completing 400 passes on 553 attempts (72.3 percent) for 4,275 yards and 36 touchdowns against the nation's toughest defenses. To put that accomplishment into perspective, in 1996, two years earlier, University of Tennessee quarterback Peyton Manning—arguably the greatest quarterback of the modern era—completed 243 passes on 380 attempts (63.9 percent) for 3,287 yards against those same SEC defenses. Couch was a finalist for the Heisman Trophy and the NFL's number-one draft pick (by the Cleveland Browns), taken ahead of such standouts as Donovan McNabb (2) and Heisman winner Ricky Williams (5).

In 1999 Kentucky once again held its own in the SEC, winning four and losing four in the conference (6-6 overall) and beating Arkansas and LSU. Tim Couch's replacement, Dusty Bonner, led the conference in passing. But the defense struggled. In three losses to Georgia, Tennessee, and Louisville, Kentucky averaged a respectable 28 points per game, while its opponents averaged 54. Still, everyone loved Hal and the team. Kentucky finished the season by playing Syracuse in the Music City Bowl, in Nashville, Tennessee, before a record crowd of 59,221, almost all of them blue-clad Kentucky fans. Everywhere the team played fans thronged to see the nation's most exciting offense. So great was the surge in home ticket sales that the University of Kentucky decided to renovate and expand its football stadium.

By then Hal was making a lot of money, too. This was the SEC, after all, not the Illini-Badger-Hawkeye Conference. His starting salary of $300,000 had been increased to $450,000 after his first season. In 1999 athletics director C. M. Newton again raised Hal's pay, this time to $800,000 on a five-year contract, making him the second-highest-paid football coach in the SEC after Florida's Steve Spurrier. With his income from his summer camps and his radio and television shows, Hal was making more than $1 million a year.

But it was just around that time that Hal's fortunes started to turn. In the 2000 season he lost most of his starters. There were now freshmen at quarterback, wide receiver, tight end, and running back; freshmen and sophomores populated most of the team's positions. The Wildcats finished 0-8 in the SEC and 2-9 overall, though they lost four games by an average of four points. It was perhaps not coincidental that this was Hal's second season without wingman Mike Leach, who had moved on to Oklahoma and Texas Tech. Hal felt his absence acutely. As a student of Civil War history, he had sometimes thought his relationship with Leach resembled the relationship between Confederate generals Robert E. Lee and Stonewall Jackson. He was of course Lee, the head coach and chief strategist, while Leach was the Jacksonian attack dog who needed to be restrained. After Leach left, Hal thought he knew how Lee might have felt when Jackson was killed. Along the now-lonely sidelines, there was no one to tell him to keep attacking, no one who would be pissed off at him when, in the fourth quarter and with the second-stringers playing in a blowout, he stopped trying to score.

In a reasonable world, 2000 would have been a rebuilding year. Hal's new quarterback, redshirt freshman Jared Lorenzen, was potentially as talented as Couch. He led the conference in passing.* Kentucky also had the strongest group of freshmen and sophomores in memory. That year its recruiting class ranked 13th in the nation.

But the world wasn't reasonable anymore. With the retirement of Newton the previous year, Hal had lost his strongest supporter in the administration. His relationship with new AD Larry Ivy was immediately contentious and difficult. Unbeknownst to Hal, Ivy

---

* Lorenzen later played for the New York Giants as backup to Eli Manning.

had been conducting an investigation since the spring into NCAA violations by the team's recruiting coordinator, Claude Bassett. This was the same man who, as a defensive coach at BYU, had helped Hal gain access to that school's coaches and camps. Working secretly with Bassett's secretary, Ivy's compliance officer had put together a list of numerous violations, including $1,400 in cash payments to high school coaches. On November 19, 2000, Ivy called Hal into his office, showed him what he had found, and told him that Bassett would have to be fired. Hal, who had a strict policy on cheating, agreed. Bassett was summoned to Ivy's office, where Ivy, in Hal's presence, demanded, and got, Bassett's resignation.

But Bassett's firing settled nothing but Bassett himself, and only for the moment. The discovery of violations, in fact, had just begun. Hal and his staff were told by the university not to speak to the media while Ivy and his associates continued to press their investigation. There were leaks to the local press. The Internet was full of talk about violations. Bassett admitted in a live television interview to delivering those cash payments, in the form of money orders, to a Memphis high school coach. "I just felt it was necessary to stand up and look people in the eye and tell them what I did," Bassett said. "Bottom line, to all the fans and to all the people that I have caused any undue hurt, I fully apologize."*

Ivy's staff, meanwhile, compiled evidence of roughly three dozen infractions that had taken place in 1999 and 2000. In addition to the cash payments to the high school coach, they included paying

---

* In an interview with the author, Bassett, who acknowledges that he violated NCAA recruiting rules, said that he believes he was a victim of the University of Kentucky's "selective compliance" with NCAA rules. Meaning that the school routinely overlooked many minor violations in the football and basketball programs, especially. He believes that he wasn't doing anything different from what other school recruiters had been doing but that he had been singled out for punishment. The reason? Bassett believes that athletics director Ivy's real target was Hal, and that Bassett was simply the vehicle for getting rid of Hal. Bassett and Hal both recall a conversation in which Bassett said, in effect, "This investigation isn't about me, this is about you." Attempts to contact Ivy were unsuccessful.

for hotel rooms for prospects; giving prospects free football jackets, shirts, and sweats; giving prospects free meals and free football tickets and paying for their in-room movies and telephone calls; assisting students with their schoolwork; and illegally soliciting contributions from boosters. The total amount involved was about $7,000. There was no evidence that Bassett had personally profited from any of it.

Embattled, silent, and increasingly the subject of wild rumors and commentary, Hal waited for the investigation to end. On February 6, 2001, the day before college recruits signed commitment letters to universities, the hammer finally fell, though not at all in the way Hal expected. In a meeting at Hal's home between him; his lawyer, Travis Bryan; Ivy; and a university lawyer, Ivy informed Hal of the conclusions of the investigation. Then he demanded Hal's resignation and offered him a severance payment of $200,000. Ivy, as it happened, was running somewhat ahead of himself. Without informing Hal, earlier that day he had appointed Hal's offensive line coach, Guy Morriss, as the new head coach of Kentucky football and had scheduled a 5:00 p.m. press conference to announce the change and Hal's resignation.

Thus began an odd negotiation. The weakness in Ivy's position was that his investigation had found no wrongdoing on Hal's part and had uncovered no evidence that he had known about or condoned Bassett's actions. Hal was vulnerable because he ran the football program, the cheating had occurred on his watch, and he had hired and promoted the cheater. He was aware, too, that he could choose to fight instead of negotiate, force Ivy to fire him, and then sue the university for breach of contract. He decided instead to spare his family the anguish and settle. By the end of the meeting, Ivy had agreed to pay Hal $1 million, and Hal had agreed, with considerable bitterness, to resign.* June cried when she heard the final terms. Hal

---

* With various other financial elements added in, Hal's final package ended up being roughly $1.6 million. The official, reported number was $1 million, roughly $3 million less than Hal was owed under his contract.

believed, and would continue to believe, that he had been unfairly forced out. That was the end of his coaching career at Kentucky. It was the last thing in the world he had ever expected.

But it was not the end of the case. Up until this point, the investigation had been conducted exclusively by Ivy and his staff. The NCAA had played no part in it. Ivy had decided to make his move against Hal well in advance of any NCAA rulings about what had happened. Yet it was the NCAA's investigating arm that posed a far larger threat to the careers and reputations of those involved and to the institution itself. In November 2001—a year after Hal had fired Bassett and more than eight months after Hal's resignation—the NCAA's Committee on Infractions finally held its own six-hour hearing on the case. On February 17, 2002, the committee published its findings. Characterizing the case as "one of the more serious it has heard in recent years in terms of scope and breadth of violations," the committee found Bassett guilty of some three dozen violations and cited the university for "lack of institutional control." It found Hal innocent of any rule violations. The committee did conclude that "from the 1998–99 to 1999–00 academic years, the head football coach failed to monitor the activities of the recruiting officer," but issued no penalties. The NCAA, however, came down hard on both Bassett and the university. It banned Bassett from coaching in the NCAA for eight years, reduced the University of Kentucky's scholarships by 19 over three years, and gave the school three years of probation, while requiring it to restructure its athletics department to prevent future cheating.

Kentucky's agonies were not quite over. Two weeks later, University of Kentucky president Lee Todd fired Ivy based on a scathing report by a five-member panel investigating the athletics department for irregularities that were not covered by the investigation into recruiting violations. In a letter to Ivy, Todd referred to "numerous violations" of Ivy's contract, "which are serious individually, and when viewed collectively leave me no choice but to take this action." The letter said further that Ivy had "violated [university policies] related to misconduct" and had "failed to report or seek approval for certain benefits." President Todd later told the *New York Times* that Ivy had controlled 165 season tickets, which he used "to barter everything." Following Ivy's departure, the university took immediate action to adopt ethics policies for the office of athletics director, as well as rules for giving and receiving gifts and the handling of conflicts of interest.*

Not that Ivy's fate meant much to Hal by this point. His adversary was gone, but so was he. He bore the stigma of having resigned in the midst of a raging ethics scandal. As sometimes happens in such affairs, his full exoneration a year later became a footnote to the larger and more entertaining story of cheating in the Kentucky football program. Everybody heard about the scandal, fewer paid attention to the verdict of innocence. It is hard to shake the whiff of cheating, even when you are not guilty of anything.

The rest of Hal's career marked a return to that harder, more-volatile, less-forgiving life of a college coach that he had temporarily transcended. He landed a job a year later as head coach at Division I-AA Southeastern Louisiana, where the football program had been eliminated in 1985. He started it up again and went 5-7 in his first year. Amazingly, that year Southeastern Louisiana ranked first in Division I-AA in both total offense and passing offense. The following year he won seven and lost four, beating sixth-ranked McNeese State, 51-17, and breaking into the national top 25 rankings. Hal had engineered another amazing turnaround. His son, Matt, who had played backup quarterback for him at Valdosta and Kentucky, was now an assistant coach. For this sparkling comeback, in 2005

---

* Ivy initially refused to resign and was accordingly fired in a letter that has become public, but later changed his mind, agreeing to resign and sign an 11-point letter stipulating among other things that he not sue the university. Ivy's firing was covered in reports in the *Louisville Courier-Journal,* based on freedom of information requests, and other newspapers.

Hal got the job as head coach at Division I-A New Mexico State University.

In retrospect, of all the job offers Hal received in a long career, this was one he probably should not have taken. NMSU was one of the worst football programs in the country and was famous as the nation's most notorious Division I-A college coaching graveyard. It had been that way for as long as anyone could remember. As *ESPN The Magazine* put it: "Few teams in the history of sports have lost more, for longer, than New Mexico State football." The Aggies had not been to a bowl game since 1960, had not won eight games in a season since 1965. In the 25 years before Hal arrived, they had won 77 games and lost 202. Every year some sportswriter wondered aloud why they even fielded a football team. What was the point?

There were problems that year that even the normally doom-stricken NMSU did not usually face. The university had jumped conferences the previous year, going from the milquetoast Sun Belt Conference to the talent-rich Western Athletic Conference, featuring bowl-bound teams like Boise State, Fresno State, and Hawaii. To add to the misery, the NCAA had just imposed penalties on NMSU based on its poor academic graduation rates, which meant that the football team would lose an average of six full scholarships a year for three years. NMSU would not only have to try to win in the unforgiving WAC, it would have to do so with significant handicaps. Most coaches would not even consider taking such a guaranteed résumé-killing job.

Of course, Hal was not like most coaches. He was anxious to get back to Division I-A, to reassert himself and rebuild his reputation at the highest level of college football. He had proved his ability to rehabilitate troubled football programs. NMSU might be a perennial cellar team; on the other hand, its football team had never run his system. It was a reasonable risk to take, or so it appeared.

But this time the magic didn't work. Recruiting was an unexpected nightmare. Hal could not get the players he wanted to come to Las Cruces, New Mexico. Though his teams at NMSU again put up big passing numbers, they continued to lose most of their games, as they always had. In 2006, for example, the year his quarterback, Chase Holbrook, was second in the nation with 4,619 passing yards, the team won only 4 of its 12 games. Though the Aggies ranked 15th in scoring, they ranked a horrific 106th in points allowed. The following year Holbrook was again among the country's top passers, but his offense, again, was consistently outscored by the opposition. That's the way it went. In four years Hal's record was 11-38. He still believed he could turn the program around. But his bosses had run out of patience. He was fired in the fall of 2008.

The following year Hal found himself right back in the world of small-college football, at McMurry University, in Abilene, Texas, a school with Methodist affiliation and 1,076 students whose football team had lost 13 straight and had not had a winning season since 2000. It was a Texas version of Iowa Wesleyan. This time it all clicked. The Air Raid offense posted its usual huge numbers. In 2011 the McMurry War Hawks had a 9-3 record, won the first round of the national D-III playoffs, and ended the season ranked 14th in the country. In 2012 they jumped to Division II, where they made a stunning 8-3 debut and beat Southern Arkansas in a bowl game. The team's success inspired a multimillion-dollar renovation of the school's stadium. Hal was on a roll again. Except the administration at McMurry decided that, after all, it did not want to place so much emphasis on football. What happened was weirdly similar to what had taken place at Iowa Wesleyan, though in this case Hal was not fired. Once again his success and his drive to win had pushed officials at a small school beyond where they wanted to go. Many of them saw football consuming resources that were better used by the chemistry or English departments. Their solution: De-emphasize football. Take it back to its scholarship-free D-III roots.

In early 2013, Hal, aware that this change was coming, and realizing it would undo most of the progress he had made, took a job as offensive coordinator at Southern Methodist University under his old friend (and Mouse Davis protégé) June Jones. He stayed a year there, helping quarterback Garrett Gilbert, a famous University of Texas washout, throw for 353 yards a game in an offense that was part run-and-shoot, part Air Raid, and too complex for Hal's liking. Then he was off to Belhaven University in Jackson, Mississippi, where he is, as of the writing of this book, head football coach. Belhaven is a small Division III Christian college with a pretty, leafy campus and a bad football team. Hal is shouldering the load once again, taking up the immense task of trying to turn a football program around. He is recruiting in Texas. He has convinced the university to build a new stadium to replace the aging high school field where the team now plays. The whole enterprise has a very familiar ring.

It also sounds very much like a descent, the reverse of his rise in the football world from Copperas Cove High School to the University of Kentucky. What it is, in fact, is a typical career path through the American football industry, where there are almost no pure, clean trajectories from the bottom to the top, and where almost no one stays at the top very long. Assistant coaches blow with the wind, moving when their bosses move. But head coaches are like corks in a raging river. From 2006 through 2010 the average turnover rate for head coaches in the Football Bowl Subdivision (FBS) was 22 percent, according to a study on ESPN.com. That means 25 vacancies every year out of 115 teams. Hidden inside that number is another discouraging trend: Coaches were increasingly being fired after two or three years, before they could even fill their teams with their own recruits.

Fired coaches, of course, almost invariably move down the industry ladder. Larry Coker took the University of Miami to a national title in 2001 and was fired in 2006 after a .500 season. He landed as coach of the start-up program at the University of Texas at San Antonio, where his teams were 26-32 in five seasons. He was fired in 2016. Down, down, and finally out of football. There is nothing fair or forgiving about the system. Frank Solich, who had an excellent 58-19 record in six years as head coach of Nebraska, appearing in six bowl games and playing for the national championship in 2001, was fired in 2003 after a couple of iffy seasons. This is the world Hal inhabits. Almost all of the coaches in it have had rough rides through their beloved sport. There is nothing more common than a former college coach now coaching at a small high school. There is nothing exceptional about a wildly successful college coach who gets to the NFL and fails spectacularly. Think of Steve Spurrier (Washington Redskins), Lou Holtz (New York Jets), and Bobby Petrino (Atlanta Falcons). It's just the business.

While he was ricocheting around the world of college football again, Hal also experienced some serious health problems. In the summer before his last season at NMSU, he had come down with an illness that was diagnosed as prostate cancer. He had surgery the following year. In 2010, at age 58, while coaching at McMurry, he underwent radiation treatments. Just prior to the start of those treatments, he and his son Matt were hit from behind in their car by a semitruck, damaging his spine in three places and causing him severe pain. (Matt sustained minor injuries.) He receives injections and takes medication to manage it. While his teams at McMurry were winning, he was often in great physical discomfort. As of this writing he is cancer-free, as is June.

Hal and June divorced in 2015. She remains in Abilene, where she is CEO and part owner of a medical imaging business. He lives in a suite at the elegant old King Edward Hotel in downtown Jackson and has a five-minute commute to his office at Belhaven. They have an amicable relationship and see their three grown children and three grandchildren frequently.

Hal remains in touch with an extraordinary number of his old coaches and players, many of whom he has close relationships with. They include Claude Bassett as well as former adversaries Bobby Wallace and Max Bowman.

Mike Leach has had his own troubles in the world of college football, despite achieving considerable fame at Texas Tech. In 2009 he became involved in a dispute involving his treatment of a player with a concussion. The player, Adam James, was the son of former football star Craig James, and the accusation, which Leach denied, was that he had punished Adam for his injury. The story became a national sensation, with Internet sentiment running overwhelmingly in Leach's favor. In the end, that didn't help him. He and his employers at Texas Tech could not agree on a resolution, and he was fired after the end of the season. After several years of job hunting, Leach was hired in 2012 as head football coach by Washington State University, where he coaches today. In 2015 his team had a 9-4 record and beat the University of Miami in the Sun Bowl. Leach was named the Pac 12's Co-Coach of the Year, an honor he shared with Stanford's David Shaw. Leach's quarterback, Luke Falk, led the nation in completions and attempts and was fifth in total passing yards. It is a measure of how Leach must now compete in the world he and Hal created that the four quarterbacks who passed for more yards than Falk—Brandon Doughty, of Western Kentucky; Matt Johnson, of Bowling Green State; Jared Goff, of California; and Patrick Mahomes of Texas Tech—are all pure Air Raid quarterbacks.[*]

Hal and Leach remain close friends and are in constant touch by phone. Sometimes they meet at Leach's place in Key West, sip drinks, listen to Jimmy Buffett, and watch the sun set over the ocean.

But wherever they are, and whatever they are doing, they talk about football. Over the years, one constant topic is their amazement at how many teams in America have adopted the plays, formations, and ideas they made famous at Kentucky and Texas Tech. They watched New England Patriots receiver Wes Welker carve up the NFL with option routes that closely resembled what Sean Pender had run at Valdosta State and that Leach later taught Welker at Texas Tech. They watched as high-speed offenses swept through

---

[*] Falk led the nation in completions and attempts even though he missed a full game and a half with injuries. Though Cal's Jared Goff led the Pac 12 in yards passing, Leach's Washington State led the Pac 12 in yards passing as a team.

college football. In 2010, two teams that played as blisteringly fast as Iowa Wesleyan—Auburn and Oregon—played for the national championship. Each weekend in the fall, Hal and Leach can turn on their television sets and watch their trademark plays—quick screens, tunnel screens, mesh, Y-sail, Y-cross, Four Verticals, and Y-stick—being executed by everyone from the San Francisco 49ers to the Bowling Green State University Falcons. By 2015, it was getting hard to find any team that did not have a least one Air Raid play in its playbook.

There are those in the football community who see Hal as a tragic figure, a brilliant coach who made it big, caught some bad breaks, then receded into the world of small-time college football while his protégés and imitators made millions and became famous running his offense. Hal does not see it that way. It is impossible for him to see it that way. He is the same man who walked into the dank old gym at Iowa Wesleyan in 1989 and started cold-calling recruits in Texas. He remains a self-described "Christian optimist." He believes he can beat teams that no one else gives him a chance to beat. He believes he can overcome large odds when no one else does. He likes small colleges and the purity and glory of the old game and the players and their parents and game days and driving all over Hell's Half-Acre looking for a high school player who can throw or catch a ball. He likes the eternal hope of spring practice. Above all he believes that if you give him enough time and a little money, he can put a team on the field that will send balls spiraling up into that blue-gray October sky and bring fans to their feet and make them scream for the sheer joyous uncertainty of it all, the possibility that anything might happen.

A Note on Sources and Methods

The Perfect Pass grew out of an interview I did with Mike Leach in Lubbock, Texas, in the spring of 2009 for a cover story in *Texas Monthly* magazine. I asked him where his radical offense had come from, and he answered by telling me a story about the miraculous, world-beating football team at tiny Iowa Wesleyan College, where he had been an assistant coach two decades before. He told me about the team's head coach, a man I had never heard of named Hal Mumme. It was a great story; it was even better because it was so wonderfully obscure.

What caught my imagination was Leach's description of his odysseys across America with Hal during the off-season. They visited everyone from professional teams and major universities to obscure junior colleges and small high schools in search of ways to perfect the forward pass. I was captivated. I didn't know football coaches did that sort of thing. Their pilgrimages looking for football's version of truth and beauty had the feel of a buddy movie. What Hal and Mike were inventing, of course, was this revolutionary passing offense that was in the process of turning the game upside down. The funny thing was: No one really knew how it worked. I certainly did not. Commentators and analysts spoke of a "system" but they quite obviously did not understand what the system consisted of or how it could deliver such stunning results year after year. What sort of dark magic was this? I wrote about those Iowa Wesleyan years briefly in my *Texas Monthly* story but did not have the time or the space in the magazine to go more deeply into the subject. I never really solved the mystery of the Air Raid.

Though I proceeded in subsequent years to write a book about the Comanche Indians (*Empire of the Summer Moon*) and a biography of Stonewall Jackson (*Rebel Yell*), I never forgot Mike's story about this unique form of American entrepreneurial technology, and I wanted some day to go back to it. I needed to figure out exactly who Hal Mumme was and how he had managed to change American football. I am grateful that Scribner's editor in chief Colin Harrison, who also happens to be my editor, let me run with my idea.

The book is drawn mostly from several hundred hours of interviews with the Air Raid's principals and supporting cast, which includes Hal and Mike, of course, plus their coaches, former players, former adversaries, current and former athletics directors, wives, secretaries, trainers, boosters, administrative colleagues, and various other hangers-on. I won't name them all—there are probably 80 of them—but they were uniformly generous with their time and in answering my persistent questions about events and places that have been long forgotten by most people. Hal was especially patient in helping me reconstruct some of his key plays, such as mesh.

Because the only writing about Hal's early teams appeared in small local newspapers, they became a key source, especially the *Mt. Pleasant News*, the *Burlington Hawk Eye*, and the *Valdosta Daily Times*. For Hal's Kentucky years, the *Lexington Herald Leader* and the *Louisville Courier-Journal* were invaluable. The reporters who crafted those stories probably had no idea that their stories would live on beyond the pages of those newspapers. But their work became critical information for me, and I thank them for it.

Books that cover this subject are extremely rare, too. June Mumme's *Play the Next Play* is an excellent account of her battle with cancer and also a good description of life as a coach's wife. *Stretch the Cornfield*, Rob Kiser's micro-history of Hal's years at Iowa Wesleyan, is well researched and was very helpful to me in trying to re-create that era. The most helpful analytical books were Tim Layden's *Blood, Sweat, and Chalk,* and two slender but insightful books by Chris B. Brown, *The Art of Smart Football* and *The Essential Smart Football.*

Magazine articles that I found useful include: Kevin Van Valkenburg's profile of Hal Mumme in the September 19, 2014, issue of *ESPN The Magazine,* "Yoda of the Air Raid Offense, He Is"; Michael Lewis's profile of Mike Leach in the December 4, 2005, issue of the *New York Times Magazine,* "Coach Leach Goes Deep, Very Deep"; and Kenny Moore's November 12, 1979, story about Mouse Davis in *Sports Illustrated,* "Of Mouse and His Men."

The bulk of articles and columns analyzing passing offenses are to be found on the Internet in one form or another. Especially useful were articles featured on *ESPN* and its (now defunct) *Grantland* blog, *Bleacher Report,* and *SB Nation.* The best analysis of the passing game by far, in my opinion, is to be found on Chris B. Brown's SmartFootball.com.

To research the book I spent time in Mount Pleasant, Iowa, and Valdosta, Georgia, and visited sources in six states for interviews. Almost none of this travel was drudgery. The people I spoke with were interesting and engaging, the subject was endlessly fascinating, and the players and coaches on those old Air Raid teams invariably felt they had been part of something very special.

Bibliography

American Football Coaches Association. *Offensive Football Strategies*. Champaign, IL: Human Kinetics, 2000.

Barra, Allen. *The Last Coach: A Life of Paul "Bear" Bryant*. New York: W. W. Norton, 2005.

Benedict, Jeff, and Arman Keteyian. *The System: The Glory and Scandal of Big-Time College Football*. New York: Doubleday, 2013.

Black, Al. *Coaching Run-and-Shoot Football*. Self-published, 1991.

Brown, Chris B. *The Essential Smart Football*. Self-published, 2012.

———. *The Art of Smart Football*. Self-published, 2015.

Bryant, Paul W., and John Underwood. *The Hard Life and Good Times of Alabama's Coach Bryant*. Boston: Little Brown, 1975.

Camp, Walter. *American Football*. New York: Harper and Bros., 1891.

Connelly, Bill. *Study Hall: College Football: Its Stats and Its Stories*. Self-published.

Edwards, LaVell. *Winning Football with the Forward Pass*. Boston: Allyn & Bacon, 1995.

Ellison, Carolyn J. *Coach the Kid, Build the Boy, Mold the Man: The Legacy of Run and Shoot Football*. Bloomington, IN: Xlibris, 2007.

Ellison, Glenn. *Run and Shoot Football: The Now Attack*. West Nyack, NY: Parker Publishing, 1985 (originally published 1965 with subtitle *The Offense of the Future*).

Falk, Gerhard. *Football and American Identity*. New York: Haworth Press, 2005.

Flynn, George L., editor. *Vince Lombardi on Football*. New York: Graphic Society and Walynn, Inc., 1973.

Franklin, Tony. *Fourth Down and Life to Go*. Lexington, KY: BadCoaches Inc., 2001.

Greenberg, Murray. *Passing Game: Benny Friedman and the Transformation of Football.* New York: Public Affairs, 2008.

Hargitt, Rich. *Coaching the Air Raid Offense.* Monterey, CA: Coaches Choice, 2014.

Jenkins, Sally. *The Real All Americans.* New York: Doubleday, 2007.

Johnson, James W. *The Wow Boys: A Coach, a Team, and a Turning Point in College Football.* Lincoln: University of Nebraska Press, 2006.

Jubera, Drew. *Must Win: A Season of Survival for a Town and Its Team.* New York: St. Martin's Press, 2012.

Kaye, Ivan N. *Good Clean Violence: A History of College Football.* Philadelphia: J. B. Lippincott, 1973.

Kemper, Kurt Edward. *College Football and American Culture in the Cold War Era.* Chicago: University of Illinois Press, 2009.

Kirwan, Pat. *Take Your Eye Off the Ball.* Chicago: Triumph Books, 2010.

Kiser, Rob. *Stretch the Cornfield.* Buffalo Gap, TX: Statehouse Press, 2013.

Lawton, James. *The All-American War Game.* Oxford, UK: Basil Blackwell, 1984.

Layden, Tim. *Blood, Sweat and Chalk: The Ultimate Football Playbook; How the Great Coaches Built Today's Game.* New York: Sports Illustrated Books, 2011.

Leach, Mike. *Swing Your Sword: Leading the Charge in Football and Life.* New York: Diversion Books, 2011.

Maggio, Frank P. *Notre Dame and the Game That Changed Football.* New York: Carroll & Graf, 2007.

Malzahn, Gus. *The Hurry-up, No-huddle: An Offensive Philosophy.* Monterey, CA: Coaches Choice, 2003.

Maraniss, David. *When Pride Still Mattered: A Life of Vince Lombardi.* New York: Simon & Schuster, 2000.

McGill, John, and Dave Baker. *Tim Couch: A Passion for the Game.* Champaign, IL: Sports Publishing Inc., 1999.

Meyer, L. R. (Dutch). *Spread Formation Football.* New York: Prentice-Hall, 1952.

Miller, John J. *The Big Scrum: How Teddy Roosevelt Saved Football.* New York: HarperCollins, 2011.

Mumme, June. *Play the Next Play.* Lexington, KY: Host Communications, 1998.

Nelson, David M. *The Anatomy of a Game: Football, the Rules, and the Men Who Made the Game.* Newark, NJ: University of Delaware Press, 1994.

Patoski, Joe Nick. *Texas High School Football: More than the Game.* Austin: University of Texas Press, 2011.

St. John, Allen, and Ainissa G. Ramirez. *Newton's Football: The Science Behind America's Game*. New York: Ballantine Books, 2013.

Schulian, John, editor. *Football: Great Writing About the National Sport*. New York: Library of America, 2014.

Shaughnessy, Clark. *Football in War and Peace (An Esquire Sports Book)*. Clinton, SC: Jacobs Press, 1943.

Sherrod, Rick. *Texas High School Football Dynasties*. Charleston, SC: History Press, 2013.

Stagg, Amos Alonzo. *Touchdown! As Told by Amos Alonzo Stagg to Wesley Winans Stout*. New York: Longmans, Green and Co., 1927.

Walsh, Bill, and Glenn Dickey. *Building a Champion: On Football and the Making of the 49ers*. New York: St. Martin's Press, 1990.

Wright, Bart. *Football Revolution: The Rise of the Spread Offense and How It Transformed College Football*. Lincoln: University of Nebraska Press, 2013.

Zimmerman, Paul. *The New Thinking Man's Guide to Pro Football*. New York: Simon & Schuster, 1984.

Index

About the Author

S. C. Gwynne is the author of the *New York Times* bestsellers *Empire of the Summer Moon*, which was a finalist for the Pulitzer Prize and the National Book Critics Circle Award, and *Rebel Yell*, which was also a finalist for the National Book Critics Circle Award and was short-listed for the PEN Literary Award for biography. He is an award-winning journalist whose work has appeared extensively in *Time*, for which he worked as bureau chief, national correspondent, and senior editor from 1988 to 2000, and in *Texas Monthly*, where he was executive editor. His work has also appeared in *Outside* magazine, the *New York Times*, the *Dallas Morning News*, the *Los Angeles Times*, the *Los Angeles Herald Examiner*, *Harper's*, and *California* magazine. He lives in Austin, Texas, with his wife, the artist Katie Maratta, and daughter, Maisie.